Prentice Hall

LITERATURE

D1568588

All-in-One
Workbook

Grade Ten

PEARSON

Upper Saddle River, New Jersey
Boston, Massachusetts
Chandler, Arizona
Glenview, Illinois

BQ Tunes Credits
Keith London, Defined Mind, Inc., Executive Producer
Mike Pandolfo, Wonderful, Producer
All songs mixed and mastered by Mike Pandolfo, Wonderful
Vlad Gutkovich, Wonderful, Assistant Engineer
Recorded November 2007 – February 2008 in SoHo, New York City, at Wonderful, 594 Broadway

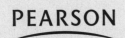

ISBN-13: 978-0-13-366815-5
ISBN-10:   0-13-366815-0

2 3 4 5 6 7 8 9 10   13 12 11 10 09

CONTENTS

UNIT 1 **Fiction and Nonfiction**

BQ Tunes 1

Big Question Vocabulary 1 2

Big Question Vocabulary 2 3

Big Question Vocabulary 3 4

Applying the Big Question 5

"Magdalena Looking" and **"Artful Research"** by Susan Vreeland

Listening and Viewing 6

Learning About Fiction and Nonfiction 7

Model Selection: Fiction 8

Model Selection: Nonfiction 9

"The Monkey's Paw" by W. W. Jacobs

Writing About the Big Question 10

Literary Analysis: Plot 11

Reading: Use Prior Knowledge to Make Predictions 12

Vocabulary Builder 13

"The Leap" by Louise Erdrich

Writing About the Big Question 14

Literary Analysis: Plot 15

Reading: Use Prior Knowledge to Make Predictions 16

Vocabulary Builder 17

"The Monkey's Paw" and **"The Leap"**

Integrated Language Skills: Grammar 18

Integrated Language Skills: Support for Writing a Story 19

from **Swimming to Antarctica** by Lynne Cox

Writing About the Big Question 20

Literary Analysis: Author's Perspective 21

Reading: Use Prior Knowledge to Make Predictions 22

Vocabulary Builder 23

"Occupation: Conductorette" *from* **I Know Why the Caged Bird Sings**
by Maya Angelou

Writing About the Big Question 24

Literary Analysis: Author's Perspective 25

Reading: Use Prior Knowledge to Make Predictions 26

Vocabulary Builder 27

from **Swimming to Antarctica and "Occupation: Conductorette"**
    Integrated Language Skills: Grammar 28
    Integrated Language Skills: Support for Extend Your Learning 29

"Marian Anderson, Famous Concert Singer" by Langston Hughes
"Tepeyac" by Sandra Cisneros
    Writing About the Big Question. 30
    Literary Analysis: Style 31
    Vocabulary Builder. 32
    Support for Writing to Compare Literary Works 33

"Contents of the Dead Man's Pocket" by Jack Finney
    Writing About the Big Question. 34
    Literary Analysis: Conflict and Resolution 35
    Reading: Reflect on Key Details to Analyze Cause and Effect 36
    Vocabulary Builder 37

"Games at Twilight" by Anita Desai
    Writing About the Big Question. 38
    Literary Analysis: Conflict and Resolution 39
    Reading: Reflect on Key Details to Analyze Cause and Effect 40
    Vocabulary Builder 41

"Contents of the Dead Man's Pocket" and **"Games at Twilight"**
    Integrated Language Skills: Grammar 42
    Integrated Language Skills: Support for Writing an Anecdote with an Ironic Ending. 43

"The Marginal World" by Rachel Carson
    Writing About the Big Question. 44
    Literary Analysis: Author's Purpose 45
    Reading: Reread Passages to Analyze Cause and Effect 46
    Vocabulary Builder 47

"Making History With Vitamin C" by Penny Le Couteur and Jay Burreson
    Writing About the Big Question. 48
    Literary Analysis: Author's Purpose 49
    Reading: Reread Passages to Analyze Cause and Effect 50
    Vocabulary Builder 51

"The Marginal World" and **"Making History With Vitamin C"**
    Integrated Language Skills: Grammar 52
    Integrated Language Skills: Support for Writing a Proposal for a Documentary 53

"Like the Sun" by R. K. Narayan
"The Open Window" by Saki

Writing About the Big Question 54

Literary Analysis: Irony and Paradox 55

Vocabulary Builder 56

Support for Writing to Compare Literary Works 57

UNIT 2   Short Stories

BQ Tunes 58

Big Question Vocabulary 1 59

Big Question Vocabulary 2 60

Big Question Vocabulary 3 61

Applying the Big Question 62

from **"The Threads of Time" by C. J. Cherryh**

Listening and Viewing 63

Learning About Short Stories 64

Model Selection: Short Story 65

"A Visit to Grandmother" by William Melvin Kelley

Writing About the Big Question 66

Literary Analysis: Characterization 67

Reading: Relate Characters and Events to Your Own Experiences to Make Inferences 68

Vocabulary Builder 69

"A Problem" by Anton Chekhov

Writing About the Big Question 70

Literary Analysis: Characterization 71

Reading: Relate Characters and Events to Your Own Experiences to Make Inferences 72

Vocabulary Builder 73

"A Visit to Grandmother" and "A Problem"

Integrated Language Skills: Grammar 74

Integrated Language Skills: Support for Writing a Retelling 75

"The Street of the Cañon" by Josephina Niggli

Writing About the Big Question 76

Literary Analysis: Setting 77

Reading: Make Inferences and Read on to Find Additional Support 78

Vocabulary Builder 79

"There Will Come Soft Rains" by Ray Bradbury

Writing About the Big Question 80

Literary Analysis: Setting 81

Reading: Make Inferences and Read on to Find Additional Support 82
Vocabulary Builder 83

"The Street of the Cañon" and "There Will Come Soft Rains"
Integrated Language Skills: Grammar 84
Integrated Language Skills: Support for Writing a Letter to a Friend and a Book Review . . 85

"One Thousand Dollars" by O. Henry
"By the Waters of Babylon" by Stephen Vincent Benét
Writing About the Big Question 86
Literary Analysis: Point of View 87
Vocabulary Builder 88
Support for Writing to Compare Literary Works 89

"How Much Land Does a Man Need?" by Leo Tolstoy
Writing About the Big Question 90
Literary Analysis: Theme and Philosophical Assumptions 91
Reading: Recognize Key Details to Draw Conclusions About Theme 92
Vocabulary Builder 93

"Civil Peace" by Chinua Achebe
Writing About the Big Question 94
Literary Analysis: Theme and Philosophical Assumptions 95
Reading: Recognize Key Details to Draw Conclusions About Theme 96
Vocabulary Builder 97

"How Much Land Does a Man Need?" and "Civil Peace"
Integrated Language Skills: Grammar 98
Integrated Language Skills: Support for Writing a Character Analysis 99

"The Masque of the Red Death" by Edgar Allan Poe
Writing About the Big Question 100
Literary Analysis: Symbolism and Allegory 101
Reading: Identify Patterns to Draw Conclusions About Symbolism 102
Vocabulary Builder 103

"The Garden of Stubborn Cats" by Italo Calvino
Writing About the Big Question 104
Literary Analysis: Symbolism and Allegory 105
Reading: Identify Patterns to Draw Conclusions About Symbolism 106
Vocabulary Builder 107

"The Masque of the Red Death" and "The Garden of Stubborn Cats"
Integrated Language Skills: Grammar 108
Integrated Language Skills: Support for Writing a Narrative 109

"The Censors" by Luisa Valenzuela

"The Leader in the Mirror" by Pat Mora

    Writing About the Big Question 110

    Literary Analysis: Tone 111

    Vocabulary Builder 112

    Support for Writing a Comparison-and-Contrast Essay 113

UNIT 3   Types of Nonfiction

    BQ Tunes 114

    Big Question Vocabulary 1 116

    Big Question Vocabulary 2 117

    Big Question Vocabulary 3 118

    Applying the Big Question 119

"Everest" *from* Touch the Top of the World by Erik Weihenmayer

    Listening and Viewing 120

    Learning About Nonfiction 121

    Model Selection: Nonfiction 122

"The Spider and the Wasp" by Alexander Petrunkevitch

    Writing About the Big Question 123

    Literary Analysis: Inductive and Deductive Reasoning in an Expository Essay 124

    Reading: Analyze Main Ideas and Supporting Details by Summarizing 125

    Vocabulary Builder 126

***from* Longitude by Dava Sobel**

    Writing About the Big Question 127

    Literary Analysis: Inductive and Deductive Reasoning in an Expository Essay 128

    Reading: Analyze Main Ideas and Supporting Details by Summarizing 129

    Vocabulary Builder 130

"The Spider and the Wasp" and *from* Longitude

    Integrated Language Skills: Grammar 131

    Integrated Language Skills: Support for Writing a Business Letter 132

"The Sun Parlor" by Dorothy West

    Writing About the Big Question 133

    Literary Analysis: Reflective Essay 134

    Reading: Ask Questions to Analyze Main Ideas and Supporting Details 135

    Vocabulary Builder 136

***from* In Commemoration: One Million Volumes by Rudolfo Anaya**

    Writing About the Big Question 137

    Literary Analysis: Reflective Essay 138

Reading: Ask Questions to Analyze Main Ideas and Supporting Details 139
Vocabulary Builder 140

"The Sun Parlor" and *from* In Commemoration: One Million Volumes

Integrated Language Skills: Grammar 141
Integrated Language Skills: Support for Writing a Memoir 142

"A Toast to the Oldest Inhabitant: The Weather of New England" by Mark Twain

"The Dog That Bit People" by James Thurber

Writing About the Big Question 143
Literary Analysis: Humorous Writing 144
Vocabulary Builder 145
Integrated Language Skills: Support for Writing to Compare Literary Works 146

"Keep Memory Alive" by Elie Wiesel

Writing About the Big Question 147
Literary Analysis: Persuasive Writing 148
Reading: Test the Writer's Logic to Evaluate Persuasive Appeals 149
Vocabulary Builder 150

from Nobel Lecture by Alexander Solzhenitsyn

Writing About the Big Question 151
Literary Analysis: Persuasive Writing 152
Reading: Test the Writer's Logic to Evaluate Persuasive Appeals 153
Vocabulary Builder 154

"Keep Memory Alive" and *from* Nobel Lecture

Integrated Language Skills: Grammar 155
Integrated Language Skills: Support for Writing a Letter 156

"The American Idea" by Theodore H. White

Writing About the Big Question 157
Literary Analysis: Analytic and Interpretive Essays 158
Reading: Distinguish Between Fact and Opinion to Evaluate Writers' Appeals 159
Vocabulary Builder 160

"What Makes a Degas a Degas?" by Richard Mühlberger

Writing About the Big Question 161
Literary Analysis: Analytic and Interpretive Essays 162
Reading: Distinguish Between Fact and Opinion to Evaluate Writers' Appeals 163
Vocabulary Builder 164

"The American Idea" and "What Makes a Degas a Degas?"

    Integrated Language Skills: Grammar 165

    Integrated Language Skills: Support for Writing a Critique 166

from **Desert Exile: The Uprooting of a Japanese-American Family**
    by Yoshiko Uchida

from **The Way to Rainy Mountain** by N. Scott Momaday

    Writing About the Big Question 167

    Literary Analysis: Author's Purpose 168

    Vocabulary Builder 169

    Support for Comparing Literary Works 170

UNIT 4   Poetry

    BQ Tunes 171

    Big Question Vocabulary 1 173

    Big Question Vocabulary 2 174

    Big Question Vocabulary 3 175

    Applying the Big Question 176

The Poetry of Cornelius Eady

    Listening and Viewing 177

    Learning About Poetry 178

    Model Selection: Poetry 179

Poetry Collection: Alexander Pushkin, Federico García Lorca, Elizabeth Bishop, Rudyard Kipling

    Writing About the Big Question 180

    Literary Analysis: Narrative and Lyric Poetry 181

    Reading: Read Aloud and Adjust Reading Rate to Read Fluently 182

    Vocabulary Builder 183

Poetry Collection: Denise Levertov, William Carlos Williams, Robert Frost, and Naomi Shihab Nye

    Writing About the Big Question 184

    Literary Analysis: Narrative and Lyric Poetry 185

    Reading: Read Aloud and Adjust Reading Rate to Read Fluently 186

    Vocabulary Builder 187

Poetry Collections: Alexander Pushkin, Federico García Lorca, Elizabeth Bishop, and Rudyard Kipling; Denise Levertov, William Carlos Williams, Robert Frost, and Naomi Shihab Nye

    Integrated Language Skills: Grammar 188

    Integrated Language Skills: Support for Writing a Lyric Poem 189

Poetry Collection: Ki Tsurayuki, Minamoto no Toshiyori, James Weldon Johnson, and Dylan Thomas

    Writing About the Big Question 190

    Literary Analysis: Poetic Form 191

    Reading: Preview a Poem to Read Fluently 192

    Vocabulary Builder 193

Poetry Collection: Priest Jakuren, Ono Komachi, Theodore Roethke, and William Shakespeare

    Writing About the Big Question 194

    Literary Analysis: Poetic Form 195

    Reading: Preview a Poem to Read Fluently 196

    Vocabulary Builder 197

Poetry Collections: Ki Tsurayuki, Minamoto no Toshiyori, James Weldon Johnson, and Dylan Thomas; Priest Jakuren, Ono Komachi, Theodore Roethke, and William Shakespeare

    Integrated Language Skills: Grammar 198

    Integrated Language Skills: Support for Writing a Tanka 199

Poetry by Gabriela Mistral, Gwendolyn Brooks, and Umberto Eco

    Writing About the Big Question 200

    Literary Analysis: Tone and Mood 201

    Vocabulary Builder 202

    Support for Writing to Compare Literary Works 203

Poetry Collection: Yusef Komunyakaa, Eve Merriam, Emily Dickinson

    Writing About the Big Question 204

    Literary Analysis: Figurative Language 205

    Reading: Picture Imagery to Paraphrase Poems 206

    Vocabulary Builder 207

Poetry Collection: Edna St. Vincent Millay, Dahlia Ravikovitch, Emily Dickinson

    Writing About the Big Question 208

    Literary Analysis: Figurative Language 209

    Reading: Picture Imagery to Paraphrase Poems 210

    Vocabulary Builder 211

Poetry Collections: Yusef Komunyakaa, Eve Merriam, and Emily Dickinson; Edna St. Vincent Millay, Dahlia Ravikovitch, and Emily Dickinson

    Integrated Language Skills: Grammar 212

    Integrated Language Skills: Support for Writing a Critical Essay 213

Poetry Collection: Langston Hughes, John McCrae, and Carl Sandburg

Writing About the Big Question 214

Literary Analysis: Sound Devices 215

Reading: Break Down Long Sentences to Paraphrase Poems 216

Vocabulary Builder 217

Poetry Collection: Alfred, Lord Tennyson, Robert Browning, and Jean Toomer

Writing About the Big Question 218

Literary Analysis: Sound Devices 219

Reading: Break Down Long Sentences to Paraphrase Poems 220

Vocabulary Builder 221

Poetry Collections: Langston Hughes, John McCrae, and Carl Sandburg; Alfred, Lord Tennyson; Robert Browning; and Jean Toomer

Integrated Language Skills: Grammar 222

Integrated Language Skills: Support for Writing a Poem 223

Poetry by Bei Dao, Shu Ting, and Billy Joel

Writing About the Big Question 224

Literary Analysis: Theme 225

Vocabulary Builder 226

Support for Writing to Compare Literary Works 227

UNIT 5 Drama

BQ Tunes 228

Big Question Vocabulary 1 231

Big Question Vocabulary 2 232

Big Question Vocabulary 3 233

Applying the Big Question 234

from **Tibet Through the Red Box** by David Henry Hwang

Listening and Viewing 235

Learning About Drama 236

Model Selection: Drama 237

Antigone, *Prologue–Scene 2,* **by Sophocles**

Writing About the Big Question 238

Literary Analysis: Greek Tragedy—The Protagonist and the Antagonist 239

Reading: List Events to Summarize 240

Vocabulary Builder 241

Integrated Language Skills: Grammar 242

Integrated Language Skills: Support for Writing an Essay 243

Antigone, *Scenes 3–5*, by Sophocles

    Writing About the Big Question 244

    Literary Analysis: Greek Tragedy—The Tragic Flaw 245

    Reading: List Events to Summarize 246

    Vocabulary Builder 247

    Integrated Language Skills: Grammar 248

    Integrated Language Skills: Support for Writing an Essay 249

from **An Enemy of the People** by Henrik Ibsen
Antigone by Sophocles

    Writing About the Big Question 250

    Literary Analysis: Universal and Culturally Specific Themes 251

    Vocabulary Builder 252

    Support for Writing a Comparative Essay 253

The Tragedy of Julius Caesar, *Act I*, by William Shakespeare

    Writing About the Big Question 254

    Literary Analysis: Exposition in Shakespeare's Tragedies 255

    Reading: Use Text Aids to Read Shakespearean Drama 256

    Vocabulary Builder 257

The Tragedy of Julius Caesar, *Act II*, by William Shakespeare

    Writing About the Big Question 258

    Literary Analysis: Blank Verse 259

    Reading: Paraphrase Shakespearean Drama 260

    Vocabulary Builder 261

The Tragedy of Julius Caesar, *Act III*, by William Shakespeare

    Writing About the Big Question 262

    Literary Analysis: Dramatic Speeches 263

    Reading: Analyze the Imagery of Shakespearean Tragedy 264

    Vocabulary Builder 265

The Tragedy of Julius Caesar, *Act IV*, by William Shakespeare

    Writing About the Big Question 266

    Literary Analysis: Conflict in Drama 267

    Reading: Read Between the Lines 268

    Vocabulary Builder 269

The Tragedy of Julius Caesar, *Act V*, by William Shakespeare

    Writing About the Big Question 270

    Literary Analysis: Shakespeare's Tragic Heroes 271

    Reading: Compare and Contrast Characters in Shakespearean Drama 272

Vocabulary Builder 273
Integrated Language Skills: Grammar 274
Integrated Language Skills: Support for Writing an Editorial 275

from **A Raisin in the Sun** by Lorraine Hansberry
The Tragedy of Julius Caesar by William Shakespeare

Writing About the Big Question 276
Literary Analysis: Character Motivation 277
Vocabulary Builder 278
Support for Writing a Comparative Essay. 279

UNIT 6 Themes in Folk Literature

BQ Tunes 280
Big Question Vocabulary 1 282
Big Question Vocabulary 2 283
Big Question Vocabulary 3 284
Applying the Big Question. 285

from **Places Left Unfinished at the Time of Creation** by John Phillip Santos

Listening and Viewing. 286
Learning About Themes in Literature. 287
Model Selection: Themes in Literature. 288

"Prometheus and the First People," Ancient Greek Myth retold by Olivia Coolidge

Writing About the Big Question 289
Literary Analysis: Myths 290
Reading: Generate Questions to Analyze Cultural Context. 291
Vocabulary Builder 292

"The Orphan Boy and the Elk Dog," Native American myth (Blackfeet)

Writing About the Big Question 293
Literary Analysis: Myths 294
Reading: Generate Questions to Analyze Cultural Context. 295
Vocabulary Builder 296

"Prometheus and the First People" and **"The Orphan Boy and the Elk Dog"**

Integrated Language Skills: Grammar 297
Integrated Language Skills: Support for Writing a Myth. 298

from **Sundiata: An Epic of Old Mali** by D. T. Niane

Writing About the Big Question 299
Literary Analysis: Epic and Epic Hero. 300
Reading: Acquire Background Knowledge to Analyze Cultural Context. 301
Vocabulary Builder 302

"Rama's Initiation" *from* **the Ramayana** by R. K. Narayan

Writing About the Big Question 303
Literary Analysis: Epic and Epic Hero 304
Reading: Acquire Background Knowledge to Analyze Cultural Context 305
Vocabulary Builder 306

from **Sundiata: An Epic of Old Mali** and **"Rama's Initiation"**

Integrated Language Skills: Grammar 307
Integrated Language Skills: Support for Writing a Newspaper Report 308

"The Love of Cupid and Psyche" retold by Sally Benson
"Ashputtle" by Jakob and Wilhelm Grimm

Writing About the Big Question 309
Literary Analysis: Archetypal Narrative Patterns 310
Vocabulary Builder 311
Support for Writing to Compare Literary Works 312

"Arthur Becomes King of Britain" *from* **The Once and Future King**
by T. H. White

Writing About the Big Question 313
Literary Analysis: Legends 314
Reading: Identify Details to Compare and Contrast Worldviews 315
Vocabulary Builder 316

"Morte d'Arthur" by Alfred, Lord Tennyson

Writing About the Big Question 317
Literary Analysis: Legends 318
Reading: Identify Details to Compare and Contrast Worldviews 319
Vocabulary Builder 320

"Arthur Becomes King of Britain" and **"Morte d'Arthur"**

Integrated Language Skills: Grammar 321
Integrated Language Skills: Support for Writing a Script for a Television News Report . . 322

from **A Connecticut Yankee in King Arthur's Court** by Mark Twain

Writing About the Big Question 323
Literary Analysis: Parody 324
Reading: Compare and Contrast to Understand Worldviews 325
Vocabulary Builder 326

from **Don Quixote** by Miguel de Cervantes

Writing About the Big Question 327
Literary Analysis: Parody 328
Reading: Compare and Contrast to Understand Worldviews 329
Vocabulary Builder 330

from **A Connecticut Yankee in King Arthur's Court** and *from* **Don Quixote**

    Integrated Language Skills: Grammar 331

    Integrated Language Skills: Support for Writing a Parody 332

"Damon and Pythias" retold by William F. Russell

"Two Friends" by Guy de Maupassant

    Writing About the Big Question 333

    Literary Analysis: Theme and Worldview 334

    Vocabulary Builder 335

    Support for Writing to Compare Literary Works 336

Reading Fluency Practice and Assessment 337

Standardized Test Practice

    Screening Test 351

    Practice Test 1 357

    Practice Test 2 363

    PSAT Practice Test 368

Answer Sheets 381

BQ Tunes

The Difference, performed by The Fake Gimms

Uncertainty. I can't be sure of what you say until I've checked it out.

Evaluate. Look through the facts just to **confirm**,

Prove what really went down.

As I weigh the situation

The **context** becomes clear.

And my **perception** strengthens as I understand

The difference between reality and truth.

Attempt to **discern**, to recognize and clearly see,

Verify and prove the truth.

Look past the lies to what is solid and **concrete**,

The **evidence** and the proof.

As I weigh the situation

The context becomes clear.

And my perception strengthens as I **comprehend**

The difference between reality and . . .

What's the **objective**?

What is your plan?

Don't be so **subjective**.

It can't only be about how you feel.

It's highly unlikely, **improbable** at best,

To **differentiate**.

To know the difference,

The difference between **reality** and truth

Song Title: **The Difference**
Artist / Performed by The Fake Gimms
Vocals & Guitar: Joe Pfeiffer
Guitar: Greg Kuter
Bass Guitar: Jared Duncan
Drums: Tom Morra
Lyrics by the Fake Gimms
Produced by the Fake Gimms
Studio Production: Mike Pandolfo, Wonderful
Executive Producer: Keith London, Defined Mind

Unit 1: Fiction and Nonfiction
Big Question Vocabulary—1

The Big Question: Is there a difference between reality and truth?

In your textbook, you learned words that are useful for talking about reality and truth. In literature as well as in our everyday lives, we sometimes struggle to identify what is real or true, as opposed to what is fictional or false.

DIRECTIONS: *Review the following definitions of words you can use when talking about reality and truth.*

comprehend: to understand the nature or meaning of something

concrete: able to be seen and touched

confirm: to verify the truth, accuracy, or genuineness of something

context: the set of circumstances that surround a particular event or situation

differentiate: to perceive the difference in or between two or more things

A. *Now, for each Big Question vocabulary word, write a synonym, an antonym, and a sentence in which you use the word correctly.*

Word	Synonym	Antonym	Example Sentence
1. comprehend			
2. concrete			
3. confirm			
4. context			
5. differentiate			

B. *Write two to three sentences in which you use three or more of the vocabulary words on this page to write a generalization about reality and truth.*

_____

_____

_____

_____

Name _____ Date _____

Unit 1: Fiction and Nonfiction
Big Question Vocabulary—2

The Big Question: Is there a difference between reality and truth?

DIRECTIONS: *Review the following definitions of words you can use when talking about reality and truth.*

discern: to recognize something as distinct or different

evaluate: to judge or determine the significance, worth, or quality of

evidence: that which tends to prove or disprove something

improbable: not likely

objective: unbiased

Now, decide whether each statement below is true or false, based on the meanings of the underlined vocabulary words. Circle T or F, and then explain any true answers. If a statement is false, rewrite it so that it is true. Do not change the underlined vocabulary words.

1. One can <u>discern</u> the truth of a situation by stating a falsehood.
   T / F _____
   _____

2. To determine whether or not a person's opinion is valid, you should <u>evaluate</u> the facts the person used to reach such a conclusion.
   T / F _____
   _____

3. In a debate, the winning side is usually the one that provides the best <u>evidence</u> to support its arguments.
   T / F _____
   _____

4. The sun rising each morning is completely <u>improbable</u>.
   T / F _____
   _____

5. An <u>objective</u> opinion is one that is based entirely on one's emotions and internal reactions to a situation.
   T / F _____
   _____

Name _____ Date _____

Unit 1: Fiction and Nonfiction
Big Question Vocabulary—3

The Big Question: Is there a difference between reality and truth?

DIRECTIONS: *Review the following definitions of words you can use when talking about reality and truth.*

perception: one's understanding of something, especially as seen through the filter of that person's emotions, experiences, and biases

reality: the state or quality of being real and provable

subjective: existing in the mind and influenced by moods, attitudes, opinions

uncertainty: the state of being in doubt or hesitant

verify: to confirm or prove the truth of something

Now, use the word or words given in parentheses to answer each question.

1. What is truth? **(verify)**

   _____

   _____

2. How can one person see something as a truth while another person does not?
   (perception)

   _____

   _____

3. How might a person's emotions influence his or her opinions on an issue?
   (perception, subjective)

   _____

   _____

4. If you are not sure about what is supposed to be real in a novel you are reading,
   how might you determine it? **(reality, uncertainty)**

   _____

   _____

5. Why is it important to understand the difference between reality and truth?
   (reality, perception, subjective)

   _____

   _____

Name _____ Date _____

Unit 1: Fiction and Nonfiction
Applying the Big Question

The Big Question: Is there a difference between reality and truth?

DIRECTIONS: *Complete the chart below to apply what you have learned about the difference between reality and truth. One row has been completed for you.*

Example	Reality	Truth	Difference Between Reality and Truth	What I Learned
From Literature	The game of hide-and-seek in "Games at Twilight" is just a game and does not really matter.	Winning the game carries a deep life lesson for Ravi about how insignificant he really is.	In reality the game is just a game, but the truth to Ravi is that the game is proof of his place in the world.	A person's perception of reality is often subjective.
From Literature				
From Science				
From Social Studies				
From Real Life				

Susan Vreeland
Listening and Viewing

Segment 1: Meet Susan Vreeland
- How did an ancient glass pitcher inspire Susan Vreeland to write about visual arts? What type of art would you like to write about?

_____

_____

_____

_____

Segment 2: Fiction and Nonfiction
- How did Susan Vreeland's nonfiction writing lead her to writing fiction about art? Why is writing descriptively important in fiction?

_____

_____

_____

_____

Segment 3: The Writing Process
- What does Susan Vreeland look to edit when revising a draft? In what ways do you agree or disagree with Susan Vreeland that revising is the most important part of the writing process?

_____

_____

_____

_____

Segment 4: The Rewards of Writing
- What does Susan Vreeland hope readers can "get out of" reading her stories? What do you think you can learn by reading books about art?

_____

_____

_____

_____

Learning About Fiction and Nonfiction

Literature may be either **fiction** or **nonfiction.** The following chart compares and contrasts these two types of literature.

Characteristics	Fiction	Nonfiction
Overall Features	Fiction is prose that tells a story from the author's imagination. The individuals who take part in the story are **characters.** They experience a series of related events called the **plot.** The plot begins with a **conflict,** or problem; rises to a **climax,** or point of great intensity; and ends with a **resolution,** or conclusion.	Nonfiction is prose that presents information about real people, events, or ideas. The author of a nonfiction work may include opinions or impressions along with facts.
Sample Forms	short stories, novellas, novels	speeches, articles, news reports, essays, biographies
Author's Purpose	to entertain	to persuade, inform, or entertain

DIRECTIONS: *Read each item. Decide whether it is a work of fiction or nonfiction, and then write fiction* or nonfiction *on the line provided.*

_____ 1. a piece of literature that tells how a real-life mystery was solved

_____ 2. a piece of literature that tries to persuade readers to plant trees

_____ 3. a piece of literature about a group of people who travel to another galaxy

_____ 4. a piece of literature that compares American pizza to Italian pizza

_____ 5. a piece of literature about highways in outer space

_____ 6. a piece of literature about an imaginary girl who lived in Spain in the 1600s

_____ 7. a piece of literature that summarizes and reviews a new work of fiction

_____ 8. a piece of literature that states the author's opinions about country music

_____ 9. a piece of literature that tells about two boys who time-travel to the year 3007

_____ 10. a piece of literature that explains how to start your own pet care business

"**Magdalena Looking**" by Susan Vreeland
Model Selection: Fiction

Fiction is prose that tells about individuals and events from the author's imagination. The individuals who take part in the story are **characters.** They experience a series of related events called the **plot.** The plot begins with a **conflict,** or problem; rises to a **climax,** or point of intensity; and ends with a **resolution,** or conclusion. The action takes place at a certain time and location, called the **setting.**

In fiction, the perspective from which a story is told is called **point of view. First-person point of view** is the perspective of a character who participates in the story. **Third-person point of view** is the perspective of a narrator outside the story. A third-person narrator might be **omniscient,** or all-knowing. The narrator might also be **limited,** reporting the perspective of only one character.

The underlying message or insight a story conveys is its **theme.** If a theme applies to all people in all cultures, it is a **universal theme.**

DIRECTIONS: *Read this passage from "Magdalena Looking," and answer the questions that follow.*

In 1696, just after their only living child, Magritte, damp with fever, stopped breathing in her arms, Magdalena read in the *Amsterdamsche Courant* of a public auction of one hundred thirty-four paintings by various artists. "Several outstandingly artful paintings," the notice said, "including twenty-one works most powerfully and splendidly painted by the late J. Vermeer of Delft, will be auctioned May 16, 1:00, at the Oude Heeren Logement." Only a week away. She thought of Hendrick [the baker]. Of course he couldn't be expected to keep those paintings forever. Hers might be there. The possibility kept her awake nights.

1. What is the setting of this passage? _____

2. What event advances the plot in this passage? _____
_____

3. A. Which characters are involved in this passage? _____
_____

   B. How does each character relate to the events that are occurring? _____
_____
_____

4. A. Is this passage told from the first-person, third-person omniscient, or third-person limited point of view? Explain. _____
_____

   B. Why do you think the author uses this point of view? _____
_____

"Artful Research" by Susan Vreeland
Model Selection: Nonfiction

Nonfiction is prose in which an author presents information about real people, events, or ideas. Unlike fiction, which contains invented characters and events, nonfiction can *only* present facts and discuss real-world ideas.

Nonfiction is presented directly by the author, whose **perspective,** or viewpoint, colors the work. Through his or her word choices and details, the author expresses a particular attitude toward the subject and the readers. This attitude is known as **tone.**

Authors of nonfiction works have a definite **purpose for writing.** Some include the following purposes:

- to explain ("How To Juggle")
- to entertain ("Life *IS* Stranger than Fiction")
- to share thoughts and experiences ("Skiing: My Downfall as an Athlete")
- to persuade ("Adopt a Pet!")
- to inform ("Why Glow Worms Glow")

DIRECTIONS: *Answer the following questions about "Artful Research."*

1. Which real people does the author mention? _____
   _____

2. From whose perspective is it told? _____

3. Summarize a real-life experience that the author shares with her readers. _____
   _____
   _____

4. List two facts that the author presents. _____
   _____
   _____

5. List two opinions that the author presents. _____
   _____
   _____

6. What is the author's attitude toward her subject? How do you explain this attitude? ____
   _____

Name _____ Date _____

Writing About the Big Question

Is there a difference between reality and truth?

Big Question Vocabulary

comprehend	concrete	confirm	context	differentiate
discern	evaluate	evidence	improbable	objective
perception	reality	subjective	uncertainty	verify

A. *Use one or more words from the list above to complete each sentence.*

1. It seemed _____ that he could win the race with a broken foot.

2. To _____ between reality and truth, consider facts objectively.

3. Sometimes your _____ of an event can be colored by emotions.

4. His behavior confused me, and I could not _____ his actions.

B. *Follow the directions in responding to each of the items below.*

1. Identify a situation in world events in which the reality of the situation might be different from the truth about the situation.

_____

_____

2. Write two sentences explaining your response in the preceding item. Use at least two of the Big Question vocabulary words.

_____

_____

_____

_____

C. *Complete the sentence below. Then, write a short paragraph in which you connect this experience to the Big Question.*

When people face personal hardship, they often _____.

_____

_____

_____

_____

_____

_____

"The Monkey's Paw" by W. W. Jacobs
Literary Analysis: Plot

A **plot** is the sequence of related events that make up a story. A typical plot concerns a **conflict**—a struggle between opposing forces—and follows a pattern.

- In the **exposition,** the writer gives background information about the characters and the situation.
- During the **rising action,** events occur that intensify the conflict.
- At the **climax,** the tension reaches its highest point because the outcome of the conflict is about to be revealed.
- The tension lessens during the **falling action.**
- The **resolution** is the final outcome of the conflict. The resolution often involves a change or an insight.

Writers use various techniques to add tension to a story. One technique is **foreshadowing**—giving details that hint at coming events. For instance, when a character leaves a door unlocked in her haste, it may foreshadow a later event—a pet getting loose, for example.

In this passage, the character Morris is speaking about a monkey's paw with a spell on it.

If you keep it, don't blame me for what happens.

Here, the author uses foreshadowing to hint at a future event relating to the monkey's paw.

DIRECTIONS: *Identify each passage below as* exposition, rising action, climax, falling action, or resolution. *Then, tell what each passage foreshadows.*

1. "Hark at the wind," said Mr. White, who, having seen a fatal mistake after it was too late, was amiably desirous of preventing his son from seeing it.

    Part of plot: _____ Foreshadows: _____

    _____

2. He wanted to show that fate ruled people's lives, and that those who interfered with it did so to their sorrow. He put a spell on it so that three separate men could each have three wishes from it.

    Part of plot: _____ Foreshadows: _____

    _____

3. "The first man had his three wishes, yes," was the reply; "I don't know what the first two were, but the third was for death."

    Part of plot: _____ Foreshadows: _____

    _____

4. Herbert sat alone in the darkness, gazing at the dying fire, and seeing faces in it. The last face was so horrible and so simian that he gazed at it in amazement.

    Part of plot: _____ Foreshadows: _____

    _____

"The Monkey's Paw" by W. W. Jacobs
Reading: Use Prior Knowledge to Make Predictions

A **prediction** is an idea about what will happen in a story. To make predictions, pay attention to story details and **use your prior knowledge.**

- Your knowledge of plot structure will help you predict that a character will experience difficulties. If you know other stories with similar plots, you might predict that similar things will happen.
- You can also use your prior knowledge of human nature. Think about how people you know react to events. Your insights into their behavior can help you predict how characters will act.

Read the following passage from "The Monkey's Paw."

"I should like to see those old temples and fakirs and jugglers," said the old man. "What was that you started telling me the other day about a monkey's paw or something, Morris?"

"Nothing," said the soldier, hastily. "Leastways nothing worth hearing."

You can use your prior knowledge of the structure of short stories to predict that the monkey's paw will play an important part in this story. The fact that the story's title is "The Monkey's Paw" and the introduction of the paw into conversation are clues to its importance.

DIRECTIONS: *Read each passage from the story. Make a prediction about what will happen based on the clues and your prior knowledge. List one clue and one piece of prior knowledge that helped you make each prediction.*

1. "It had a spell put on it by an old fakir," said the sergeant major, "a very holy man. He wanted to show that fate ruled people's lives, and that those who interfered with it did so to their sorrow."

   Prediction: _____

   Clue: _____

   Prior knowledge: _____

2. A fine crash from the piano greeted the words, interrupted by a shuddering from the old man. His wife and son ran toward him.

   "It moved," he cried with a glance of disgust at the object as it lay on the floor. "As I wished it twisted in my hand like a snake."

   Prediction: _____

   Clue: _____

   Prior knowledge: _____

3. "The paw!" she cried wildly. "The monkey's paw!"

   He started up in alarm. "Where? Where is it? What's the matter?"

   She came stumbling across the room toward him. "I want it," she said quietly.

   Prediction: _____

   Clue: _____

   Prior knowledge: _____

"The Monkey's Paw" by W. W. Jacobs
Vocabulary Builder

Word List

apathy   credulity   furtively   grave   maligned   oppressive

A. DIRECTIONS: *Think about the meaning of each italicized word. Then, answer the question.*

1. If you saw someone moving *furtively* around your home, what should you do?

   _____

2. If a new movie was *maligned* by a critic, would you want to see it? Why or why not?

   _____

3. If voters had *apathy* toward a political candidate, what do you think would happen in the election?

4. If a coach had a *grave* expression at the end of a game, did the team win or lose? Explain.

   _____

5. Will your *credulity* cause you to question every claim made by a politician?

   _____

6. If an employer's work load is *oppressive*, how does that person probably feel about the job?

   _____

B. WORD STUDY: The Latin root *-cred-* means "believe." Answer the following questions using one of these words that contain the root *-cred-*: *credence, credo, discredit.*

1. Would you have *credence* in a report presented by someone known for giving false information?

2. If your *credo* is "Live and Let Live," are you a tolerant person?

3. Why would you be unhappy if someone tried to *discredit* your results on a test?

Name _____ Date _____

"The Leap" by Louise Erdrich
Writing About the Big Question

Is there a difference between reality and truth?

Big Question Vocabulary

comprehend	concrete	confirm	context	differentiate
discern	evaluate	evidence	improbable	objective
perception	reality	subjective	uncertainty	verify

A. *Use one or more words from the list above to complete each sentence.*

1. The events surrounding the election gave us a _____ in which to consider her remarks.

2. It is sometimes difficult to take a(n) _____ view of someone you know well.

3. Your personal feelings about your loved ones often lead to a _____ view of their actions.

B. *Follow the directions in responding to each of the items below.*

1. List a time when you learned that the reality you knew about a person was not the same as the truth about that person.

   _____

   _____

2. Write two sentences explaining your response in the preceding item. Use at least two of the Big Question vocabulary words.

   _____

   _____

   _____

   _____

C. *Complete the sentence below. Then, write a short paragraph in which you connect this situation to the Big Question.*

The choices people make can have a variety of effects on _____

_____

_____

_____

_____

_____

"The Leap" by Louise Erdrich
Literary Analysis: Plot

A **plot** is the sequence of related events that make up a story. A typical plot concerns a **conflict**—a struggle between opposing forces—and follows a pattern.

- In the **exposition,** the writer gives information about the characters and the situation.
- During the **rising action,** events occur that intensify the conflict.
- At the **climax,** the tension reaches its highest point because the outcome of the conflict is about to be revealed.
- The tension lessens during the **falling action.**
- The **resolution** is the final outcome of the conflict. It often involves a change or an insight.

Writers use various techniques to add tension to a story. One technique is **foreshadowing**—giving details that hint at coming events. For instance, when a character leaves a door unlocked in her haste, it may foreshadow a later event—a pet getting loose, for example.

Read the following passage from "The Leap."

> When extremes of temperature collide, a hot and cold front, winds generate instantaneously behind a hill and crash upon you without warning.

Here, the author uses foreshadowing to hint at an event caused by weather later in the story.

DIRECTIONS: *Identify each passage below as* exposition, rising action, climax, falling action, *or* resolution. *Then, tell what each passage foreshadows.*

1. I would, in fact, tend to think that all memory of double somersaults and heart-stopping catches had left her arms and legs were it not for the fact that sometimes, as I sit sewing in the room of the rebuilt house where I slept as a child, I hear the crackle, catch a whiff of smoke from the stove downstairs, and suddenly the room goes dark, the stitches burn beneath my fingers, and I am sewing with a needle of hot silver, a thread of fire.

   Part of plot: _____   Foreshadows: _____

   _____

2. My mother once said that I'd be amazed at how many things a person can do within the act of falling.

   Part of plot: _____   Foreshadows: _____

   _____

3. That is the debt we take for granted since none of us asks for life. It is only once we have it that we hang on so dearly.

   Part of plot: _____   Foreshadows: _____

   _____

4. She has never upset an object or as much as brushed a magazine onto the floor. She has never lost her balance or bumped into a closet door left carelessly open.

   Part of plot: _____   Foreshadows: _____

   _____

"**The Leap**" by Louise Erdrich
Reading: Use Prior Knowledge to Make Predictions

A **prediction** is an idea about what will happen in a story. To make predictions, pay attention to story details and **use your prior knowledge.**

- Your knowledge of plot structure will help you predict that a character will experience difficulties. If you know other stories with similar plots, you might predict that similar things will happen.
- You can also use your prior knowledge of human nature. Think about how people you know react to events. Your insights into their behavior can help you predict how characters will act.

Read the following passage from "The Leap."

My mother is the surviving half of a blindfold trapeze act, not a fact I think about much even now that she is sightless, the result of encroaching and stubborn cataracts.

You can use your prior knowledge of the structure of short stories to predict that the story will tell about the death of the other half of the trapeze act.

DIRECTIONS: *Read each passage from the story. Make a prediction about what will happen based on the clues and your prior knowledge. List one clue and one piece of prior knowledge that helped you make each prediction.*

1. In one news account it says, "The day was mildly overcast, but nothing in the air or temperature gave any hint of the sudden force with which the deadly gale would strike."

   Prediction: _____

   Clue: _____

   Prior knowledge: _____

   _____

2. In the town square a replica tent pole, cracked and splintered, now stands cast in concrete.

   Prediction: _____

   Clue: _____

   Prior knowledge: _____

   _____

3. Outside, my mother stood below my dark window and saw clearly that there was no rescue.

   Prediction: _____

   Clue: _____

   Prior knowledge: _____

   _____

"The Leap" by Louise Erdrich
Vocabulary Builder

Word List

commemorates   constricting   encroaching   extricating   perpetually   tentative

A. DIRECTIONS: *Think about the meaning of each italicized word. Then, answer the question.*

1. If night is *encroaching* on daylight, what will happen in the next few minutes?

   _____

2. If a person takes a *tentative* step onto a diving board, what is he or she probably feeling?

   _____

3. If firefighters are involved in *extricating* people from a building, what are they doing?

   _____

4. If a statue in your city *commemorates* fire fighters, is it a serious or funny piece of art?

   _____

5. Would someone who *perpetually* trips be a good choice to carry trays of dishes?

   _____

B. WORD STUDY: The Latin root -*strict*- means "confine" or "squeeze." Answer the following questions using one of these words that contain the root -*strict*-: *district, restrict, stricture.*

1. If you won the spelling bee for your *district*, did you compete against students from across the country?

   _____

2. If you *restrict* your diet to apples, what are you eating?

   _____

3. When a team receives a *stricture* from the referee, should the team be worried?

   _____

"The Monkey's Paw" by W. W. Jacobs
"The Leap" by Louise Erdrich
Integrated Language Skills: Grammar

Common and Proper Nouns

A **common noun** is a general name for any one of a group of people, places, or things. A **proper noun** names a particular person, place, or thing. A proper noun always begins with a capital letter.

Examples

Common Nouns: student, teacher, country, skyscraper, book

Proper Nouns: Will Fordham, Ms. Ruiz, Japan, Empire State Building, *The Outsiders*

A. DIRECTIONS: *In each of the following sentences from the selections, identify the underlined nouns as common or proper. For each common noun, name a proper noun that could take its place. For each proper noun, name a common noun that could take its place.*

1. Mrs. White drew back with a grimace.

   Type of noun: _____

   Substitute noun: _____

2. The soldier regarded him in the way that middle age is wont to regard presumptuous youth.

   Type of noun: _____

   Substitute noun: _____

3. "I was to say that Maw and Meggins disclaim all responsibility," continued the other.

   Type of noun: _____

   Substitute noun: _____

4. "You're afraid of your own son," she cried, struggling.

   Type of noun: _____

   Substitute noun: _____

B. DIRECTIONS: *Rewrite each of the following sentences by correcting any errors in capitalization. Make sure that proper nouns are capitalized.*

1. The narrator's Mother was one-half of a blindfolded Trapeze Act.

   _____

2. Mr. and mrs. white are horrified by the outcome of their Wishes.

   _____

3. Louise erdrich writes about a definitive moment in Her own life.

   _____

4. The Monkey's Paw brings bad luck to anyone who uses it.

   _____

"The Monkey's Paw" by W. W. Jacobs
"The Leap" by Louise Erdrich

Integrated Language Skills: Support for Writing a Sequel

Use the following flowchart to write the plot details for a sequel to the story you read.

Exposition:

↓

Rising Action:

↓

Climax:

↓

Falling Action:

↓

Resolution:

Now, use the details from your flowchart to write a sequel to "The Monkey's Paw" or "The Leap."

from **Swimming to Antarctica** by Lynne Cox

Writing About the Big Question

Is there a difference between reality and truth?

Big Question Vocabulary

comprehend	concrete	confirm	context	differentiate
discern	evaluate	evidence	improbable	objective
perception	reality	subjective	uncertainty	verify

A. *Use one or more words from the list above to complete each sentence.*

1. _____ facts should be easy to believe, but they can obscure the truth.

2. Your physical senses can help you _____ what you *think* you know.

3. Facing _____ can make you doubt what is real.

4. People must face challenges in order to _____ the truth about what they can really do.

B. *Follow the directions in responding to each of the items below.*

1. List two different times when you learned the truth about what you could accomplish.

   _____

   _____

2. Write two sentences explaining one of the experiences you listed in your response, and describe the results. Use at least two of the Big Question vocabulary words.

   _____

   _____

   _____

   _____

C. *Complete the sentence below. Then, write a short paragraph in which you connect this situation to the Big Question.*

People often learn deep truths about themselves when facing _____

   _____.

   _____

   _____

from **Swimming to Antarctica** by Lynne Cox
Literary Analysis: Author's Perspective

The **author's perspective** in a literary work includes the judgments, attitudes, and experiences the author brings to the subject.

- An author's perspective determines which details he or she includes. For example, a writer with firsthand experience of an event might report his or her own reactions as well as generally known facts. A writer with a positive view of a subject may emphasize its benefits.
- A work may combine several perspectives. For example, a writer may tell what it felt like to live through an event. In addition, the writer may express his or her present views of the experience.

In the following passage from *Swimming to Antarctica*, Lynne Cox states facts about her test swim in cold water and expresses her reactions to it.

I had mixed feelings about the test swim. In some ways, it had given me confidence; I now knew that I could swim for twenty-two minutes in thirty-three-degree water. But it had also made me feel uncertain.

DIRECTIONS: *For each of the following passages, write what facts the writer includes. Then, write the author's reactions.*

1. When I hit the water, I went all the way under. I hadn't intended to do that; I hadn't wanted to immerse my head, which could over-stimulate my vagus nerve and cause my heart to stop beating. Dog-paddling as quickly as I could, I popped up in the water, gasping for air. I couldn't catch my breath. I was swimming with my head up, hyperventilating. I kept spinning my arms, trying to get warm, but I couldn't get enough air. I felt like I had a corset tightening around my chest. I told myself to relax, take a deep breath, but I couldn't slow my breath.

Facts	Author's Reactions

2. I put my head down, and something suddenly clicked. Maybe it was because I knew shore was within reach, or maybe because I got a second wind; I don't know. But I was finally swimming strongly, stretching out and moving fluidly. My arms and legs were as cold as the sea, but I felt the heat within my head and contained in my torso and thrilled to it, knowing my body had carried me to places no one else had been in only a bathing suit.

Facts	Author's Reactions

All-in-One Workbook

from **Swimming to Antarctica** by Lynne Cox
Reading: Use Prior Knowledge to Make Predictions

As you read, **make predictions,** or educated guesses, about what will happen next based on your own experience and details in a text. **Verify,** or confirm, predictions by comparing the outcome you predicted to the actual outcome. **Revise,** or adjust, your predictions as you gather more information.

- **Strategy:** To help you make, verify, and revise predictions, **ask questions,** such as *Will the main character succeed?*
- For each question you ask, record your predictions and how they change with new information.

Read the following passage from the excerpt from *Swimming to Antarctica.*

The water temperature on the big swim would be a degree colder. Thirty-two degrees. That was a magic number, the temperature at which freshwater froze. I wondered if in thirty-two-degree water the water in my cells would freeze, if my body's tissues would become permanently damaged.

You can make a prediction about the rest of the selection by asking yourself a question such as this: *Will the one-degree difference make the swim impossible?*

DIRECTIONS: *Make a prediction about each of the following passages from the text. Write the details from the text and from your own experiences that helped you make your prediction.*

1. Dr. Block caught me at the top of the stairs, just before we stepped out the door and onto the ramp, and asked if I would sit down on a step so he could trace two veins on my hands with a blue Magic Marker. It was just a precaution, he said, in case I needed emergency assistance. . . . Why did he have to do this now, right before I swam? Didn't he realize this kind of stuff psyches people out?

   Predict: Will the author be psyched out by the doctor's action? _____

   _____

   Details from the text that support my prediction: _____

   _____

   My own experiences that support my prediction: _____

   _____

2. An icy wave slapped my face: I choked and felt a wave of panic rise within me. My throat tightened. I tried to clear my throat and breathe. My breath didn't come out. I couldn't get enough air in to clear my throat. I glanced at the crew. They couldn't tell I was in trouble. If I stopped, Dan would jump in and pull me out.

   Predict: Will the author stop swimming? _____

   Details from the text that support my prediction: _____

   _____

   My own experiences that support my prediction: _____

   _____

from **Swimming to Antarctica** by Lynne Cox
Vocabulary Builder

Word List

abruptly   buffer   equilibrium   gauge   prolonged   venturing

A. DIRECTIONS: *Think about the meaning of each italicized word. Then, answer the question.*

1. If someone endures *prolonged* exposure to the sun, what will probably happen to him or her?

   _____

2. If a dancer loses her *equilibrium* during a recital, what might happen?

   _____

3. If a friend uses you to *buffer* himself from a group of other people, how does he probably feel about the other people?

   _____

4. If your sister *abruptly* hung up the telephone during a conversation, how does she probably feel?

   _____

5. If you want to *gauge* the warmth of a body of water, what should you do?

   _____

B. WORD STUDY: The Latin prefix *pro-* means "forth" or "forward." Answer each of the following questions using one of these words containing *pro-*: *pronounce, profess, project.*

1. What are you doing if you *pronounce* your name? _____

   _____

2. If you *profess* your support for your local animal shelter, do you support it? _____

   _____

3. When actors *project* their voices, do they whisper? _____

   _____

"Occupation: Conductorette" *from* **I Know Why the Caged Bird Sings** by Maya Angleou
Writing About the Big Question

Is there a difference between reality and truth?

Big Question Vocabulary

comprehend	concrete	confirm	context	differentiate
discern	evaluate	evidence	improbable	objective
perception	reality	subjective	uncertainty	verify

A. *Use one or more words from the list above to complete each sentence.*

1. When she finally stood at the podium, the _____ of the event was so overwhelming she lost her voice.

2. Discrimination is so puzzling that it is difficult to _____.

3. Sometimes people will not face the truth even when presented with _____ facts.

B. *Follow the directions in responding to each of the items below.*

1. List two different times when you encountered an unexpected and harsh reality.

   _____

   _____

   _____

   _____

2. Write two sentences explaining one of the experiences you listed in your response, and describe how you felt. Use at least two of the Big Question vocabulary words.

   _____

   _____

   _____

   _____

C. *Complete the sentence below. Then, write a short paragraph in which you connect this experience to the Big Question.*

People who see the truth behind problems in society must decide whether to

   _____

   _____

   _____

   _____

"Occupation: Conductorette" from I Know Why the Caged Bird Sings by Maya Angelou

Literary Analysis: Author's Perspective

The **author's perspective** in a literary work includes the judgments, attitudes, and experiences the author brings to the subject.

- An author's perspective determines which details he or she includes. For example, a writer with firsthand experience of an event might report his or her own reactions as well as generally known facts. A writer with a positive view of a subject may emphasize its benefits.
- A work may combine several perspectives. For example, a writer may tell what it felt like to live through an event. In addition, the writer may express his or her present views of the experience.

In the following passage from "Occupation: Conductorette," Maya Angelou recalls her reaction to being told that African Americans could not work on streetcars.

> I would like to claim an immediate fury which was followed by the noble determination to break the restricting tradition. But the truth is, my first reaction was one of disappointment.

The author tells how she reacted at the time of the incident, and she also expresses her current attitude about the event.

DIRECTIONS: *For each of the following passages, write the author's reactions to the incident at the time and her present-day attitude toward the event.*

1. The next three weeks were a honeycomb of determination with apertures for the days to go in and out. The Negro organizations to whom I appealed for support bounced me back and forth like a shuttlecock on a badminton court. Why did I insist on that particular job? Openings were going begging that paid nearly twice the money. The minor officials with whom I was able to win an audience thought me mad. Possibly I was.

Author's Reaction at the Time	Author's Attitude Today

2. "I am applying for the job listed in this morning's *Chronicle* and I'd like to be presented to your personnel manager." While I spoke in supercilious accents, and looked at the room as if I had an oil well in my own backyard, my armpits were being pricked by millions of hot pointed needles.

Author's Reaction at the Time	Author's Attitude Today

Name _____ Date _____

"Occupation: Conductorette" from I Know Why the Caged Bird Sings by Maya Angelou
Reading: Use Prior Knowledge to Make Predictions

As you read, **make predictions,** or educated guesses, about what will happen next based on your own experience and details in a text. **Verify,** or confirm, predictions by comparing the outcome you predicted to the actual outcome. **Revise,** or adjust, your predictions as you gather more information.

- **Strategy:** To help you make, verify, and revise predictions, **ask questions,** such as *Will the main character succeed?*
- For each question you ask, record your predictions and how they change with new information.

Read the following passage from "Occupation: Conductorette."

In the offices of the Market Street Railway Company, the receptionist seemed as surprised to see me there as I was surprised to find the interior dingy and the décor drab. Somehow I had expected waxed surfaces and carpeted floors. If I had met no resistance, I might have decided against working for such a poor-mouth-looking concern.

You can make a prediction about the rest of the selection by asking yourself a question such as this: *Will the receptionist make it impossible for the author to get a job?*

DIRECTIONS: *Make a prediction about each of the following passages from the text. Write the details from the text and from your own experiences that helped you make your prediction.*

1. I wouldn't move into the streetcar but stood on the ledge over the conductor, glaring. My mind shouted so energetically that the announcement made my veins stand out, and my mouth tighten into a prune.

   I WOULD HAVE THE JOB. I WOULD BE A CONDUCTORETTE.

   Predict: Will the author keep trying to get the job? _____

   _____

   Details from the text that support my prediction: _____

   _____

   My own experiences that support my prediction: _____

   _____

2. On my way out of the house one morning she said, "Life is going to give you just what you put in it. Put your whole heart in everything you do, and pray, then you can wait." Another time she reminded me that "God helps those who help themselves."

   Predict: Will the author take her mother's advice? _____

   _____

   Details from the text that support my prediction: _____

   _____

   My own experiences that support my prediction: _____

   _____

Name _____ Date _____

"Occupation: Conductorette" from I Know Why the Caged Bird Sings by Maya Angelou
Vocabulary Builder

Word List

dexterous   dingy   hypocrisy   indignation   self-sufficiency   supercilious

A. DIRECTIONS: *Think about the meaning of each italicized word. Then, answer the question.*

1. If a friend wants to prove her *self-sufficiency* to you, what will she probably say when you offer to help her?

   _____

2. If an actor has a *supercilious* attitude during an interview, what might the interviewer write about him?

   _____

3. What needs to be done to a room that is *dingy*?

   _____

4. If someone's remarks cause you to feel *indignation*, what might that person have said?

   _____

5. What could a vegetarian do that would reveal his or her *hypocrisy*?

   _____

6. Your friend is very *dexterous* in language arts, so what does she probably like to do?

   _____

B. WORD STUDY: The Latin prefix *super-* means "above." Provide an explanation for your answer to each question containing a word with the prefix *super-*: *superfluous, supersede, superscript*

1. If you have *superfluous* paper in your backpack, do you need to save it?

   _____

2. If you want a new piece of your artwork to *supercede* the picture on the wall, what will you do?

   _____

3. When you write a *superscript* on a journal entry, what have you done?

   _____

from **Swimming to Antarctica** by Lynne Cox
"Occupation: Conductorette" *from* **I Know Why the Caged Bird Sings** by Maya Angelou
Integrate Language Skills: Grammar

Concrete and Abstract Nouns

A **concrete** noun is a word that names a specific person, place, or thing that can be seen or recognized through any of the five senses. An **abstract noun** is a word that names an idea, an action, a condition, or a quality that cannot be seen, heard, smelled, tasted, or touched. The following are examples of concrete and abstract nouns.

Concrete nouns: desk, window, hallway, Tom, closet, wife, Times Square
Abstract nouns: tomorrow, conscience, deceit, intention, fear

A. DIRECTIONS: *Read the following sentences from the excerpt from* Swimming to Antarctica *and from "Occupation Conductorette." Underline the nouns. Write* **C** *above each concrete noun and* **A** *above each abstract noun.*

1. I had mixed feelings about the test swim.

2. I stared across the icy water at Neko Harbor's beach and felt excitement building within me.

3. She comprehended the perversity of life, that in the struggle lies the joy.

4. I choked and felt a wave of panic rise within me.

5. The next three weeks were a honeycomb of determination with apertures for the days to go in and out.

B. Writing Application: *Write a brief paragraph in which you summarize Lynne Cox's swim. Use a combination of abstract and concrete nouns, including at least four of the following words:* cold, water, exhaustion, penguins, excitement, beach.

_____

_____

_____

_____

_____

_____

Name _____   Date _____

from **Swimming to Antarctica** by Lynne Cox
"Occupation: Conductorette" from **I Know Why the Caged Bird Sings** by Maya Angelou
Integrated Language Skills: Support for Writing a Description

DIRECTIONS: *A description should appeal to the senses. Fill in the following chart with details you might observe in Antarctica or on a streetcar in the 1940s that appeal to each of the five senses. Use precise words.*

Details I Might See	
Details I Might Smell	
Details I Might Hear	
Details I Might Touch	
Details I Might Taste	

Now, use the details you have collected to write your description.

"Marian Anderson, Famous Concert Singer" by Langston Hughes
"Tepeyac" by Sandra Cisneros

Writing About the Big Question

Is there a difference between reality and truth?

Big Question Vocabulary

comprehend	concrete	confirm	context	differentiate
discern	evaluate	evidence	improbable	objective
perception	reality	subjective	uncertainty	verify

A. *Circle the word or phrase that is closer in meaning to the underlined word.*

1. **evaluate:** judge; increase

2. **verify:** to make real; to prove

3. **discern:** to see something concealed; to reject

4. **comprehend:** to capture; to understand

5. **uncertainty:** being in doubt; unaltered

B. *Follow the directions in responding to each of the items below.*

1. Describe a memory from childhood that you believed was real until you later found out it was not a true memory.

   _____

   _____

   _____

   _____

2. In one or two sentences, explain how the memory you described above was different from the truth.

   _____

   _____

   _____

   _____

C. *Complete the sentence below. Then, write a short paragraph in which you connect this experience to the Big Question.*

   One person's idea of the truth can be challenged when _____

   _____

   _____

   _____

All-in-One Workbook
30

"Marian Anderson, Famous Concert Singer" by Langston Hughes
"Tepeyac" by Sandra Cisneros
Literary Analysis: Style

A writer's **style** consists of the features that make his or her expression of ideas distinctive. Writers may write on the same topic, or even tell the same story, in very different styles. Two important elements of style are diction and syntax.

Diction, or word choice, is the type of words the writer uses. One writer might like to use everyday words, while another might prefer scholarly ones. In "Marian Anderson," for example, Langston Hughes writes that the singer *broke* her ankle rather than *fractured* it. This word choice reflects the author's straightforward style.

Syntax is the way an author arranges words into sentences. A single sentence might express one distinct thought, or it might express several related ones. In "Tepeyac," Cisneros weaves words and phrases together to form rich, rolling sentences that overflow with ideas and images.

A. DIRECTIONS: *Read each of the following passages. Then, answer the questions.*

from "Tepeyac" by Sandra Cisneros

Green iron gates that arabesque and scroll like the initials of my name, familiar whine and clang, familiar lacework of ivy growing over and between except for one small clean square for the hand of the postman whose face I have never seen, up the twenty-two steps we count out loud together— *uno, dos, tres*—to the supper of *sopa de fideo* and *carne guisada*. . . .

from "Marian Anderson, Famous Concert Singer" by Langston Hughes

Marian Anderson's mother was a staunch church worker who loved to croon the hymns of her faith about the house, as did the aunt who came to live with them when Marian's father died. Both parents were from Virginia. Marian's mother had been a schoolteacher there, and her father a farm boy.

1. A. Which author's style is more direct and down-to-earth? _____

   B. Identify two words in the passage that contribute to this style. _____

   _____

2. A. Which author's style is more descriptive and poetic? _____

   B. Identify two words in the passage that contribute to this style. _____

   _____

   _____

3. Compare the kinds of sentences each author uses. Consider sentence length and the number of ideas expressed in each sentence. _____

   _____

   _____

B. DIRECTIONS: *A writer's style can be affected by his or her **purpose,** or reason for writing. Choose one of the works in this pair. On a separate sheet of paper, state one purpose the author might have had for writing the work. Explain how this purpose influenced the author's style.*

"Marian Anderson, Famous Concert Singer" by Langston Hughes
"Tepeyac" by Sandra Cisneros

Vocabulary Builder

Word List

canopied	debut	dimpled	irretrievable
lucrative	repertoire	staunch	

A. DIRECTIONS: *Complete each sentence so that it makes sense.*

1. Isabel received two job offers. She decided to accept the more *lucrative* one because

   _____

2. I am glad our patio is *canopied* because _____

   _____

3. The toddler's *repertoire* consisted of _____

   _____

4. The *irretrievable* balloon _____

   _____

5. A *staunch* fan of the football team, Jackson _____

   _____

6. An hour before her *debut*, Ava felt _____ because _____

   _____

7. My little brother's face becomes *dimpled* when he_____

   _____

B. DIRECTIONS: *Circle the letter of the word or phrase closest in meaning to the vocabulary word.*

1. canopied
   A. folded   B. shredded   C. covered   D. decorated
2. staunch
   A. firm   B. hostile   C. disappointed   D. cheerful
3. repertoire
   A. old clothes   B. small books   C. odd beliefs   D. ready songs
4. irretrievable
   A. unclear   B. lost   C. astonishing   D. careful

"Marian Anderson, Famous Concert Singer" by Langston Hughes
"Tepeyac" by Sandra Cisneros
Support for Writing to Compare Literary Works

Before you draft your essay evaluating the effectiveness of each author's style, complete the following graphic organizer.

Cisneros's Purpose:

_____

Examples of Style Elements That Help Achieve Purpose

Diction:

Syntax:

Examples of Style Elements That Get in the Way

Diction:

Syntax:

Hughes's Purpose:

_____

Examples of Style Elements That Help Achieve Purpose

Diction:

Syntax:

Examples of Style Elements That Get in the Way

Diction:

Syntax:

Now, use your notes to write an essay that evaluates how well each author's style advances his or her purpose.

Name _____ Date _____

"Contents of the Dead Man's Pocket" by Jack Finney

Writing About the Big Question

Is there a difference between reality and truth?

Big Question Vocabulary

comprehend	concrete	confirm	context	differentiate
discern	evaluate	evidence	improbable	objective
perception	reality	subjective	uncertainty	verify

A. *Write the word from the list above that best fits each definition.*

1. the part of a passage, in which a word is used, that defines that word's meaning _____

2. to detect or see something that is concealed _____

3. to see or show the difference between two or more things _____

4. not based on emotion or prejudice _____

5. personal, or taking place within an individual's mind _____

B. *Follow the directions in responding to each of the items below.*

1. Write one or two sentences describing a time or an event in people's lives that might make them look at the reality about themselves and change their perception about what is really important.

   _____

   _____

   _____

2. Write a sentence describing how the perceptions or attitudes of people you described above might have changed. Use one or two Big Question vocabulary words.

   _____

   _____

   _____

C. *Complete the sentence below. Then, write a short paragraph in which you connect this experience to the Big Question.*

   The most important thing in life is _____

   _____

   _____

   _____

"Contents of the Dead Man's Pocket" by Jack Finney
Literary Analysis: Conflict and Resolution

Conflict is the struggle between two forces. In an **external conflict,** a character struggles against an outside force, such as an element of nature or another character. In an **internal conflict,** a character struggles with his or her own opposing desires, beliefs, or needs. A **resolution** occurs when the conflict is settled or resolved.

Writers use **suspense,** a rising curiosity or anxiety in readers, to build interest in a conflict. To accomplish this, writers may hint at events to come or "stretch out" action that leads up to an important moment in the story.

A. DIRECTIONS: *Answer the following questions about conflict and suspense in "Contents of the Dead Man's Pocket."*

1. Both internal conflict and external conflict are present in "Contents of the Dead Man's Pocket." Find one sentence in the story that shows internal conflict and one that shows external conflict and write them on the following lines.

   Internal conflict: _____

   _____

   External conflict: _____

   _____

2. If Finney had chosen to focus only on the external conflict and had not included internal conflict at all, how would the story have been affected? _____

   _____

   _____

3. How does the title "Contents of the Dead Man's Pocket" contribute to the story's suspense?

   _____

   _____

B. DIRECTIONS: *Write a brief alternative ending for "Contents of the Dead Man's Pocket" in which Tom Benecke's internal conflict is resolved differently than it was in Finney's version.*

_____

_____

_____

_____

_____

_____

_____

_____

"Contents of the Dead Man's Pocket" by Jack Finney

Reading: Reflect on Key Details to Analyze Cause and Effect

A **cause** is an event, an action, or a situation that produces a result. An **effect** is the result produced. To better follow a story, **analyze causes and effects** as you read, determining which earlier events lead to which later events. To analyze causes and effects, **reflect on key details**, details that the writer spends time explaining or describing.

Example of a cause-and-effect sequence from "Contents of the Dead Man's Pocket":

Cause: As he picks up the paper, Tom looks down between his legs and sees the street far below.

Effect 1:   He instantly becomes terrified and loses his deftness.

Effect 2:   The trip back to the window is much more difficult than the trip to the paper had been.

A. DIRECTIONS: *Complete the following organizer by filling in the boxes with the events that resulted from Tom Benecke's decision to go out on the ledge.*

Cause

Tom decides to go out on the ledge to get the yellow paper.

⬇

Effect 1

⬇

Effect 2

⬇

Effect 3

B. DIRECTIONS: *Describe three future effects that may result from Tom's realizations about his wife and his job at the end of the story.*

_____

_____

_____

_____

_____

_____

_____

_____

_____

"Contents of the Dead Man's Pocket" by Jack Finney
Vocabulary Builder

Word List

convoluted   deftness   imperceptibly   interminable   reveling   verified

A. DIRECTIONS: *For each of the following items, think about the meaning of the italicized word, and then answer the question in a complete sentence.*

1. Which is more likely to be *convoluted:* a pebble or a seashell? Why?

   _____

2. If a factory worker completes her tasks with *deftness*, how do you think her supervisor feels about her work?

   _____

3. What is an example of something that happens *imperceptibly*?

   _____

4. If your wait in a doctor's reception area is *interminable*, was the doctor prompt in seeing you? Why or why not?

   _____

5. Why is it important that your identity be *verified* when you are cashing a check?

   _____

6. Do you think you would be *reveling* if you received a perfect score on a test? Why or why not?

   _____

B. WORD STUDY: The Latin root *-ver-* means true. Define each word showing how *-ver-* contributes to the meaning.

1. **verity:**

   _____

2. **veracious:**

   _____

3. **very:**

   _____

Name _____ Date _____

"Games at Twilight" by Anita Desai

Writing About the Big Question

Is there a difference between reality and truth?

Big Question Vocabulary

comprehend	concrete	confirm	context	differentiate
discern	evaluate	evidence	improbable	objective
perception	reality	subjective	uncertainty	verify

A. *Write the word from the list above that best completes each sentence.*

1. Ravi felt it was _____ that he would be found in his hiding place.

2. He had feelings of _____ while waiting to be found.

3. Ravi could not _____ that he could be so easily forgotten.

4. In the dim twilight, it was difficult to _____ the faces of the children.

5. Ravi looked for some _____ in their faces that they were glad to see him.

B. *Follow the directions in responding to each of the items below.*

1. Write two sentences describing two ways in which a person might not see the reality of his or her own limitations.

   _____

   _____

2. In one or two sentences, describe a situation in which the person described above might learn the truth about himself or herself. Use one or two Big Question vocabulary words.

   _____

   _____

C. *Complete the sentence below. Then, write a short paragraph in which you connect this situation to the Big Question.*

You can tell how people really see you when _____

_____

_____

_____

_____

_____

All-in-One Workbook

"Games at Twilight" by Anita Desai
Literary Analysis: Conflict and Resolution

Conflict is the struggle between two forces. In an **external conflict,** a character struggles against an outside force, such as an element of nature or another character. In an **internal conflict,** a character struggles with his or her own opposing desires, beliefs, or needs. A **resolution** occurs when the conflict is settled or resolved.

Writers use **suspense,** a rising curiosity or anxiety in readers, to build interest in a conflict. To accomplish this, writers may hint at events to come or "stretch out" action that leads up to an important moment in the story.

A. DIRECTIONS: *Answer the following questions about conflict and suspense in "Games at Twilight."*

1. Both an internal and an external conflict are present in "Games at Twilight." Find one sentence in the story that shows internal conflict and one that shows external conflict and write them on the following lines.

   Internal conflict: _____

   _____

   External conflict: _____

   _____

2. If Desai had chosen to focus only on the external conflict and had not included internal conflict at all, how would the story have been affected? _____

   _____

   _____

3. Identify a moment of great suspense in the story. How does this suspenseful moment help to build your interest in the conflict? _____

   _____

   _____

B. DIRECTIONS: *Write a brief alternative ending for "Games at Twilight" in which Ravi's internal conflict is resolved differently than it was in Desai's version.*

_____

_____

_____

_____

_____

_____

_____

_____

Name _____ Date _____

Reading: Reflect on Key Details to Analyze Cause and Effect

A **cause** is an event, an action, or a situation that produces a result. An **effect** is the result produced. To better follow a story, **analyze causes and effects** as you read, determining which earlier events lead to which later events. To analyze causes and effects, **reflect on key details,** details that the writer spends time explaining or describing.

Example of a cause-and-effect sequence from "Games at Twilight":

Cause: Ravi hides in the shed to escape Raghu.

Effect 1:   Raghu does not find him and moves away.

Effect 2:   Ravi is encouraged by Raghu's inability to find him and becomes excited about the idea of winning the game.

A. DIRECTIONS: *Complete the organizer by filling in the boxes with the events that resulted from Ravi's decision to run to the "den" to win the game.*

Cause	Ravi runs to the veranda in tears.

↓

Effect 1	

↓

Effect 2	

↓

Effect 3	

B. DIRECTIONS: *Describe three possible future effects that may result from Ravi's new awareness of his own insignificance.*

_____

_____

_____

_____

_____

_____

"Games at Twilight" by Anita Desai
Vocabulary Builder

Word List

defunct   dejectedly   dogged   elude   intervened   livid

A. DIRECTIONS: *For each of the following items, think about the meaning of the italicized word, and then answer the question.*

1. If Sara's father's face becomes *livid* upon seeing her report card, what kind of grades do you think she made?

_____

2. What should you do with a *defunct* television?

_____

3. If Gilberto runs a marathon in a *dogged* way, is he likely to finish the course? Why or why not?

_____

4. What might you do if your best friend is behaving *dejectedly*?

_____

5. If your parent *intervened* in an argument between you and your sister, how would you feel? Why?

_____

6. Why might a person try to *elude* someone?

_____

B. WORD STUDY: The Latin root *-ven-* means "come" or "go." Define each word showing how *-ven-* contributes to the meaning.

1. **convent:**

_____

2. **ventilate:**

_____

3. **convene:**

_____

Name _____ Date _____

"Contents of the Dead Man's Pocket" by Jack Finney
"Games at Twilight" by Anita Desai
Integrated Language Skills: Grammar

Personal Pronouns

A **pronoun** is a word that is used in place of a noun or in place of words that work together as a noun. The most commonly used pronouns are personal pronouns, which refer to the person speaking (first-person pronouns), the person spoken to (second-person pronouns), or the person, place, or thing spoken about (third-person pronouns).

Personal Pronouns

	Singular	Plural
First Person	I, me, my, mine	we, us, our, ours
Second Person	you, your, yours	you, your, yours
Third Person	he, him, his, she, her, hers, it, its	they, them, their, theirs

A. PRACTICE: *The following sentences are taken from "Contents of the Dead Man's Pocket" or "Games at Twilight." Circle each first-person pronoun, draw a box around each second-person pronoun, and underline each third-person pronoun.*

Example: Tom looked regretful when she kissed him good-bye. "I wish I could go with you," he said, "but I have to work."

1. "What are you doing here?" she whispered, surprised to see him as he sat down next to her in the dark theater. He smiled at her and kissed her cheek, "I just missed you, Clare."

2. When they returned to their apartment, she was very surprised to see the broken glass. It was all over the living room floor.

3. "You were acting like such a baby, Ravi," she said later. "I was embarrassed for you."

4. The next time they played hide-and-seek, he did not play. He claimed his head was hurting, but it really wasn't.

5. It would bother him for many years. How could they have forgotten him?

B. Writing Application: *Rewrite each of the following sentences. Replace each underlined word or group of words with an appropriate personal pronoun.*

1. Tom did not want to lose the paper because Tom had worked on the paper for months.

_____

2. Tom tried to get the neighbors' attention, but none of the neighbors noticed Tom out on the ledge.

_____

"**Contents of the Dead Man's Pocket**" by Jack Finney
"**Games at Twilight**" by Anita Desai
Integrated Language Skills: Support for Writing an Anecdote with an Ironic Ending

For your anecdote with an ironic ending, use the following graphic organizer to help you come up with a character, a conflict, an expected outcome, and an unexpected outcome. Use the bottom portion of the organizer to brainstorm details to set your reader up for the expected outcome and hints that could explain the unexpected outcome.

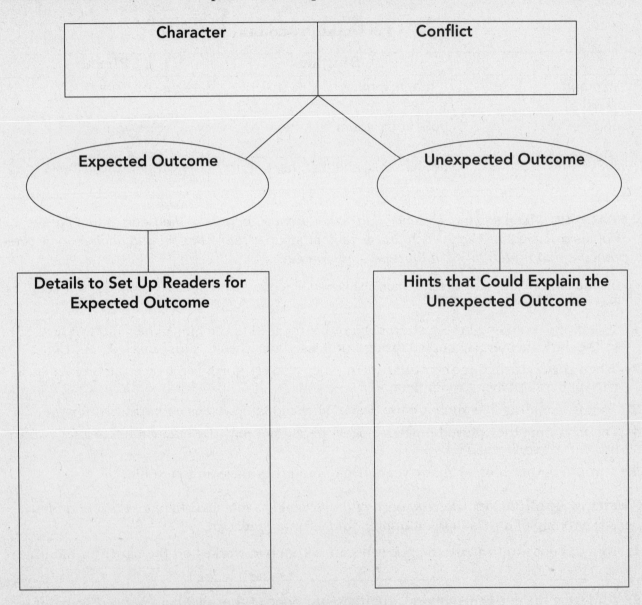

Now, use your notes to write an anecdote with an ironic ending.

"The Marginal World" by Rachel Carson

Writing About the Big Question

Is there a difference between reality and truth?

Big Question Vocabulary

comprehend	concrete	confirm	context	differentiate
discern	evaluate	evidence	improbable	objective
perception	reality	subjective	uncertainty	verify

A. *Use one or more words from the list above to complete each sentence.*

1. Rachel Carson's observations were often _____ and personal, help-ing her see truth in a nonscientific way.

2. Scientists have to _____ their findings to make sure they are true.

3. The _____ of life for creatures in the ocean is very different from the experience of life on land.

4. Scientists try to _____, or understand, how sea creatures survive in difficult conditions.

B. *Follow the directions in responding to each of the items below.*

1. In several sentences, describe a time when what appeared to be the reality of a situa-tion was not really the truth. Use one or two of the Big Question vocabulary words.

_____

_____

2. Write one or two sentences explaining how you and others reacted to the situation you describe in the preceding item. Use one or two Big Question vocabulary words.

_____

_____

C. *Complete the sentence below. Then, write a short paragraph in which you connect this experience to the Big Question.*

Reality is sometimes best discovered by _____

_____

_____

_____

_____

_____

"The Marginal World" by Rachel Carson
Literary Analysis: Author's Purpose

An **author's purpose** is his or her main reason for writing. An author may seek to inform, explain, persuade, describe, or entertain, or he or she may combine a variety of these purposes in a single work. To convey his or her purpose, an author may include specific details—a moving description or persuasive passages, for example. Recognizing the importance of certain details will help you to understand an author's purpose.

If the author's primary purpose is to inform or persuade, he or she presents a **thesis**—the main point the writer wants to make about the subject. To explain and prove the thesis, the author supplies support in the form of evidence, facts, and other details confirming the thesis.

A. DIRECTIONS: *Identify Carson's purpose for including the details in the following sentences from "The Marginal World."*

1. In this difficult world of the shore, life displays its enormous toughness and vitality by occupying almost every conceivable niche. _____
_____
_____

2. The shore is an ancient world, for as long as there has been an earth and sea there has been this place of the meeting of land and water. _____
_____
_____

3. I have seen hundreds of ghost crabs in other settings, but suddenly I was filled with the odd sensation that for the first time I knew the creature in its own world—that I understood, as never before, the essence of its being. _____
_____
_____

4. Here were creatures so exquisitely fashioned that they seemed unreal, their beauty too fragile to exist in a world of crushing force. Yet every detail was functionally useful, every stalk and hydranth and petallike tentacle fashioned for dealing with the realities of existence. _____
_____
_____

B. DIRECTIONS: *Identify Carson's thesis and then explain how the following sentence supports her thesis.*

I have seen hundreds of ghost crabs in other settings, but suddenly I was filled with the odd sensation that for the first time I knew the creature in its own world—that I understood, as never before, the essence of its being.

_____
_____
_____

Name _____ Date _____

Reading: Reread Passages to Analyze Cause and Effect

A **cause** is an event, an action, or a situation that produces a result. An **effect** is the result produced. To better follow a story, **analyze causes and effects** as you read, determining which earlier events cause which later events.

To analyze causes and effects, **reread** passages to determine whether they involve sequences of events or changing situations. Ask yourself whether the writer indicates any causes and effects in these sequences. Look for terms that signal cause or effect—*because, as a result, for that reason,* and so on.

In "The Marginal World," Carson often implies cause-and-effect connections by describing sequences of events that clearly lead from one to another.

Example of a cause-and-effect sequence from "The Marginal World":

One of them [a willet] stood at the edge of the water and gave its loud, urgent cry; an answer came from far up the beach and the two birds flew to join each other.

In this sentence, Carson implies the cause-and-effect relationships between the birds' actions. One willet cried out, which caused another willet to answer. This in turn caused the two willets to join each other (the effect).

DIRECTIONS: *Reread the following sentences from "The Marginal World." On the lines following each sentence, explain the cause-and-effect relationships you see.*

1. "I knew that if the wind held from the northwest and no interfering swell ran in from a distant storm the level of the sea should drop below the entrance to the pool." _____

   _____

   _____

2. "They were horn shells, and when I saw them I had a nostalgic moment when I wished I might see what Audubon saw, a century and more ago." _____

   _____

   _____

3. "Soon I found the tracks of a shore bird, probably a sanderling, and followed them a little; then they turned toward the water and were lost, for the tide had erased them and made them as though they had never been." _____

   _____

   _____

"The Marginal World" by Rachel Carson
Vocabulary Builder

Word List

elusive   ephemeral   manifestations   marginal   mutable

A. DIRECTIONS: *In each of the following items, think about the meaning of the italicized word. Then, on the lines provided, write a new sentence in which you use the italicized word correctly.*

1. The weather in this area is *mutable*, so what starts out as a sunny day may end up in a hailstorm.

   _____

2. The joy we felt after our team's victory was *ephemeral*, for we lost the very next game.

   _____

3. Due to my home's *marginal* location, I do not know which school I should attend.

   _____

4. Two foggy circles on the cold glass were the *manifestations* of our anxious breathing as we waited for our father to pull into the driveway.

   _____

5. Sand crabs are *elusive* creatures that can be difficult to capture.

   _____

B. WORD STUDY: The Latin prefix *inter-* means "between" or "among," as in the word intertidal. Fill in each blank in the following sentences with the correct word from the list.

intermission   international   interscholastic   interrupt

1. Jan was named captain of the school's _____ basketball team.
2. The _____ flight made stops in three different countries.
3. It is rude to _____ when someone else is speaking.
4. The play stopped for an _____ after the second act.

Name _____ Date _____

"Making History With Vitamin C" by Penny Le Couteur and Jay Burreson
Writing About the Big Question

Is there a difference between reality and truth?

Big Question Vocabulary

comprehend   concrete   confirm   context   differentiate
discern   evaluate   evidence   improbable   objective
perception   reality   subjective uncertainty   verify

A. *Explain why the underlined word in each sentence is used correctly or incorrectly.*

1. Ships' captains had to <u>evaluate</u> whether the claim for citrus juice as a cure for scurvy was the truth or a coincidence.

_____

2. Doctors in the past experienced <u>uncertainty</u> about the real causes of scurvy.

_____

3. A solution as simple as citrus juice seemed <u>improbable</u> as a cure for the ugly reality of the disease scurvy.

_____

4. His ideas about disease were <u>concrete</u>, and everyone seemed to think he was talking about something that lacked reality.

_____

B. *Follow the directions in responding to each of the items below.*

1. Think about some of the diseases you have learned about from history. Write one or two sentences explaining what people of the time thought about the reality of the disease.

_____

_____

2. Write one or two sentences explaining what truth about the disease you discussed above was later discovered.

_____

_____

C. *Complete the sentence below. Then, write a short paragraph in which you connect this situation to the Big Question.*

Ship's captains treated scurvy as _____

_____

_____

Name _____ Date _____

"**Making History with Vitamin C**" by Penny Le Couteur and Jay Burreson

Literary Analysis: Author's Purpose

An **author's purpose** is his or her main reason for writing. An author may seek to inform, explain, persuade, describe, or entertain, or he or she may combine a variety of these purposes in a single work. To convey his or her purpose, an author may include specific details—a moving description or persuasive passages, for example. Recognizing the importance of certain details will help you to understand an author's purpose.

If the author's primary purpose is to inform or persuade, he or she, presents a **thesis**—the main point the writer wants to make about the subject. To explain and prove the thesis, the author supplies support in the form of evidence, facts, and other details confirming the thesis.

A. DIRECTIONS: *Identify the authors' purpose for including the details in the following sentences from "Making History with Vitamin C."*

1. Changes in bone structure in Neolithic remains are thought to be compatible with scurvy, and hieroglyphs from ancient Egypt have been interpreted as referring to it. _____

   _____

   _____

2. It is estimated that for centuries scurvy was responsible for more death at sea than all other causes; more than the combined total of naval battles, piracy, shipwrecks, and other illnesses. _____

   _____

   _____

3. Astonishingly, preventives and remedies for scurvy during these years were known—but largely ignored. _____

   _____

4. Thanks to vitamin C, the ascorbic acid molecule, Cook was able to compile an impressive list of accomplishments: the discovery of the Hawaiian Islands and the Great Barrier Reef, the first circumnavigation of New Zealand, the first charting of the coast of the Pacific Northwest, and the first crossing of the Antarctic Circle. _____

   _____

   _____

B. DIRECTIONS: *Identify the authors' thesis and then explain how the following sentence supports this thesis.*

Thanks to vitamin C, the ascorbic acid molecule, Cook was able to compile an impressive list of accomplishments: the discovery of the Hawaiian Islands and the Great Barrier Reef, the first circum-navigation of New Zealand, the first charting of the coast of the Pacific Northwest, and the first crossing of the Antarctic Circle.

_____

_____

_____

"**Making History with Vitamin C**" by Penny Le Couteur and Jay Burreson
Reading: Reread Passages to Analyze Cause and Effect

A **cause** is an event, an action, or a situation that produces a result. An **effect** is the result produced. To better follow a story, **analyze causes and effects** as you read, determining which earlier events cause which later events.

To analyze causes and effects, **reread** passages to determine whether they involve sequences of events or changing situations. Ask yourself whether the writer indicates any causes and effects in these sequences. Look for terms that signal cause or effect—*because, as a result, for that reason,* and so on.

In "Making History with Vitamin C," Le Couteur and Burreson often imply cause-and-effect connections by describing sequences of events that clearly lead from one to another.

Example of a cause-and-effect sequence from "Making History with Vitamin C":

In the fourteenth and fifteenth centuries, as longer voyages were made possible by the development of more efficient sets of sails and fully rigged ships, scurvy became commonplace at sea.

In this sentence, the authors explain how more efficient ships caused longer voyages to become possible. The effect of longer voyages was an increase in the number of cases of scurvy.

DIRECTIONS: *Reread the following passages from "Making History with Vitamin C." On the lines that follow each passage, explain the cause-and-effect relationships you see.*

1. Anyone who showed signs of scurvy was dosed with three teaspoons of lemon juice every morning. On arrival at the Cape of Good Hope, none of the men on board the Dragon was suffering from scurvy, but the toll on the other three ships was significant. _____

_____

_____

2. A healthy, well-functioning crew was essential for Cook to accomplish what he did on his voyages. This fact was recognized by the Royal Society when it awarded him its highest honor, the Copley gold medal, not for his navigational feats but for his demonstration that scurvy was not an inevitable companion on long ocean voyages. _____

_____

_____

3. He records that a 'Sour Kroutt' prepared from local plants was initially made available only to the officers; within a week the lower ranks were clamoring for their share. _____

_____

_____

Name _____ Date _____

"Making History with Vitamin C" by Penny Le Couteur and Jay Burreson
Vocabulary Builder

Word List

alleviate   compulsory   deficiency   incessant   obscured   replenished

A. DIRECTIONS: *In each of the following items, think about the meaning of the italicized word. Then, on the lines provided, write a new sentence in which you use the italicized word correctly.*

1. A *deficiency* of water causes dehydration.

   _____

2. I took a part-time job and *replenished* my bank account after buying new school clothes.

   _____

3. My sister's *incessant* interruptions last night made it difficult for me to finish my homework.

   _____

4. The thick curtains *obscured* the bright sun and kept the room cool and dark.

   _____

5. Since attendance at the meeting was *compulsory*, we had to go.

   _____

6. This ointment will *alleviate* the pain of the scratch.

   _____

B. WORD STUDY: *The Latin prefix* ob- *means "against or inverse." Fill in the blanks in the following sentences with the correct word from the list.*

object   obsolete   obliterate

1. Your teammates will _____ if you decide to quit the team.
2. The authorities are going to use explosives to _____ the old building.
3. The technology from the 1990s is _____.

"Making History with Vitamin C" by Penny Le Couteur and Jay Burreson
"The Marginal World" by Rachel Carson
Integrated Language Skills: Grammar

Relative Pronouns

Pronouns are words that are used in place of or refer to nouns or other pronouns. A relative pronoun is a pronoun that connects one part of a sentence, called a subordinate clause, to the noun or pronoun that the clause tells more about.

RELATIVE PRONOUNS
that   which   who   whom   whose

Examples: In the following sentences, relative pronouns (boldfaced) connect a subordinate clause (underlined) to a word (in italics).

Rachel Carson, **whose** life's work was studying and writing about nature, felt that the shore was a particularly magical place.

The *creatures* **that** live at the edge of the sea are hardy and adaptable.

PRACTICE: *The following sentences are based on "The Marginal World" or "Making History with Vitamin C." Circle each relative pronoun, underline each subordinate clause, and draw an arrow from the relative pronoun to the noun to which it refers.*

1. The hidden cave, which is visible only at the lowest of the year's low tides, is a place of special beauty.

2. The little crab that Carson saw on the beach one night became a symbol for life itself.

3. For decades, sailors ignored proven remedies that could prevent or cure scurvy.

4. Sailors who were used to hardtack and salted meat did not want to eat fresh fruits and vegetables.

5. Captain Cook, who insisted on cleanliness and a good diet on his ships, lost very few men to disease.

"The Marginal World" by Rachel Carson
"Making History With Vitamin C" by Penny Le Couteur and Jay Burreson
Integrated Language Skills: Support for Writing a Proposal for a Documentary

For your documentary proposal, use the following graphic organizer to help you come up with a thesis, supporting scenes, and topics for discussion or commentary. Your thesis should be the point you are trying to make in your documentary. It should be similar to the authors' thesis in "The Marginal World" or "Making History with Vitamin C" since your documentary will be based on one of the essays. Choose visuals, action, and comments that clearly support your thesis.

Thesis:
Scenes or items to film:
Topics to be covered or commented upon:

Now, use your notes to write your proposal for a documentary on life at the edge of the sea or on Cook's efforts to solve the problem of scurvy.

Name _____ Date _____

Writing About the Big Question

Is there a difference between reality and truth?

Big Question Vocabulary

comprehend	concrete	confirm	context	differentiate
discern	evaluate	evidence	improbable	objective
perception	reality	subjective	uncertainty	verify

A. *Write the word from the list above that is a* synonym *for the underlined phrase or word in each sentence.*

1. Noah's <u>way of seeing</u> things sometimes led him to make mistakes about other people's intentions. _____

2. Some people are unable to <u>tell the difference</u> between truth and lies. _____

3. Framton did not <u>verify</u> that Vera was telling the truth. _____

4. Jessica tries to remain <u>unprejudiced</u> about a situation even when she is angry. _____

5. The <u>details that furnish proof</u> of a crime can sometimes be misleading. _____

B. *Follow the directions in responding to each of the items below.*

1. In a short paragraph, describe a time when your perception of reality about a situation was affected by your belief about that situation.

   _____

   _____

2. In one or two sentences, explain how you learned the truth about the situation, which was different from your first perception.

   _____

   _____

C. *Complete the sentence below. Then, write a short paragraph in which you connect this experience to the Big Question.*

When things do not turn out as you plan, _____

_____

_____

_____

_____

Name _____ Date _____

"**Like the Sun**" by R.K. Narayan
"**The Open Window**" by Saki
Literary Analysis: Irony and Paradox

Irony is the effect created when a writer makes a forceful contrast between words or expectations and reality.

- In **situational irony,** something happens that directly contradicts strong expectations. For example, if you go through a door expecting a surprise party and instead find an empty room, you actually *will* be surprised.
- In **verbal irony,** words are used to "say" the opposite. If it starts to rain, and you say, "Oh, this is *great*" to mean "Oh, this is *awful*," you are using verbal irony.
- In **dramatic irony,** the reader or audience knows something that a character or speaker does not. In "Like the Sun," for example, the reader knows about Sekhar's experiment, but the headmaster does not.

Another kind of contrast writers use is **paradox.** A paradox expresses two contradictory ideas and yet also reveals a truth. "You must sometimes be cruel to be kind" is one example of a paradox.

A. DIRECTIONS: *Explain what is ironic in each of the following passages from "Like the Sun" and "The Open Window." Then identify the type of irony in each passage.*

"Like the Sun"

1. "No. I want it immediately—your frank opinion. Was it good?" "No, sir. . ." Sekhar replied.

   _____

   _____

   Type of irony: _____

"The Open Window"

2. "My aunt will be down presently, Mr. Nuttel," said a very self-possessed young lady of fifteen; "in the meantime you must try and put up with me."

   _____

   _____

   Type of Irony: _____

B. DIRECTIONS: *Explain how each paradox is illustrated in "Like the Sun" or "The Open Window."*

"Like the Sun"

1. "You have to be cruel to be kind." _____

   _____

"The Open Window"

2. "One would think he had seen a ghost." _____

   _____

Name _____ Date _____

"Like the Sun" by R.K. Narayan
"The Open Window" by Saki
Vocabulary Builder

Word List

delusion   endeavored   falteringly   ingratiating   scrutinized   tempering

A. DIRECTIONS: *Write a complete sentence to answer each question. For each item, use a word from the Word List in place of the underlined word(s) with a similar meaning.*

Example: Why might belief in Martian invaders be considered a <u>false belief</u>?

Answer: Belief in Martian invaders might be considered a <u>delusion</u> since there is no evidence for them.

1. When can <u>softening</u> your tone come in handy?

   _____

2. Why might a person's signature be <u>closely examined</u>?

   _____

3. Why do many people find behavior <u>intended to win someone's favor</u> annoying?

   _____

4. How would you feel if someone <u>tried to</u> harm you?

   _____

5. Why might a person speak with <u>a wavering voice</u>?

   _____

B. DIRECTIONS: *On the line, write the letter of the word that is most nearly* opposite *in meaning to the word in CAPITAL LETTERS.*

____ 1. SCRUTINIZED:
    A. punished   B. celebrated   C. purchased   D. ignored

____ 2. TEMPERING:
    A. moderating   B. increasing   C. reducing   D. frightening

____ 3. FALTERINGLY:
    A. angrily   B. strongly   C. plainly   D. weakly

____ 4. INGRATIATING:
    A. civilized   B. thankful   C. disrespectful   D. soothing

"**Like the Sun**" by R.K. Narayan
"**The Open Window**" by Saki

Integrated Language Skills: Support for Writing to Compare Literary Works

Before you draft your essay comparing and contrasting the ideas of honesty and deception in these two stories, complete the graphic organizer below.

	"Like the Sun"	"The Open Window"
Examples of a character's honesty or deception		
How a character's attitude toward honesty or deception changes		
Resulting ironies or paradoxes		
Important idea(s) the author wants to convey		

Now, use your notes to write an essay comparing and contrasting the authors' ideas about honesty and deception. In your essay, examine how each author uses irony or paradox to express these ideas.

No Easy Way Out, performed by The Dave Pittenger Band

It started with the news that she was sick

and the doctors said her chances were looking pretty slim

They told her to resist it—she'd regain her strength

and find **reconciliation,** to try to find some peace

She'd have to fight and **oppose**—it doesn't come easily (easily . . .)

Growth takes **change**

So we fight and strive and **struggle** to achieve it

Adversity is the mountain that we learn to climb

Oooo . . . Oooo . . .

The **debate** was raging on

People questioned if she had the **motivation,** had the drive to beat the odds

She strengthened her **resolve,** from that moment said she's never grant **concession**

Said she'd never give in

We **unify** to support and give her what she needs (what she needs . . .)

Growth takes **change**

So we fight and strive and **struggle** to achieve it

Adversity is the mountain that we learn to climb

Oooo . . . Oooo . . .

Confrontation leads to trouble

We **negotiate,** together seek solutions

Radical events challenge the way that we live

Compromise brings **progress** and moves us ahead

Song Title: **No Easy Way Out**

Artist / Performed by The Dave Pittenger Band

Vocals & Guitar: Dave Pittenger

Bass Guitar: Jon Price

Drums: Josh Dion

Lyrics by Dave Pittenger

Music composed by Dave Pittenger

Produced by Mike Pandolfo, Wonderful

Executive Producer: Keith London, Defined Mind

Name _____ Date _____

The Big Question: Can progress be made without conflict?

In your textbook, you learned words that are useful for talking about conflict, the struggle between opposing forces. Life is full of conflict, and so are stories, novels, movies, TV shows, sports, and games.

DIRECTIONS: *Review the following definitions of words you can use when talking about conflict.*

compromise: an agreement reached by each party giving something up or adjusting its expectations; meeting in the middle

contradictory: logically opposite

deference: respectful and courteous willingness to give in to another's will or opinion

negotiate: to bargain with another in order to reach an agreement

change: to make different

dissonance: disagreement, particularly in the sense of a loud argument

Now rewrite each sentence by replacing each underlined word or phrase with a vocabulary word from the list above that has a similar meaning.

1. In order to reach <u>an agreement</u>, the two groups had to <u>bargain</u> for hours and <u>alter</u> their demands several times.

   _____

   _____

2. People were shouting angrily at each other, and those contributing to the <u>loud disagreement</u> were making <u>logically opposite</u> statements and refusing to <u>reach an agreement</u>.

   _____

   _____

   _____

3. I always show <u>respect</u> for my grandparents by doing what they ask.

   _____

4. Showing <u>respect</u> for another person's opinions is one way to end a conflict and open a <u>discussion</u> that might help to end the <u>disagreement</u>.

   _____

   _____

Unit 2: Short Stories
Big Question Vocabulary—2

The Big Question: Can progress be made without conflict?

DIRECTIONS: *Review the following definitions of words you can use when talking about conflict.*

strategy: a plan for achieving a specific goal
evolve: to grow, change, or develop in some way
tumultuous: disorderly, noisy, emotional, turbulent
war/battle: armed conflict or fighting
treaty: a written agreement between combatants to end fighting
motive: reason for doing something

Now, complete the graphic organizer below by filling in a synonym and an antonym for each vocabulary word.

Synonym	Word	Antonym
	1. strategy	
	2. evolve	
	3. tumultuous	
	4. battle	
	5. treaty	
	6. motive	

Unit 2: Short Stories
Big Question Vocabulary—3

The Big Question: Can progress be made without conflict?

DIRECTIONS: *Review the following definitions of words you can use when talking about conflict.*

neutrality: an unwillingness to take sides in a conflict

struggle: *n.* a difficult situation in which a person must make a great effort; *v.* to make a great effort in a difficult situation

adversity: challenging circumstances

radical: extreme or drastic

aggression: offensive action or attack; starting a conflict

resolution: the solution of a problem; the ending of a conflict

Now, read each sentence and use the context clues and the definitions above to help you rewrite the definition of each underlined word in your own words.

Sentence	Definition in Your Own Words
1. You can count on Mina's <u>neutrality</u> since she never takes sides in her friends' arguments.	
2. The protagonist in the movie I saw last night had to <u>struggle</u> against the forces of evil to save the world.	
3. Everyone faces <u>adversity</u> at some point in their lives and must find a way to overcome such challenges.	
4. A politician should not take <u>radical</u> positions on many issues because he or she must try to appeal to most voters.	
5. The dictator's <u>aggression</u> caused the leaders of neighboring countries to increase their armies.	
6. The <u>resolution</u> of our argument over the music player came when we agreed to take turns with it during the car trip.	

Name _____ Date _____

Unit 2: Short Stories
Applying the Big Question

The Big Question: Can progress be made without conflict?

DIRECTIONS: *Complete the chart below to apply what you have learned about how progress is made. One row has been completed for you.*

Example	Type of Conflict	Who won or lost	Is progress made?	Did conflict contribute to progress?	What I learned
From Literature	Ivan Markovitch's fight with the uncles over Sasha in "A Problem"	Ivan won because Sasha will not have a trial.	Ivan makes progress with the uncles but not with Sasha.	Because of the long, intense argument, the uncles change their minds about Sasha.	Sometimes a conflict can lead to progress for some but not for others.
From Literature					
From Science					
From Social Studies					
From Real Life					

C. J. Cherryh
Listening and Viewing

Segment 1: Meet C. J. Cherryh

- In addition to writing, C. J. Cherryh keeps busy with many other activities. What hobbies and interests does C. J. Cherryh explore? How do you think her willingness to explore new activities affects her writing?

_____

_____

_____

Segment 2: The Short Story

- According to C. J. Cherryh, what is the difference between fantasy and science-fiction stories? Why do you think a short story is an effective way of writing science-fiction and fantasy stories?

_____

_____

_____

_____

Segment 3: The Writing Process

- What does C. J. Cherryh mean by her motto "write garbage but edit brilliantly"? Do you agree with her that revising is the most "magical" step in the writing process? Explain why you agree or disagree.

_____

_____

_____

Segment 4: The Rewards of Writing

- Why do you think students should read science-fiction stories? Why is it important for writers to write for readers of the future as well as for readers of today?

_____

_____

_____

_____

Learning About Short Stories

A **short story** is a brief work of fiction. The following chart shows the key elements of a short story.

Element	Definition
Plot	The events that make up the action: introduction, rising action, climax, and falling action.
Conflict	External conflict: a struggle between two characters, a character and a group, or a character and a force Internal conflict: a struggle within the mind of a character
Character	An individual who participates in the action Direct characterization: developed through statements about a character's personality, habits, goals, values, or beliefs Indirect characterization: developed through a character's words, thoughts, actions, and interaction
Setting	The time and place of the action
Theme	The central message or insight about life in a story Stated theme: expressed directly by the author Implied theme: suggested indirectly through characters' experiences or events and setting

DIRECTIONS: *Read each item. Write which of the following it describes—internal conflict, external conflict, direct characterization, indirect characterization, setting, stated theme, or implied theme.*

1. Julian was painfully shy. _____

2. "I refuse to babysit Taisha tonight!" Frida told her mother. _____

3. The house was cold and gloomy in the winter wind. _____

4. Be careful what you wish for; you just might get it. _____

5. People looked through Bobby as if he did not exist. _____

6. Mindy worried about whether to invite Luisa. _____

7. It had been a hundred years since the last war. _____

8. "Carmen can dish it out, but she sure cannot take it," Sammy said. _____

9. "The wind is too strong!" I shouted. "I cannot control the boat!" _____

10. At last, summer had come. We had two whole months of freedom. _____

from "The Threads of Time" by C. J. Cherryh
Model Selection: Short Story

A **short story** is a brief work of fiction. It includes a series of events called the **plot.** The plot centers on conflict. An **external conflict** is a conflict between characters, between an individual and a group, or between a character and a force. An **internal conflict** occurs within a character's mind. The conflict develops to a **climax** and is then sorted out in a **resolution.**

The **characters** in a short story are the individuals who participate in the plot. Writers reveal **character development** through **direct characterization,** or statements about the characters, and **indirection characterization,** a character's words, thoughts, and actions. The story's **setting** is the time and place in which it occurs. Its **theme** is the central message or insight about life it provides. The theme can be **stated** or **implied.**

A. DIRECTIONS: *"The Threads of Time" is a short story. Use the following chart to list details of its conflicts, climax, resolution, characters, and setting.*

Element	Details
Conflict	
Climax	
Resolution	
Character	
Setting	

B. DIRECTIONS: *Most short stories contain a **theme,** a message about life. A theme can be **stated,** or expressed directly by the author. It can also be **implied,** or suggested indirectly by events, setting, or experiences of the characters. What is the theme of "The Threads of Time"? Is it stated or implied? Support your answer with details from the story.*

_____

_____

_____

_____

_____

_____

_____

_____

_____

Name _____ Date _____

Writing About the Big Question

Can progress be made without conflict?

Big Question Vocabulary

adversity	change	compromise	concession	confrontation
debate	motive	negotiate	oppose	progress
radical	reconciliation	resolve	struggle	unify

A. *Use one or more words from the list above to complete each sentence.*

1. The flood was a disaster, but she faced _____
   by helping others.

2. We often will not _____ our opinion of people
   even when we learn new information about them.

3. Settling a quarrel between family members can lead to a
   _____ that brings everyone together.

4. We all _____ with our feelings when someone
   we love disappoints us.

B. *Follow the directions in responding to each of the items below.*

1. List two conflicts you have experienced.

   _____

   _____

2. Write two sentences explaining the outcome of one of the experiences you listed in
   your response. Use at least two of the Big Question vocabulary words.

   _____

   _____

   _____

C. *Complete the sentence below. Then, write a short paragraph in which you connect this
experience to the Big Question.*

   Someone who directly engages another person in a conflict often must _____

   _____

   _____

   _____

   _____

   _____

"A Visit to Grandmother" by William Melvin Kelley
Literary Analysis: Characterization

Characters are the people, animals, or objects that perform the actions and experience the events of a story. An author reveals the personalities of characters in a story by using **direct** or **indirect characterization.** With direct characterization, an author makes direct statements about a character. With indirect characterization, the author reveals a character's traits through his or her **dialogue,** actions, thoughts, and appearance and through what other people in the story think of the character.

Think about the information you learn about characters and how you learn it. Think also about **character development**—changes the character undergoes through the course of the story or new information that the author reveals about the character.

A. DIRECTIONS: *Complete this chart with examples from the story of direct and indirect characterization of each character listed. If there is no example of either direct or indirect characterization, explain why you think the author chose not to use that form of characterization.*

Character	Examples of Direct Characterization	Examples of Indirect Characterization
Example: GL	GL is said to be part con man, part practical joker, and part Don Juan.	He is wearing brown and white two-tone shoes with very pointed toes and a white summer suit. His smile is innocent and open, like a five-year-old's.
1. Charles		
2. Chig		
3. Mama		

B. DIRECTIONS: *In a brief essay, indicate whether direct or indirect characterization makes you feel you know a character better. Explain your answer.*

_____

_____

_____

_____

_____

_____

_____

Name _____ Date _____

"A Visit to Grandmother" by William Melvin Kelley
Reading: Relate Characters and Events to Your Own Experiences to Make Inferences

An **inference** is something you figure out about information that is not directly stated in a story. One way to make inferences is to **relate characters and events to your own experiences.** For example, when Rose offers to make dinner, Mama says, "You can do the cooking if you promise it ain't because you think I can't." By thinking about a strong aging person in your own family, you might be able to infer that Mama is very proud and wants people to understand that she is not feeble. Or you might think about a time when you were hurt or sick and hated having to rely on others to take care of you. Personal observations and experiences such as these can help you better understand characters in literature.

DIRECTIONS: *Complete the following chart with personal experiences you can relate to each passage and an inference you are able to make based on your experiences. If you do not have a personal experience you can directly relate to the passage, make an educated guess based on observations of people you know.*

Passage From Story	Personal Experience Related to Passage	Inference
1. But when he had bent to kiss the old lady's black face, something new and almost ugly had come into his eyes: fear, uncertainty, sadness, and perhaps even hatred.		
2. Aunt Rose, over Chig's weak protest, was spooning mashed potatoes onto his plate.		
3. Chig turned to his father and found his face completely blank, without even trace of a smile or a laugh.		
4. He [GL] stood in the doorway, smiling broadly, an engaging, open, friendly smile, the innocent smile of a five-year-old.		

"A Visit to Grandmother" by William Melvin Kelley
Vocabulary Builder

Word List

    engaging   fraud   grimacing   indulgence   meager   trace

A. DIRECTIONS: *Provide an explanation for your answer to each question.*

1. If you show *indulgence* toward your little sister, will you be angry when she loses your soccer ball?

   _____

   _____

2. If you are *grimacing* in your school photograph, do you have a big smile?

   _____

   _____

3. Will a *meager* bag of apples feed the entire school?

   _____

   _____

4. Will a *trace* of rain flood the corn fields?

   _____

   _____

5. If someone uses *fraud* to win an election, what should happen to that person?

   _____

   _____

6. Do you want to talk to someone who has an *engaging* personality?

   _____

   _____

B. WORD STUDY: The Latin suffix *-ence* means "quality of" or "state of." Revise each sentence so that the underlined word containing the suffix *-ence* is used logically. Be sure not to change the underlined word.

1. Her <u>fraudulence</u> made us trust her even more.

   _____

   _____

2. His <u>resurgence</u> as a great player caused him to retire.

   _____

   _____

3. Her <u>diligence</u> worried her teachers, because she never worked hard enough.

   _____

   _____

Name _____ Date _____

"A Problem" by Anton Chekhov
Writing About the Big Question
Can progress be made without conflict?

Big Question Vocabulary

adversity	change	compromise	concession	confrontation
debate	motive	negotiate	oppose	progress
radical	reconciliation	resolve	struggle	unify

A. *Use one or more words from the list above to complete each sentence.*

1. The uncles _____ for hours, arguing back and forth, about Sasha's debt.

2. A group of uncles _____ Ivan Markovitch, disagreeing with his position.

3. Sasha will never _____, choosing instead to remain a scoundrel.

4. A crisis can sometimes _____ a family, but it can also drive them apart.

B. *Follow the directions in responding to each of the items below.*

1. Identify a time when you tried to convince someone to support your point of view.

   _____

   _____

2. Write two sentences explaining the outcome of your experience, describing whether you won the support of the person. Use at least two Big Question vocabulary words.

   _____

   _____

   _____

C. *Complete the sentence below. Then, write a short paragraph in which you connect this experience to the Big Question.*

When a person wants to help a troubled loved one who may not want to be helped, that person must often _____

   _____

   _____

   _____

   _____

"A Problem" by Anton Chekhov
Literary Analysis: Characterization

Characters are the people, animals, or objects that perform the actions and experience the events of a story. An author reveals the personalities of characters in a story by using **direct** or **indirect characterization.** With direct characterization, an author makes direct statements about a character. With indirect characterization, the author reveals a character's traits through his or her **dialogue,** actions, thoughts, and appearance, as well as what other people in the story think of the character.

To better understand characters, think about the information you learn about characters and how you learn it. Think also about **character development**—changes the character undergoes through the course of the story or new information that the author reveals about the character.

A. DIRECTIONS: *Complete the following chart with examples from the story of direct and indirect characterization of each character listed. If there is no example of either direct or indirect characterization, explain why you think the author chose not to use that form of characterization.*

Character	Examples of Direct Characterization	Examples of Indirect Characterization
Example: The Treasury official	The author describes him as taciturn, dull-witted, and rheumatic.	He sits mostly silent and fails to support his opinion; he mutters his replies to the Colonel.
1. Sasha		
2. The Colonel		
3. Ivan Markovitch		

B. DIRECTIONS: *In a brief essay, indicate whether direct or indirect characterization makes you feel you know a character better. Explain your answer.*

_____

_____

_____

_____

_____

_____

Name _____ Date _____

Reading: Relate Characters and Events to Your Own Experiences to Make Inferences

An **inference** is something you figure out about information that is not directly stated in a story. One way to make inferences is to **relate characters and events to your own experiences.** For example, at the beginning of the story the author states that the family was careful to keep something secret from the servants. Though you may not have servants, you might be able to relate to the desire to keep your family's personal business within the family. By thinking about a similar situation in your own life, it can help you infer that the Uskov family is dealing with something they feel might be embarrassing if it is made public. Personal observations and experiences such as these can help you better understand characters in literature.

DIRECTIONS: *Complete the following chart with personal experiences you can relate to each passage and an inference you are able to make based on your experiences. If you do not have a personal experience you can directly relate to the passage, make an educated guess based on observations of people you know.*

Passage From Story	Personal Experience Related to Passage	Inference
1. "Shall we be false to civic duty," Ivan Markovitch exclaimed passionately, "if instead of punishing an erring boy we hold out to him a helping hand?"		
2. Every minute he [Sasha] was on the point of jumping up, bursting into the study and shouting in answer to the detestable metallic voice of the Colonel: "You are lying!"		
3. But then he [Sasha] remembered he had not a farthing, that the companions he was going to would despise him at once for his empty pockets. He must get hold of some money, come what may!		
4. But debt is not a crime, and it is unusual for a man not to be in debt.		

"A Problem" by Anton Chekhov
Vocabulary Builder

Word List

candid   detestable   edifying   lofty   pretense   subdued

A. DIRECTIONS: *Provide an explanation for your answer to each question.*

1. If he maintained a *pretense* of enjoying math, was math his favorite subject?

   _____

   _____

2. Would you want a president who gives a *candid* answer to a question?

   _____

   _____

3. Should a government try to attain *lofty* goals?

   _____

   _____

4. Would you be eager to meet a classmate with *detestable* behavior?

   _____

   _____

5. How does a *subdued* person behave?

   _____

   _____

6. Does an *edifying* speech have a positive or negative message?

   _____

   _____

B. WORD STUDY: The Latin suffix *-able* means "capable of being." Revise each sentence so that the underlined word containing the suffix *-able* is used logically. Be sure not to change the underlined word.

1. She was always <u>reliable</u>, so we knew we could not count on her.

   _____

   _____

2. The contract was <u>negotiable</u>, so we knew we could not change it.

   _____

   _____

3. His artwork was <u>remarkable</u>, so the teacher passed it over with no commentary.

   _____

   _____

"A Visit to Grandmother" by William Melvin Kelley
"A Problem" by Anton Chekhov

Integrated Language Skills: Grammar

Regular Verbs

A verb has four principal parts: the present, the present participle, the past, and the past participle. The present and past forms function as verbs. The present participle and the past participle can also act as adjectives. Most of the verbs in the English language are regular; the past and past participle of a regular verb are formed by adding *-ed* or *-d* to the present form. The past and past participle of regular verbs have the same form. The following chart lists the principal parts of two verbs—*visit* and *discuss*.

Principal Parts of Regular Verbs

Present	Present Participle	Past	Past Participle
visit	(is, are, was, were) visiting	visited	(has, have, had) visited
discuss	(is, are, was, were) discussing	discussed	(has, have, had) discussed

A. PRACTICE: *Identify the principal part used to form each of the underlined verbs.*

Example:

__past__ Chig <u>noticed</u> an ugly look on his father's face.

_____ 1. Ronald is <u>cooking</u> dinner while the children talk.

_____ 2. Charley had <u>wanted</u> to go to college.

_____ 3. Lucille <u>asked</u> her mother to ride in the car with her.

_____ 4. "I <u>believe</u> their behavior will improve," Jennifer said.

B. Writing Application: *Write sentences according to the instructions.*

Example: Write a sentence using the past participle form of the verb *prepare*.
Sasha <u>had prepared</u> himself for the possibility that he might have to go to court.

1. Write a sentence using the past participle of the verb *talk*.

_____

2. Write a sentence using the present form of the verb *agree*.

_____

3. Write a sentence using the present participle of the verb *decide*.

_____

4. Write a sentence using the past of *laugh*.

_____

"A Visit to Grandmother" by William Melvin Kelley
"A Problem" by Anton Chekhov
Integrated Language Skills: Support for Writing a Retelling

For your retelling, use the following story map to list the main events of "A Visit to Grandmother" or "A Problem."

The Main Conflict or Problem:

Event 1:	Event 2:	Event 3:

Event 4:	Event 5:	Event 6:

The Resolution or Solution to the Problem:

The Ending:

Now, use this story map to help you retell the story from either Mama's point of view and then from GL's viewpoint **or** from the moneylender's point of view and then from the perspective of Sasha as an old man.

Name _____ Date _____

"The Street of the Cañon" by Josephina Niggli
Writing About the Big Question

Can progress be made without conflict?

Big Question Vocabulary

adversity	change	compromise	concession	confrontation
debate	motive	negotiate	oppose	progress
radical	reconciliation	resolve	struggle	unify

A. *Write the word that best matches each definition.*

1. to make a firm decision _____

2. to transform _____

3. extreme _____

4. to strenuously engage against a problem or opponent _____

5. the act of giving up something _____

B. *Follow the directions in responding to each of the items below.*

1. From history or from your own experience, describe a long-lasting conflict between two people or two groups. Use complete sentences and at least one Big Question vocabulary word.

   _____

   _____

2. Explain how this conflict was settled, or how it might be settled.

   _____

   _____

   _____

C. *Complete the sentence below. Then, write a short paragraph in which you connect this experience to the Big Question.*

One possible motive for using humor during a quarrel is _____

_____

_____

_____

_____

_____

_____

All-in-One Workbook

Name _____ Date _____

"The Street of the Cañon" by Josephina Niggli
Literary Analysis: Setting

All stories have a **setting**—the time and the place of the story's events. To establish a setting, writers use **descriptions,** or word-pictures, to appeal to the senses. Settings shape stories by helping to determine plot as well as characters' concerns and values.

A story may have an overall setting as well as specific settings. There may be more than one setting as the action moves from place to place, and from one time to another. In Shakespeare's *Romeo and Juliet,* for example, the overall setting is Verona, Italy, in the sixteenth century, but the specific time and place changes from scene to scene.

A. DIRECTIONS: *In the "Setting" column, fill in the overall time, overall place, specific time, and specific place in "The Street of the Cañon." In the "Evidence" column, fill in the detail from the story that gives you the information for the setting. In the "Impact" column, write how overall and specific times and places matter to the story. What effect, if any, does each have?*

"The Street of the Cañon"			
	Setting	**Evidence**	**Impact**
Overall Time:			
Overall Place:			
Specific Time:			
Specific Place:			

B. DIRECTIONS: *Write a brief summary of a version of "The Street of the Cañon" set today in your region of the United States. To adapt the story to its new setting, think about situations that can cause rivalries or competition between communities.*

_____

_____

_____

_____

_____

_____

_____

Name _____ Date _____

"**The Street of the Cañon**" by Josephina Niggli

Reading: Make Inferences and Read on to Find Additional Support

An **inference** is an insight, based on stated details, about information that is not stated. As you read, check your inferences against new information and revise them if needed.

DIRECTIONS: *For each passage from the story, write an inference you can draw from it. Then, write a detail from later in the story that either proves or disproves your inference.*

Example: A tall slender man, a package clutched tightly against his side, slipped from shadow to shadow. Once a dog barked, and the man's black suit merged into the blackness of a wall. But no voice called out, and after a moment he slid into the narrow dirt-packed street again. . . .

Inference: The man is frightened of someone and is trying to escape.

Detail that proves or disproves the inference: The man enters a party, so he does not seem to be trying to escape after all. He was being sneaky, but he was not frightened.

1. The fan in her small hand snapped shut. She tapped its parchment tip against her mouth and slipped away to join the dancing couples in the front room. The gestures of a fan translate into a coded language on the frontier. The stranger raised one eyebrow as he interpreted the signal.

   Inference: _____

   Detail that proves or disproves your inference: _____

   _____

2. This request [to dance] startled her [Sarita's chaperone's] eyes into popping open beneath the heavy brows. "So, my young rooster, would you flirt with me, and I old enough to be your grandmother?"

   Inference: _____

   Detail that proves or disproves your inference: _____

   _____

3. His eyes on the patio, he asked blandly, "You say the leader was one Pepe Gonzalez? The name seems to have a familiar sound."

   Inference: _____

   Detail that proves or disproves your inference: _____

   _____

4. "This is no cheese from Linares. . . . Years ago, when the great Don Rómolo Balderas was still alive, we had such cheese as this—ay, in those days we had it."

   Inference: _____

   Detail that proves or disproves your inference: _____

   _____

"The Street of the Cañon" by Josephina Niggli
Vocabulary Builder

Word List

apprehension   audaciously   disdain   imperiously   nonchalantly   plausibility

A. DIRECTIONS: *Revise or rewrite each sentence so that the underlined vocabulary word is used logically. Be sure to keep the vocabulary word in your revision.*

> **Example:** The stranger from Hidalgo walked <u>cautiously</u> down the streets of the village, not concerned at all about anyone seeing him.
>
> The stranger from Hidalgo walked <u>cautiously</u> down the streets of the village, hoping no one would see him.

1. The polite party guests thanked their host <u>imperiously</u> for his hospitality.

   _____

2. Due to the <u>plausibility</u> of his story, not a single person there believed him.

   _____

3. Accustomed to getting good grades, she glanced <u>nonchalantly</u> at the D- she received on her research paper.

   _____

4. Even though Joe had some <u>apprehension</u>, he was a little bit afraid to enter the cave.

   _____

5. He looked at her with <u>disdain</u>, a friendly smile spreading across his face.

   _____

6. Mary Ann entered the room <u>audaciously</u>, tiptoeing quietly to avoid being noticed.

   _____

B. WORD STUDY: *The Latin suffix -ity means "the quality of or state of being." Add the suffix -ity to each of the following words (change the ending where necessary), and then write a sentence using each word.*

1. acceptable: _____

   _____

2. desirable: _____

   _____

3. possible: _____

   _____

Name _____ Date _____

"There Will Come Soft Rains" by Ray Bradbury
Writing About the Big Question

Can progress be made without conflict?

Big Question Vocabulary

adversity	change	compromise	concession	confrontation
debate	motive	negotiate	oppose	progress
radical	reconciliation	resolve	struggle	unify

A. *Write the word from the list above that best completes each sentence.*

1. In "There Will Come Soft Rains," technological _____
   leads to terrible consequences.

2. Humans have always had to _____ to change
   their environment.

3. Human beings are often able to overcome _____.

4. After Janet and Lisa argued, they both secretly hoped for a _____.

B. *Follow the directions in responding to each of the items below.*

1. In one or two sentences, explain what you feel is one of the most important technological advances humans have made. Use at least one Big Question vocabulary word.

   _____

   _____

2. From your own experience or knowledge of history, explain how this advance has led to conflict.

   _____

   _____

C. *Complete the sentence below. Then, write a paragraph in which you connect this experience to the Big Question.*

   A benefit of technological progress is _____

   _____

   _____

   _____

   _____

   _____

   _____

   _____

Name _____ Date _____

"There Will Come Soft Rains" by Ray Bradbury
Literary Analysis: Setting

All stories have a **setting**—the time and the place of the story's events. To establish a setting, writers use **descriptions,** or word-pictures, to appeal to the senses. Settings shape stories by helping to determine plot as well as characters' concerns and values.

A story may have an overall setting as well as specific settings. There may be more than one setting as the action moves from place to place, and from one time to another. In Shakespeare's *Romeo and Juliet,* for example, the overall setting is Verona, Italy, in the sixteenth century, but the specific time and place changes from scene to scene.

You should pay attention to details about the setting, just as you pay attention to other information in the story. What details give you information about the time and place of a story, and what is the effect of those details? Use the following charts to organize what you learn about the settings of the story.

A. DIRECTIONS: *In the "Setting" column, fill in the overall time, overall place, specific time, and specific place in "There Will Come Soft Rains." In the "Evidence" column, fill in the detail from the story that gives you the information for the setting. In the "Impact" column, write how overall and specific times and places matter to the story. What effect, if any, does each have on the story?*

"There Will Come Soft Rains"			
	Setting	**Evidence**	**Impact**
Overall Time:			
Overall Place:			
Specific Time:			
Specific Place:			

B. DIRECTIONS: *How might "There Will Come Soft Rains" have been different if set in a different time and place? How might it have been the same? Write a brief summary of the story as it would be if its setting were today in your region of the United States.*

_____

_____

_____

_____

"There Will Come Soft Rains" by Ray Bradbury

Reading: Make Inferences and Read on to Find Additional Support

An **inference** is an insight, based on stated details, about information that is not stated. Making inferences helps you make connections between facts or events. After making an inference, **read on** to find additional support. If other details disprove your inference, change it.

DIRECTIONS: *On the lines following each passage from the story, write an inference you can draw from it. Then, write a detail from later in the story that either proves or disproves your inference.*

Example: In the living room the voice-clock sang, *"Tick-tock, seven o'clock, time to get up, time to get up, seven o'clock!"* as if it were afraid that nobody would. The morning house lay empty.

Inference: The family that lives in the house has gone away on vacation.

Detail that proves or disproves the inference: A few paragraphs later, it is revealed that the family's car is still in the garage. It is unlikely that they left without it, so something is probably wrong.

1. In the kitchen the breakfast stove gave a hissing sigh and ejected from its warm interior eight pieces of perfectly browned toast, eight eggs sunnyside up, sixteen slices of bacon, two coffees, and two cool glasses of milk.

   Inference: _____

   Detail that proves or disproves your inference: _____

   _____

2. The entire west face of the house was black, save for five places. Here the silhouette in paint of a man mowing a lawn. Here, as in a photograph, a woman bent to pick flowers. Still farther over, their images burned on wood in one titanic instant, a small boy, hands flung into the air; higher up, the image of a thrown ball, and opposite him a girl, hands raised to catch a ball which never came down.

   Inference: _____

   Detail that proves or disproves your inference: _____

   _____

3. The dog, once huge and fleshy, but now gone to bone and covered with sores, moved in and through the house, tracking mud.

   Inference: _____

   Detail that proves or disproves your inference: _____

   _____

Name _____ Date _____

"There Will Come Soft Rains" by Ray Bradbury
Vocabulary Builder

Word List

fluttered   manipulated   oblivious   paranoia   titanic   tremulous

A. DIRECTIONS: *Revise or rewrite each sentence so that the underlined vocabulary word is used logically. Be sure to keep the vocabulary word in your revision.*

Example: The house <u>shuddered</u> as it went peacefully through its morning routine.
The house <u>shuddered</u> as the fire ate away at its walls.

1. The large rock in the front yard <u>fluttered</u> in the afternoon sunshine.

   _____

2. Her voice was loud and <u>tremulous</u> as she confidently gave the best speech of her life.

   _____

3. The pebble made a <u>titanic</u> splash as it hit the surface of the pond.

   _____

4. Her <u>paranoia</u> made her a very trusting person.

   _____

5. He was <u>oblivious</u> to the speaker, paying close attention to every word.

   _____

6. The mother <u>manipulated</u> her children, letting them do exactly as they pleased.

   _____

B. WORD STUDY: *The Latin suffix -ic means "having the characteristic of or pertaining to." Add the suffix -ic to each of the following words (change the ending where necessary), and then write a sentence using each word.*

1. hero: _____

   _____

2. specify: _____

   _____

3. metal: _____

   _____

   _____

"The Street of the Cañon" by Josephina Niggli
"There Will Come Soft Rains" by Ray Bradbury
Integrated Language Skills: Grammar

Irregular Verbs

A verb has four principal parts: the present, the present participle, the past, and the past participle. Many very common verbs are irregular. This means that the past and past participle are not formed by adding *-ed* or *-d* to the present form. The past and the past participle of irregular verbs are formed in various ways. Two irregular verbs, *spend* and *bring*, are shown in the following chart.

Principal Parts of Irregular Verbs

Present	Present Participle	Past	Past Participle
spend	(is, are, was, were) spending	spent	(has, have, had) spent
bring	(is, are, was, were) bringing	brought	(has, have, had) brought

A. PRACTICE: *Identify the principal part used to form each underlined verb.*

Example:

___past___ Pepe <u>kept</u> the package under his arm until he reached the table.

____ 1. Pepe <u>laid</u> the cheese on the table where he knew people would find it.

____ 2. When Pepe left the party, he <u>had taught</u> the people of San Juan Iglesias that he did not look or act like the devil they thought he was.

____ 3. San Juan Iglesias <u>is keeping</u> the bones of the famous historian.

____ 4. An atomic bomb <u>struck</u> the city.

____ 5. The house <u>had kept</u> its peace for many days.

____ 6. The sun <u>will rise</u> again over the ruined city.

B. Writing Application: *Write sentences according to the instructions. Check a dictionary if you are unsure of the correct irregular forms.*

   Example: Write a sentence using the past participle form of the verb *write*.
      Ray Bradbury <u>has written</u> many stories about the consequences of future technological growth.

1. Write a sentence using the past participle form of the verb *shrink.*

   _____

2. Write a sentence using the present form of the verb *freeze.*

   _____

3. Write a sentence using the present participle form of the verb *burst.*

   _____

Name _____ Date _____

"The Street of the Cañon" by Josephina Niggli
"There Will Come Soft Rains" by Ray Bradbury
Integrated Language Skills: Support for Writing a Letter to a Friend and a Book Review

Fill in the story map below to help you summarize "The Street of the Cañon" or "There Will Come Soft Rains."

The Main Conflict or Problem:

Event 1:	Event 2:	Event 3:

Event 4:	Event 5:	Event 6:

The Resolution or Solution to the Problem:

The Ending:

Now, use your completed story map to help you write your personal letter and book review. Remember to use language appropriate for each audience and provide information that each audience would expect and find interesting.

Name _____   Date _____

Writing About the Big Question

Can progress be made without conflict?

Big Question Vocabulary

adversity	change	compromise	concession	confrontation
debate	motive	negotiate	oppose	progress
radical	reconciliation	resolve	struggle	unify

A. *Write the word from the list above that best completes each sentence.*

1. Bobby had an unselfish _____ for his actions.

2. After the disaster, people had to _____ to survive.

3. Even though they suffered great _____, they built a new life.

4. The disaster caused a dramatic _____ from the previous civilization to the new way of life.

5. Bobby's uncle hoped that Bobby would make a _____ change in behavior.

B. *Follow the directions in responding to each of the items below.*

1. In several sentences, describe an internal conflict that you experienced in the past. Use one or two Big Question vocabulary words from the list.

   _____

   _____

   _____

2. Write a sentence or two describing how you were able to resolve the conflict.

   _____

   _____

C. *Complete the sentence below. Then, write a short paragraph in which you connect this experience to the Big Question.*

To deal with life's challenges, you should _____.

   _____

   _____

   _____

   _____

"One Thousand Dollars" by O. Henry
"By the Waters of Babylon" by Stephen Vincent Benét
Literary Analysis: Point of View

Point of view is the perspective from which a story is told. Most stories are told from either first-person point of view or third-person point of view.

In **first-person point of view,** the narrator is one of the characters and refers to himself or herself with the pronouns *I* or *me.* In "By the Waters of Babylon," for example, the story's narrator is also its main character, John.

In **third-person point of view,** the narrator does not participate in the action. Instead, the narrator refers to characters by the third-person pronouns *he, she, him, her, they,* and *them.* "One Thousand Dollars" is told in third-person point of view. A narrator outside the story tells about the actions and experiences of the main character, Bob Gillian.

Sometimes, a writer gives the reader more information than the narrator or a character has. By doing so, the writer creates **dramatic irony,** a forceful contrast between what the reader knows to be true and what the narrator or character believes.

DIRECTIONS: *Write your answers to the following questions.*

1. How can you tell that "One Thousand Dollars" is told in third-person point of view? _____

_____

2. At the end of "One Thousand Dollars," what do Gillian and the reader know that the lawyers do *not* know? _____

_____

3. Reread the last sentence of "One Thousand Dollars." How does this sentence create dramatic irony? _____

_____

4. Does this dramatic irony make you see other people in a new light? Why or why not?

_____

5. **A.** Give one quote from "By the Waters of Babylon" that helps you identify John as the story's first-person narrator. _____

_____

   B. Now, circle the word or words in the quote that reveal the point of view.

6. What does John know that the reader does *not* know? _____

_____

7. Give one detail from "By the Waters of Babylon" about which the reader has more knowledge than John does. _____

_____

8. What mood is created by the story's dramatic irony? _____

_____

Name _____ Date _____

Vocabulary Builder

Word List

nevertheless   prudence   prudent   purification   purified   stipulates

A. DIRECTIONS: *Each sentence below features a word from the Word List. Explain whether each sentence makes sense, given the meaning of the underlined word. If it does not make sense, write a new sentence using the word correctly.*

1. Lake water should be <u>purified</u> before it is consumed.

   _____

   _____

2. It was <u>prudent</u> of James to rollerblade without a helmet.

   _____

   _____

3. Greta is sleepy; <u>nevertheless</u>, she wants to go to bed.

   _____

   _____

4. The entry form <u>stipulates</u> that all contestants must be under 18 years of age.

   _____

   _____

5. Jack exercised <u>prudence</u> in refusing to spend his savings to go to the movies.

   _____

   _____

6. When the water <u>purification</u> plant closed, the water tasted fresher.

   _____

   _____

B. DIRECTIONS: *Write each word from the Word List next to its correct definition.*

_____ 1. exercising sound judgment; cautious

_____ 2. in spite of that; however

_____ 3. cleansed; made pure

_____ 4. includes specifically as part of an agreement

_____ 5. the process of getting rid of impurities

_____ 6. good judgment

Name _____   Date _____

"One Thousand Dollars" by O. Henry
"By the Waters of Babylon" by Stephen Vincent Benét

Integrated Language Skills: Support for Writing to Compare Literary Works

Before you draft your essay comparing how each author uses point of view to create irony, complete the graphic organizers below.

One Thousand Dollars
What truth is revealed at the end of the story?
Who sees the truth? (Consider the narrator, the story's characters, and the reader.) Who does not?
What is ironic about the story's ending? (Do the reader, the characters, or the narrator continue to hold any wrong assumptions?) How does the ironic ending affect the way you see yourself, the world, or others?

By the Waters of Babylon
What truth is revealed at the end of the story?
Who sees the truth? (Consider the narrator, the story's characters, and the reader.) Who does not?
What is ironic about the story's ending? (Do the reader, the characters, or the narrator continue to hold any wrong assumptions?) How does the ironic ending affect the way you see yourself, the world, or others?

Now, use your notes to write an essay comparing how point of view creates irony in each story. In your essay, explain which use of irony you found more effective, and why.

All-in-One Workbook
© Pearson Education, Inc. All rights reserved.
89

Name _____ Date _____

Writing About the Big Question

Can progress be made without conflict?

Big Question Vocabulary

adversity	change	compromise	concession	confrontation
debate	motive	negotiate	oppose	progress
radical	reconciliation	resolve	struggle	unify

A. *Write a sentence explaining whether the underlined word in each sentence is used correctly or incorrectly.*

1. The two friends reached a <u>reconciliation</u> after not speaking to each other for weeks.

   _____

2. Because of their <u>compromise,</u> their disagreement continued for months.

   _____

3. Barry tried to <u>negotiate</u> with his little brother about who could use the computer first.

   _____

4. Because of all the <u>progress</u> they made, nothing changed.

   _____

5. Everyone was happy about the <u>confrontation</u> between Janet and her teacher.

   _____

B. *Follow the directions in responding to each of the items below.*

1. In "How Much Land Does a Man Need?" the main character has an internal conflict about how much land he should try to earn. Write a sentence describing a conflict in which a person must weigh his or her desire against what is reasonable. Use one or two Big Question vocabulary words.

   _____

   _____

2. Based on your description above, explain what you might have done in the same situation.

   _____

   _____

C. *Complete the sentence below. Then, write a short paragraph in which you connect this experience to the big question.*

In "How Much Land Does a Man Need?" a man must decide what to do when he has conflict with his neighbors over land. Complete this sentence:

Options for dealing with conflict in the community include: _____

_____

Name _____   Date _____

"How Much Land Does a Man Need?" by Leo Tolstoy
Literary Analysis: Theme and Philosophical Assumptions

The **theme** of a literary work is the central message it communicates. To express a theme, a writer may take one of these approaches: (1) directly state the theme of the work, or have a character directly state it; or (2) create patterns of story elements to suggest a larger meaning. Themes that appeal to all times and cultures are universal themes.

In many cases, a theme reflects a **philosophical assumption**—the writer's basic beliefs about life. The writer's literary work may reflect these beliefs.

A. DIRECTIONS: *Write Tolstoy's philosophical assumption in "How Much Land Does a Man Need?" Then, explain how three major events in the story reflect this philosophical assumption. Finally, write the central theme in your own words.*

Philosophical assumption: _____

_____

First major event and how it reflects Tolstoy's assumption: _____

_____

_____

_____

Second major event and how it reflects Tolstoy's assumption: _____

_____

_____

_____

Third major event and how it reflects Tolstoy's assumption: _____

_____

_____

_____

Theme: _____

_____

B. DIRECTIONS: *Tolstoy's theme in "How Much Land Does a Man Need?" is a universal theme. In other words, it has meaning in all times and for all cultures. Explain how this theme applies to modern life in the United States.*

_____

_____

_____

_____

"How Much Land Does a Man Need?" by Leo Tolstoy
Reading: Recognize Key Details to Draw Conclusions About Theme

To identify the **theme** of a story, pay attention to **key details.** Combine later details with earlier ones to **draw a conclusion** about the author's message. There might be more than one theme in a story, but there is usually one central theme that is the guiding message the author intends to communicate. If the theme is not directly stated by the author or a character in the story, look for clues to help determine the theme. Clues can be found in details such as dialogue, setting, symbolism, conflict, plot action, and more.

DIRECTIONS: *Write the theme of "How Much Land Does a Man Need?" on the lines below. Then complete the chart by explaining how each detail helps a reader draw a conclusion about the theme of the story.*

Theme: _____

_____

Detail	Conclusion
Example: At the beginning of the story, the Devil hears Pahom thinking that, if he had enough land, he would fear nothing, not even the Devil.	By having the Devil listen in on Pahom's thoughts, Tolstoy shows that he thinks greed for property is a path to evil.
1. Pahom begins to argue with his neighbors and the judges because people are trespassing on his land. His place in the community gets worse, even though he is a landowner now.	
2. Pahom almost makes a deal for more land in his second home, when a passing dealer tells him about the land of the Bashkirs. He cancels his deal and goes to see the Bashkirs' land for himself.	
3. The night before he marks his land claim, Pahom does not sleep well. He dreams that every person who has tempted him with the promise of more land was the Devil in disguise.	
4. While Pahom is marking off the land he wants to claim, he cannot resist including a damp hollow where he believes flax would grow well.	
5. Pahom's servant buries him. All the land that Pahom needs in the end is a grave long enough for him to lie in—six feet.	

Name _____ Date _____

"How Much Land Does a Man Need?" by Leo Tolstoy
Vocabulary Builder

Word List

    aggrieved   arable   discord   forbore   piqued   prostrate

A. DIRECTIONS: *Fill in the following chart with at least one synonym, at least one antonym, and an example sentence for each word.*

Word	Synonym	Antonym	Example Sentence
1. piqued			
2. forbore			
3. aggrieved			
4. arable			
5. discord			
6. prostrate			

B. WORD STUDY: *The Latin prefix dis- means "apart or separation" or "not." Write an original sentence using each of the following words.*

    1. **disenchanted:** _____

    _____

    2. **disembark:** _____

    _____

    3. **disregard:** _____

    _____

All-in-One Workbook
93

Name _____ Date _____

"**Civil Peace**" by Chinua Achebe

Writing About the Big Question

Can progress be made without conflict?

Big Question Vocabulary

adversity	change	compromise	concession	confrontation
debate	motive	negotiate	oppose	progress
radical	reconciliation	resolve	struggle	unify

A. *Use one or more words from the list above to complete each sentence.*

1. Jonathan felt his conflict with the thieves was _____

2. Civil war can cause people to _____

3. The children settled their argument over the ball by _____

   _____

4. Abby wanted to learn to play chess, so she _____

B. *Follow the directions in responding to each of the items below.*

1. Using two or more of the Big Question vocabulary words, describe a recent cata-
   strophic event that has challenged people's survival.

   _____

   _____

2. Using the description above, explain what specific challenges people might face due
   to the event, and how they might overcome them.

   _____

   _____

C. *Complete the sentence below. Then, write a short paragraph in which you connect this
experience to the Big Question.*

   To use war as a path to progress, a person must _____

   _____

   _____

   _____

All-in-One Workbook
© Pearson Education, Inc. All rights reserved.

94

Name _____ Date _____

Literary Analysis: Theme and Philosophical Assumptions

The **theme** of a literary work is the central message it communicates. To express a theme, a writer may take one of these approaches: (1) directly state the theme of the work, or have a character directly state it; or (2) create patterns of story elements to suggest a larger meaning. Themes that appeal to all times and cultures are universal themes.

In many cases, a theme reflects a **philosophical assumption**—the writer's basic beliefs about life. The writer's literary work may reflect these beliefs.

A. DIRECTIONS: *Write Achebe's philosophical assumption in "Civil Peace." Then, explain how three major events in the story reflect this philosophical assumption. Finally, write the central theme in your own words.*

Philosophical assumption: _____

_____

First major event and how it reflects Achebe's assumption: _____

_____

_____

_____

Second major event and how it reflects Achebe's assumption: _____

_____

_____

_____

Third major event and how it reflects Achebe's assumption: _____

_____

_____

_____

Theme: _____

_____

B. DIRECTIONS: *Achebe's theme in "Civil Peace" is a universal theme. In other words, it has meaning in all times and for all cultures. Explain how this theme applies to modern life in the United States.*

_____

_____

_____

_____

"Civil Peace" by Chinua Achebe

Reading: Recognize Key Details to Draw Conclusions About Theme

To identify the **theme** of a story, pay attention to **key details**. Combine later details with earlier ones to **draw a conclusion** about the author's message. There might be more than one theme in a story, but there is usually one central theme that is the guiding message the author intends to communicate. If the theme is not directly stated by the author or a character in the story, look for clues to help determine the theme. Clues can be found in details such as dialogue, setting, symbolism, conflict, plot action, and more.

DIRECTIONS: *Write the theme of "Civil Peace" on the lines below. Then, complete the chart by explaining how each detail helps a reader draw a conclusion about the theme of the story.*

Theme: _____

_____

_____

Detail	Conclusion
Example: At the beginning of the story, Jonathan Iwegbu is thankful for his five remaining family members.	The author puts Jonathan's life in perspective by showing readers the violence and brutality of the war that has recently ended. Jonathan regards it as a miracle and a blessing that five members of his family managed to stay alive.
1. Jonathan discovers that his house is still standing. He is overwhelmed with disbelief and joy.	
2. Jonathan sells palm-wine, and his wife sells breakfast akara balls.	
3. Jonathan receives twenty pounds as an *egg-rasher* payment. He thinks that it is like Christmas to receive this money.	
4. Thieves come to take Jonathan's money. He does not fight them and makes a deal with them to give him his *egg-rasher* if they will not hunt him and his family.	
5. Jonathan's neighbors feel sorry for him, but he says, "I count it as nothing." He points out that he survived without the money before he got it.	

"Civil Peace" by Chinua Achebe
Vocabulary Builder

Word List

amenable   commiserate   destitute   disreputable   dissent   inaudibly

A. DIRECTIONS: *Fill in the following chart with at least one synonym, at least one antonym, and an example sentence for each word.*

Word	Synonym	Antonym	Example Sentence
1. disreputable			
2. amenable			
3. destitute			
4. commiserate			
5. inaudibly			
6. dissent			

B. WORD STUDY: *The Latin prefix com- means "together" or "with." Write an original sentence using each of the following words.*

1. **compassion:** _____

_____

2. **combat:** _____

_____

3. **commerce:** _____

_____

"How Much Land Does a Man Need?" by Leo Tolstoy
"Civil Peace" by Chinua Achebe

Integrated Language Skills: Grammar

Action and Linking Verbs

An **action verb** shows physical or mental action. A **linking verb** expresses a state of being or tells what the subject is by linking it to one or more words in the predicate. The most common linking verbs are forms of *be* (*is, are, was, were,* and so on). Other verbs are linking verbs if they can be replaced with a form of *be* and the sentence still makes sense.

Action verbs: Pahom *buys* some land from his neighbor. [shows physical action; cannot be replaced with a form of *be*]

Jonathan *values* his family's lives more than anything else. [shows mental action; cannot be replaced with a form of *be*]

Linking verbs: Pahom *is* content with his new farm for a while. [links *Pahom* to *content; is* is a form of *be*]

Jonathan *feels* grateful for his family's survival. [links *Jonathan* to *grateful;* can be replaced with *is*]

A. PRACTICE: *The following sentences are based on "How Much Land Does a Man Need?" or "Civil Peace." Identify each verb as either a linking verb or an action verb by writing LV or AV on the line before each sentence.*

Example:

_AV_ Pahom listened to his wife's discussion with her sister.

____ 1. The Devil was thrilled about Pahom's boast.

____ 2. The Devil gained power over Pahom through his greed for more land.

____ 3. Pahom remained unhappy, even with a larger farm.

____ 4. Jonathan seemed genuinely happy to find his home mostly intact.

____ 5. The Iwegbu family worked hard to get by after the war.

____ 6. The thieves took Jonathan's "egg-rasher" money.

B. Writing Application: *Write a paragraph based on either "How Much Land Does a Man Need?" or "Civil Peace." Use both action and linking verbs. Circle each verb and label it with LV or AV.*

_____

_____

_____

_____

_____

_____

_____

"**How Much Land Does a Man Need?**" by Leo Tolstoy
"**Civil Peace**" by Chinua Achebe

Integrated Language Skills: Support for Writing a Character Analysis

For your character analysis, use the following graphic organizer to help you identify the main traits that define Pahom or Jonathan Iwegbu. Then, fill in examples of incidents and descriptions in the story that show these traits.

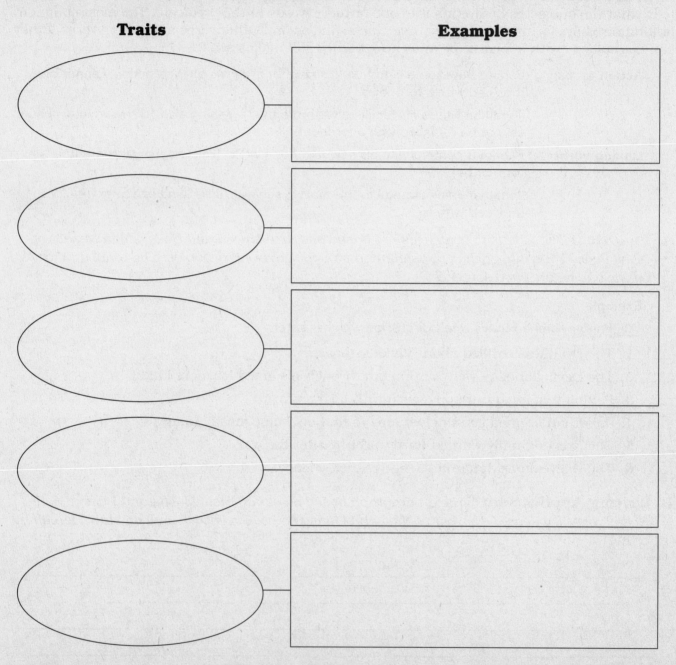

Now, use this graphic organizer to help you write a brief character analysis of Pahom or Jonathan.

Name _____   Date _____

"The Masque of the Red Death" by Edgar Allan Poe
Writing About the Big Question
Can progress be made without conflict?

Big Question Vocabulary

adversity	change	compromise	concession	confrontation
debate	motive	negotiate	oppose	progress
radical	reconciliation	resolve	struggle	unify

A. *Write the word from the list above that best completes each sentence.*

1. People of the Middle Ages had to face the terrible _____ of the plague.

2. The prince's _____ for shutting himself in his abbey was fear.

3. The School Council will hold a _____ among candidates for council president.

4. When Andy lost the election, he gave a very generous _____ speech.

5. The new president must _____ and work with a variety of groups to reach a compromise among those who all want to put their interests first.

B. *Follow the directions in responding to each of the items below.*

1. In a sentence or two, describe an event, either historical or from your own experience, when someone struggled to overcome almost certain defeat.

   _____

   _____

2. Based on your description above, explain the outcome of the struggle. Use one or two Big Question vocabulary words in your answer.

   _____

   _____

C. *Complete the sentence below. Then, write a short paragraph in which you connect this experience to the Big Question.*

   The best way to resolve a dangerous situation is _____

   _____

   _____

   _____

Name _____ Date _____

Literary Analysis: Symbolism and Allegory

Symbolism is a writer's use of symbols. A **symbol** is a character, place, thing, or event in a literary work that stands for a larger idea. For example, a raven in a story might stand for death, or a doorway might stand for a new opportunity. To make a particular character or thing into a symbol, a writer may use these common strategies: (1) calling on traditional associations, such as a branching pathway that represents a choice in life; or (2) creating new associations, such as a character becoming more noble after choosing a path, which in turn helps the reader understand that the path represents courage or bravery.

A story in which all characters and settings are clearly symbolic is called an **allegory**.

DIRECTIONS: *Complete the following chart. Explain what you think each symbol in "The Masque of the Red Death" represents and how it helps teach the lesson of the story.*

Symbol	What it represents	How it helps teach the lesson
Example: dreams	masqueraders, fantasies	Shows us that life is fleeting; forebodes the grim ending to the story
1. the masked visitor		
2. the black chamber		
3. the music		
4. the clock		

Name _____ Date _____

Reading: Identify Patterns to Draw Conclusions About Symbolism

When you **draw a conclusion,** you make a decision or form an opinion based on facts and details in a text. To draw a conclusion about the meaning of a symbol, **identify patterns** that suggest the nature of an object's greater importance.

DIRECTIONS: *List three details from the story that have to do with each symbol. Then identify a pattern created by these details in regard to the symbol. Finally, draw a conclusion about what the symbol means based on the pattern you discover.*

1. Symbol: the masked visitor
   Three details about this symbol:

   A. _____

   B. _____

   C. _____

   Pattern: _____

   _____

   Meaning: _____

   _____

   _____

2. Symbol: the black chamber
   Three details about this symbol:

   A. _____

   B. _____

   C. _____

   Pattern: _____

   _____

   Meaning: _____

   _____

   _____

Name _____   Date _____

Word List

august   cessation   decorum   impeded   profuse   tangible

A. DIRECTIONS: *In each of the following items, think about the meaning of the italicized word, and then answer the question.*

1. If a home has an *august* appearance, what kind of people would you assume live there? Why?

   _____

2. If Lindsey went to a baseball game and something *impeded* her view of the field, do you think she enjoyed the game? Why or why not?

   _____

3. If you hear the *cessation* of your air conditioner on an extremely hot day, how might you feel? Why?

   _____

4. If you received a *profuse* number of birthday gifts, would you be pleased? Why or why not?

   _____

5. If you had a friend who always behaved with *decorum*, would your parents approve? Why or why not?

   _____

6. If there were *tangible* evidence against a person accused of a crime, how should that person be treated? Why?

   _____

B. WORD STUDY: *The Latin suffix -tion means "the act, process, or fact of." Write the definition of each of the following words based on the meaning of the suffix -tion.*

1. **restoration:** _____

   _____

2. **hesitation:** _____

   _____

3. **recommendation:** _____

   _____

"The Garden of Stubborn Cats" by Italo Calvino

Writing About the Big Question

Can progress be made without conflict?

Big Question Vocabulary

adversity	change	compromise	concession	confrontation
debate	motive	negotiate	oppose	progress
radical	reconciliation	resolve	struggle	unify

A. *Circle the word or phrase that is closest in meaning to the underlined word.*

1. <u>unify:</u> settle; bring together

2. <u>reconciliation:</u> a reestablishment of friendship; a compromise

3. <u>radical:</u> emerging; extreme

4. <u>confrontation:</u> proof of wrong; face-off

5. <u>oppose:</u> resist; persecute

B. *Follow the directions in responding to each of the items below.*

1. Write one or two sentences describing an event in which an older structure or undeveloped land was cleared to make way for something new over the objections of some community members. Use at least one Big Question vocabulary word.

   _____

   _____

   _____

2. In a few sentences, explain whether you think this progress was worth the conflict.

   _____

   _____

   _____

C. *Complete the sentence below. Then, write a short paragraph in which you connect this experience to the Big Question.*

   When confronted with force, it is best to _____

   _____

   _____

   _____

   _____

   _____

"The Garden of Stubborn Cats" by Italo Calvino
Literary Analysis: Symbolism and Allegory

Symbolism is a writer's use of symbols. A **symbol** is a character, place, thing, or event in a literary work that stands for a larger idea. For example, a raven in a story might stand for death, or a doorway might stand for a new opportunity. To make a particular character or thing into a symbol, a writer may use these common strategies: (1) calling on traditional associations, such as a branching pathway that represents a choice in life; or (2) creating new associations, such as a character becoming more noble after choosing a path, which in turn helps the reader understand that the path represents courage or bravery.

A story in which all characters and settings are clearly symbolic is called an **allegory.**

DIRECTIONS: *Complete the following chart. Explain what you think each symbol in "The Garden of Stubborn Cats" represents and how it helps teach the lesson of the story.*

Symbol	What it represents	How it helps teach the lesson
Example: cats	mischief and mystery	Shows us that cats are clever and adaptable creatures; their society is mysterious to humans and has its own rules
1. the fish Marcovaldo catches		
2. the garden		
3. the cat lovers		
4. those who dislike the cat garden		

"**The Garden of Stubborn Cats**" by Italo Calvino
Reading: Identify Patterns to Draw Conclusions About Symbolism

When you **draw a conclusion,** you make a decision or form an opinion based on facts and details in a text. To draw a conclusion about the meaning of a symbol, **identify patterns** that suggest the nature of an object's greater importance.

DIRECTIONS: *List three details from the story that have to do with each symbol. Then identify a pattern created by these details in regard to the symbol. Finally, draw a conclusion about what the symbol means based on the pattern you discover.*

1. Symbol: the "city of cats"
    Three details about this symbol:

    A. _____

    B. _____

    C. _____

    Pattern: _____

    _____

    Meaning: _____

    _____

    _____

2. Symbol: the Marchesa
    Three details about this symbol:

    A. _____

    B. _____

    C. _____

    Pattern: _____

    _____

    Meaning: _____

    _____

    _____

Name _____   Date _____

"The Garden of Stubborn Cats" by Italo Calvino
Vocabulary Builder

Word List

consigned   futile   indigence   intrigues   itinerary   squalid

A. DIRECTIONS: *In each of the following items, think about the meaning of the italicized word, and then answer the question.*

1. If you went on a vacation to a foreign country, would you be likely to see more sights with or without an *itinerary*? Why?

   _____

   _____

2. What kind of person might be involved in *intrigues*? In what kinds of intrigues might such a person participate?

   _____

   _____

3. If the national economy is improving, is the level of *indigence* likely to increase? Why or why not?

   _____

   _____

4. Would you be happy to live in a *squalid* home? Why or why not?

   _____

   _____

5. If a package were *consigned* to someone, how might that person respond?

   _____

   _____

6. If someone told you that pursuing your dreams was *futile*, how would you react?

   _____

   _____

B. WORD STUDY: *The Latin suffix -id means "the body of or related to." Write the definition of each of the following words based on the meaning of the suffix -id.*

1. **horrid:** _____

   _____

2. **morbid:** _____

   _____

3. **livid:** _____

   _____

"The Masque of the Red Death" by Edgar Allan Poe
"The Garden of Stubborn Cats" by Italo Calvino
Integrated Language Skills: Grammar

Active and Passive Voice

A verb is in the **active voice** when the subject performs the action. A verb is in the **passive voice** when the action is performed on the subject. Verbs in the passive voice consist of a form of *be* used as a helping verb followed by the past participle of the main verb. Passive voice is used when the writer wants to emphasize the recipient of the action. Passive voice is also used when the subject performing the action is unknown. However, you should choose the active voice whenever possible because it is more direct and less wordy than passive voice.

Active voice:	Marcovaldo *followed* the tabby.
Passive voice:	The tabby *was followed* by Marcovaldo.
Active voice:	The Red Death *frightened* Prince Prospero.
Passive voice:	Prince Prospero *was frightened* of the Red Death.

A. PRACTICE: *Identify each verb or verb phrase as active or passive by writing AV or PV on the line before each sentence.*

Example:

 PV Prospero's guests were given a safe place to stay.

_____ 1. A fish *was caught* by Marcovaldo.

_____ 2. Marcovaldo *followed* the fishing line to the Marchesa's garden.

_____ 3. The Marchesa *was cooking* the fish.

_____ 4. An elaborate masquerade *was thrown* by Prospero for his guests.

B. Writing Application: *Rewrite each sentence below, changing it from passive to active voice.*

1. Marcovaldo was told that the cats were never fed by the Marchesa.

   _____

2. Construction is stopped by the mischievous cats.

   _____

3. The Red Death is characterized by bleeding from the pores.

   _____

4. The Red Death, though a fictitious disease, is based on the real Black Death of the 1300s.

   _____

Name _____ Date _____

"The Masque of the Red Death" by Edgar Allan Poe
"The Garden of Stubborn Cats" by Italo Calvino
Integrated Language Skills: Support for Writing a Narrative

Use the graphic organizer below to help you come up with an animal to use as a symbol in your narrative. To show what the animal stands for, first describe it using vivid adjectives that suggest the qualities it symbolizes. Then, provide information about its situation and actions. Give it a name that hints at what it represents.

Finally, plan how you will link it to important events in your story.

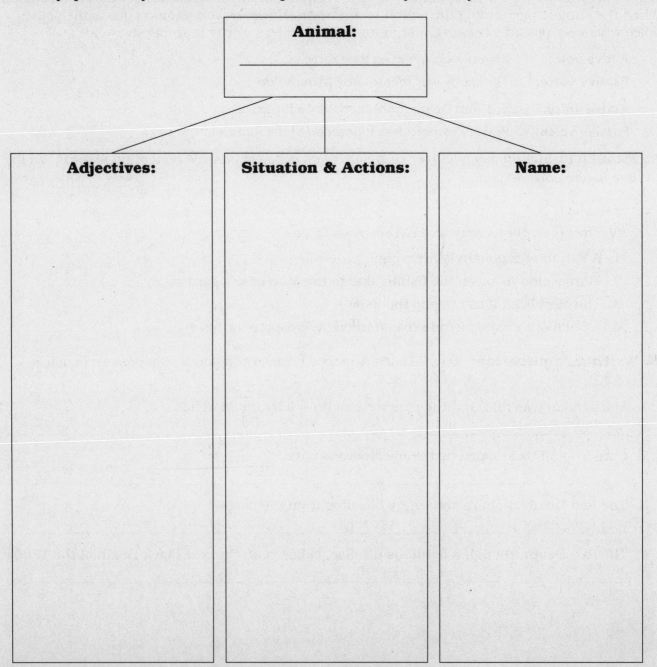

Now, use this graphic organizer to help you write your brief narrative using an animal as a symbol.

All-in-One Workbook
© Pearson Education, Inc. All rights reserved.
109

Name _____ Date _____

"The Censors" by Luisa Valenzuela
"The Leader in the Mirror" by Pat Mora

Writing About the Big Question

Can progress be made without conflict?

Big Question Vocabulary

adversity	change	compromise	concession	confrontation
debate	motive	negotiate	oppose	progress
radical	reconciliation	resolve	struggle	unify

A. *Write the word from the list above that best fits each definition.*

1. to go against _____

2. to argue or disagree with _____

3. to settle differences or to end a problem _____

4. the giving up of something to another _____

5. to discuss issues with another in an attempt to settle differences _____

B. *Follow the directions in responding to each of the items below.*

1. In both selections, an individual experiences conflict with society in one form or another. In one or two sentences, describe another type of conflict that an individual might have with society. Use one or more Big Question vocabulary words.

   _____

   _____

   _____

2. Describe a time when a conflict between individuals or groups and the larger society resulted in progress for society.

   _____

   _____

C. *Complete the sentence below. Then, write a short paragraph in which you connect this experience to the Big Question.*

   If you had no challenges in your life, _____

   _____

   _____

   _____

   _____

   _____

"**The Censors**" by Luisa Valenzuela
"**The Leader in the Mirror**" by Pat Mora
Literary Analysis: Tone

The **tone** of a work is the writer's attitude toward his or her subject and audience. Tone is closely related to **voice**, the personality that a writer shows to readers. For example, in "The Censors," Louisa Valenzuela uses a matter-of-fact tone. Her voice is calm and detached. Pat Mora, on the other hand, uses a serious, somewhat formal tone in "The Leader in the Mirror." Her voice is respectful.

Tone may be conveyed by several elements, including the details the writer chooses to include: the **diction**, or word choice, that the writer uses, and the direct statements of the writer's feelings. When Mora writes that her speech to young people would be an "occasion for reflection," she chooses words that reflect the seriousness of the task—and also of the essay that she is writing.

DIRECTIONS: *Answer the following questions to help you analyze the tone of "The Censors" and "The Leader in the Mirror."*

1. Which selection's tone makes you feel as if you are chatting with the author at a party?

    _____

    Write two sentences from the selection that make you feel this way.

    _____

    _____

    Now circle two words in these sentences that reflect the author's diction. What kinds of words are these? Write an adjective to describe them.

    _____

2. Which selection's tone is at odds with what is being discussed or described?

    _____

    Write two sentences from the selection that make you feel this way.

    _____

    _____

    Now circle two words in these sentences that reflect the author's diction. What kinds of words are these? Write an adjective to describe them.

    _____

"The Censors" by Luisa Valenzuela
"The Leader in the Mirror" by Pat Mora
Vocabulary Builder

Word List

aspirations   aspire   catalyst   heritage

inheritance   irreproachable   staidness   ulterior

A. DIRECTIONS: *Write a complete sentence to answer each question. For each item, use a word from the Word List in place of the underlined word(s) with a similar meaning.*

Example: What might you <u>wish to achieve</u> in your life?

Answer: I might <u>aspire</u> to becoming an Olympic gold medalist.

1. What motive <u>beyond</u> kindness might a person have for doing a good deed?

_____

2. What could be <u>something that makes</u> your dog begin barking?

_____

3. What do some people do with the <u>money and property left to them by their parents?</u>

_____

4. Why might a person who is <u>blameless</u> make a poor leader?

_____

5. In what kind of situation would a <u>state of seriousness or somberness</u> be appropriate?

_____

6. Do you think a person with a <u>strong desire to do something</u> will accomplish much?

_____

7. Why is it important to protect <u>the things passed down to us from previous generations?</u>

_____

B. DIRECTIONS: *On the line, write the letter of the word that is most nearly* opposite *in meaning to the word in CAPITAL LETTERS.*

____ 1. ASPIRE:
     A. hope   B. breathe   C. despair   D. encourage

____ 2. STAIDNESS:
     A. restlessness   B. weakness   C. oddness   D. gentleness

____ 3. IRREPROACHABLE:
     A. distant   B. guilty   C. harmless   D. calm

____ 4. CATALYST:
     A. producer   B. chemical   C. outcome   D. degenerator

"The Censors" by Luisa Valenzuela
"The Leader in the Mirror" by Pat Mora
Support for Writing a Comparison-and-Contrast Essay

Before you draft your essay comparing and contrasting the ideas of honesty and deception in these two selections, complete the graphic organizer below.

	"The Censors"	**"The Leader in the Mirror"**
Tone		
Major Points the Author Makes		
Details, Diction, or Direct Statements That Convey Tone		
How Tone Affects My Reaction		

Now, use your notes to write an essay comparing your reactions to the tone in each selection.

Palm of Our Hands, performed by Polina Goudieva

I'm waiting for the day I get out of this grind

A way to **adapt**, and to change, something to open my mind

Awareness of unfairness / I see

Makes me wanna cry sometimes

So many problems, we're facing it's crazy and nobody knows how to solve

I figure it's either I move to the moon or we all gotta learn to adapt and **evolve**

How we're spinning around (it's a mystery)

If we're **ignorant** of **history**

Looking for some peace and **understanding**

Asking all these **question**s without end

Looking for some love and **empathy**

Do you feel what I feel

Looking for some peace and **understanding**

Asking all these **questions** without end

Looking for the mind that knows it all

Enlightenment it's in the palm of my hands

I'm growing and not just in height

The truth about **growth** is it only comes from **insight**

Reflecting, thinking about what

Is wrong and what is right

The **influence** of science is in us—even the food's **modified**

Genetics and ethics are changing, we expect it all to be **revised**

How we're spinning around (it's a mystery)

If we're **ignorant** of **history**

Looking for some peace and **understanding**

Asking all these **question**s without end

Looking for some love and **empathy**

Do you feel what I feel

Continued

Looking for some peace and **understanding**

Asking all these **questions** without end

Looking for the mind that knows it all

Enlightenment it's in the palm of my hands

Palm of my hands, palm of my hands, palm of my hands,

It's in the palm of my hands, palm of my hands, palm of my hands,

palm of my hands

So many problems, we're facing it's crazy and nobody knows how to solve

I figure it's either I move to the moon or we all gotta learn to adapt and **evolve**

How we're spinning around (it's a mystery)

If we're **ignorant** of **history**

Song Title: **Palm of Our Hands**
Artist / Performed by Polina Goudieva
Lyrics by Polina Goudieva
Music composed and produced by Polina Goudieva and Dimitiri Ehrlich
Post production: Mike Pandolfo, Wonderful
Executive Producer: Keith London, Defined Mind

All-in-One Workbook
115

Name _____ Date _____

Unit 3: Types of Nonfiction
Big Question Vocabulary—1

The Big Question: What kind of knowledge changes our lives?

In your textbook, you learned words that are useful for talking about information and how it changes our understanding of ourselves and the world around us.

DIRECTIONS: *Review the following definitions of words you can use when talking about information and change.*

adapt: to adjust or modify to suit new conditions

awareness: the state of having knowledge of or alertness to a situation

empathy: the ability to imagine how another person feels or thinks

enlighten: to make someone aware or to impart knowledge to others

evolve: to grow, change, or develop in some way

On the lines provided, write an answer to each question. Refer to the meanings of the underlined vocabulary words in your responses.

1. How might a person <u>adapt</u> after moving to a new town and a new school?

   _____

   _____

2. How does the audience at a sporting event show its <u>awareness</u> of what is going on in the game?

   _____

   _____

3. What is an example from your life in which you or someone you know displayed <u>empathy</u> toward another person?

   _____

   _____

4. What is one method that a teacher might use to <u>enlighten</u> her students about a literary selection they are reading?

   _____

   _____

5. How might learning new information about an issue cause a person's opinion on that issue to <u>evolve</u>?

   _____

   _____

Unit 3: Types of Nonfiction
Big Question Vocabulary—2

The Big Question: What kind of knowledge changes our lives?

DIRECTIONS: *Review the following definitions of words you can use when talking about information and change.*

growth: a gradual development or increase

history: a record of past events

ignorance: the state of being uneducated or of lacking knowledge

influence: to change the actions, behavior, or opinions of others

insight: an understanding of the true nature or underlying truth of a thing

Create two different sentences for each of the following words. Try to use the word to explain something entirely different in your second sentence.

1. **growth**

   _____

   _____

2. **history**

   _____

   _____

3. **ignorance**

   _____

   _____

4. **influence**

   _____

   _____

5. **insight**

   _____

   _____

Name _____ Date _____

Unit 3: Types of Nonfiction
Big Question Vocabulary—3

The Big Question: What kind of knowledge changes our lives?

DIRECTIONS: *Review the following definitions of words you can use when talking about information and change.*

modified: changed somewhat or partially altered

question: *n.* a matter or problem of some uncertainty; *v.* to challenge or dispute a conclusion

reflect: to think deeply about something

revise: to modify or change something, especially to improve it

understanding: comprehension; knowing

On the lines below, write a paragraph about how learning new information about a situation has changed how you felt or behaved. Use at least three of the Big Question vocabulary words.

_____

_____

_____

_____

_____

_____

_____

_____

_____

_____

_____

_____

_____

_____

_____

_____

Unit 3: Types of Nonfiction
Applying the Big Question

The Big Question: What kind of knowledge changes our lives?

DIRECTIONS: *Complete the chart below to apply what you have learned about how knowledge can change your life One row has been completed for you.*

Example	Type of knowledge	What was learned?	Who acquired knowledge	Lives changed? Who?	What I learned
From Literature	Knowledge learned from experience in "Keep Memory Alive"	Silence about brutality to others harms everyone.	Elie Wiesel	Yes, Wiesel's life was changed, and his story changed others.	One person's knowledge can affect the world.
From Literature					
From Science					
From Social Studies					
From Real Life					

Name _____   Date _____

Erik Weihenmayer
Listening and Viewing

Segment 1: Meet Erik Weihenmayer
- According to Weihenmayer, why is writing more challenging than mountain climbing? Does his point of view surprise you? Why or why not?

_____

_____

_____

_____

Segment 2: The Essay
- According to Weihenmayer, why is honesty important in writing? Why is honesty important when you are conveying your ideas in an essay?

_____

_____

_____

_____

Segment 3: The Writing Process
- How does Weihenmayer prepare to write? How do you prepare to write?

_____

_____

_____

_____

Segment 4: The Rewards of Writing
- Does Weihenmayer's attitude toward writing make you think differently about the importance of literature? Why or why not?

_____

_____

_____

_____

Learning About Nonfiction

Essays and speeches are short works of nonfiction. An **essay** is a written work in which the author examines a topic and often presents his or her views. A **speech** is delivered orally to an audience. Both essays and speeches include these elements:

- **Style:** the distinctive way in which an author uses language
- **Tone:** the author's attitude toward his or her subject and audience
- **Perspective:** the viewpoint or opinion that the author expresses
- **Purpose:** the author's reason for writing or speaking

This list presents different kinds of essays and speeches:

- **Narrative essay:** the presentation of real events or personal experiences
- **Descriptive essay:** an impression about a person, an object, or an experience
- **Expository essay:** the presentation of information or the explanation of a process
- **Persuasive essay:** an attempt to persuade readers to act or think in a certain way
- **Reflective essay:** a writer's thoughts about an experience or an idea
- **Address:** a formal, prepared speech that is usually delivered by an important person
- **Talk:** an informal speech that is delivered in a conversational tone
- **Oration:** an eloquent speech that is delivered on a formal occasion
- **Lecture:** a prepared speech with which the speaker instructs or informs his or her audience

A. DIRECTIONS: *Read the description of each work. Then, identify it. Choose from the terms in boldface type in the preceding list.*

1. a short, written work that tells readers why they should buy a small car
   _____

2. a short, written work that tells about the writer's encounter with a shark
   _____

3. a short, formal work delivered orally by the winner of the Nobel peace prize at the awards
   ceremony _____

4. a short, written work that tells what Costa Rica's rain forest looks like _____

5. a short, written work that tells how to make pizza _____

6. a short work about Renaissance art delivered orally by a professor to his or her students
   _____

B. DIRECTIONS: *The following paragraph opens a speech or an essay. Identify the kind of work it begins. Explain your answer.*

Hi. I am glad you could come today. I just wanted to say a few words about the literary magazine and what we are trying to do. And I want to encourage you to speak out if you have ideas about how to make it better.

_____

_____

"Everest" *from* **Touch the Top of the World** by Erik Weihenmayer
Model Selection: Nonfiction

"Everest" is a **narrative essay,** an essay that tells about an experience that the writer, Erik Weihenmayer, has had. Like all essays, it expresses the writer's style, tone, and perspective. **Style** may be defined as the way in which the writer uses language. It involves level of formality; the use of figurative language, word choice, and sentence patterns; and methods of organization. **Tone** is the writer's attitude toward his or her subject and audience. **Perspective** is the writer's point of view or opinion.

A. DIRECTIONS: *On the chart, write details from "Everest" that reveal Weihenmayer's style, tone, and perspective.*

Style:
Tone:
Perspective:

B. DIRECTIONS: *Although "Everest" is a narrative essay, it includes elements of other types of essays. Briefly explain the ways in which "Everest" is characteristic of each of the following types of essay.*

1. **Expository:** _____

_____

2. **Reflective:** _____

_____

3. **Descriptive:** _____

_____

4. **Persuasive:** _____

_____

Name _____ Date _____

Writing About the Big Question

What kind of knowledge changes our lives?

Big Question Vocabulary

adapt	awareness	empathy	enlighten	evolve
growth	history	ignorance	influence	insight
modified	question	reflect	revise	understanding

A. *Use one or more words from the list above to complete each sentence.*

1. Animals must _____ , changing in the face of insurmountable odds, to survive.

2. The spider usually has a delicate sense of touch, so its _____ of the wasp's presence is striking.

3. The wasp has no _____ for the spider and is focused only on a home for her egg.

4. The _____ of the wasp larva toward adulthood means the death of the spider.

B. *Follow the directions in responding to each of the items below.*

1. List two pieces of knowledge about current events you acquired this week.

_____

_____

2. Choose one piece of knowledge you listed and explain whether it changed your life. Use at least two of the Big Question vocabulary words.

_____

_____

C. *Complete the sentence below. Then, write a short paragraph in which you connect this experience to the big question.*

Concrete information can be overruled by a gut reaction when _____

_____

_____

_____

Name _____   Date _____

"The Spider and the Wasp" by Alexander Petrunkevitch
Literary Analysis: Inductive and Deductive Reasoning in an Expository Essay

An **expository essay** is a brief nonfiction work that informs, defines, explains, or discusses a particular topic. Often, an expository essay includes a conclusion the writer reaches through reasoning. The writer's reasoning may be inductive or deductive. In "The Spider and the Wasp," Alexander Petrunkevitch uses both inductive and deductive reasoning.

With **inductive reasoning,** the writer reviews a number of cases and then makes a generalization from them.

In **deductive reasoning,** the writer proves that a conclusion is true by applying a general principle to a specific case.

DIRECTIONS: *Fill in the chart below to show how Petrunkevitch uses inductive and deductive reasoning to draw conclusions about whether tarantulas and wasps act instinctively or intelligently.*

	Spider	**Wasp**
Rule or Evidence	The spider will react defensively if approached from above.	Wasps will not attack the wrong species of tarantula.
Rule or Evidence		
Rule or Evidence		
Rule or Evidence		
Conclusion: Intelligent or Instinctive? (Circle One)	Intelligent Instinctive	Intelligent Instinctive

Name _____   Date _____

"The Spider and the Wasp" by Alexander Petrunkevitch

Reading: Analyze Main Ideas and Supporting Details by Summarizing

To fully understand an essay, **analyze main ideas and supporting details.** In other words, recognize each main point the writer makes and identify its relation to the ideas or facts that explain or illustrate it. To help you organize your thoughts and remember the relationships you identify, pause occasionally to summarize. To **summarize,** restate main ideas in your own words. Begin by stating the main idea and then tell the most important facts or examples that support this idea.

A. DIRECTIONS: *Use the graphic organizer below to identify the main idea and a few important supporting details in "The Spider and the Wasp."*

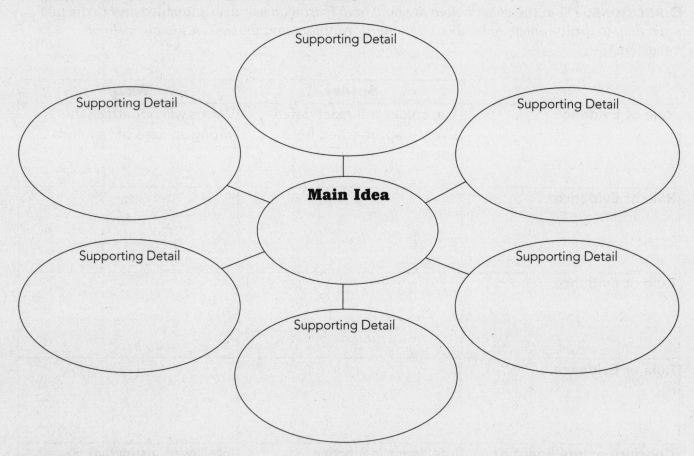

B. DIRECTIONS: *Use your completed graphic organizer to help you summarize "The Spider and the Wasp" on the lines below.*

_____

_____

_____

_____

_____

"The Spider and the Wasp" by Alexander Petrunkevitch
Vocabulary Builder

Word List

customarily   distinct   evoking   formidable   instinct   tactile

A. DIRECTIONS: *Create two different sentences for each of the following words. You may use a different form of the word in your second sentence if you wish.*

Example: Wasps use <u>instinct</u> to release a strong odor when they feel threatened.

If approached from above, the spider <u>instinctively</u> reacts with a threatening posture.

1. customarily

_____

_____

2. distinct

_____

_____

3. tactile

_____

_____

4. formidable

_____

_____

5. evoking

_____

_____

B. WORD STUDY: The **Latin root -tact-** means "touch." Answer the following questions using one of these words that contain the root -tact-: *tactless, contact, intact.*

1. How would a *tactless* person behave if someone fell into a mud puddle?
2. How could you make *contact* with a friend who lives in another city?
3. Why would you be happy if you dropped a glass and it remained *intact*?

from **Longitude** by Dava Sobel
Writing About the Big Question

What kind of information changes our lives?

Big Question Vocabulary

adapt	awareness	empathy	enlighten	evolve
growth	history	ignorance	influence	insight
modified	question	reflect	revise	understanding

A. *Use one or more words from the list above to complete each sentence.*

1. The _____ of longitude is filled with jealousy, deception, and perseverance.

2. Construction of clocks had to _____ from pendulum clocks to portable time pieces.

3. Our _____ for Harrison is great, because we, too, would want recognition for a great achievement.

4. The _____ of how to compute longitude was asked by many scientists.

B. *Follow the directions in responding to each of the items below.*

1. List an area of study that has the potential to change our lives.

   _____

   _____

2. Write two sentences explaining how knowledge gained in that area of study can be life-changing. Use at least two Big Question vocabulary words.

   _____

   _____

C. *Complete the sentence below. Then, write a short paragraph in which you connect this experience to the big question.*

Information that changes the world often deals with _____

_____

_____

_____

Name _____ Date _____

from **Longitude** by Dava Sobel
Literary Analysis: Inductive and Deductive Reasoning in an Expository Essay

An **expository essay** is a brief nonfiction work that informs, defines, explains, or discusses a particular topic. Often, an expository essay includes a conclusion the writer reaches through reasoning. The writer's reasoning may be inductive or deductive. In this excerpt from *Longitude*, Dava Sobel uses both inductive and deductive reasoning.

With **inductive reasoning,** the writer reviews a number of cases and then makes a generalization from them.

In **deductive reasoning,** the writer proves that a conclusion is true by applying a general principle to a specific case.

DIRECTIONS: *Fill in the chart below to show how Sobel uses inductive and deductive reasoning to draw conclusions about the importance of clocks in measuring longitude.*

	Importance of Accurate Clocks in Navigation	**How Harrison's Clock Solved the Longitude Problem**
Rule or Evidence	Distances in longitude are proportionate to hours in the day.	Design modifications enabled the clock to be mass produced.
Rule or Evidence		
Rule or Evidence		
Rule or Evidence		
Conclusion		

from **Longitude** by Dava Sobel

Reading: Analyze Main Ideas and Supporting Details by Summarizing

To fully understand an essay, **analyze main ideas and supporting details.** In other words, recognize each main point the writer makes and identify its relation to the ideas or facts that explain or illustrate it. To help you organize your thoughts and remember the relationships you identify, pause occasionally to summarize. To **summarize,** restate main ideas in your own words. Begin by stating the main idea and then tell the most important facts or examples that support this idea.

A. DIRECTIONS: *Use the graphic organizer below to identify the main idea and a few important supporting details in Sobel's essay from* Longitude.

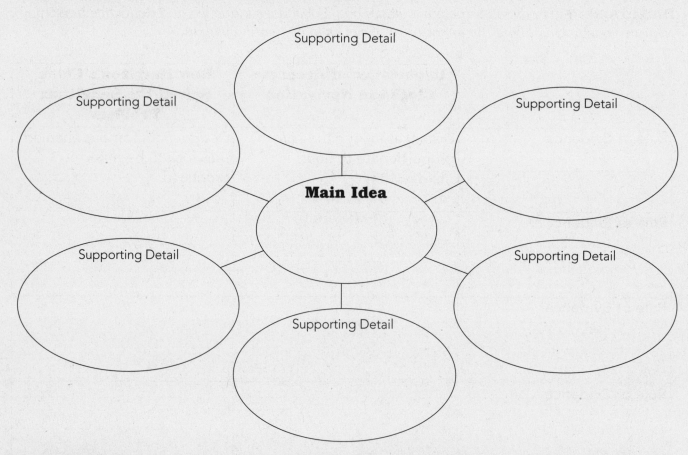

B. DIRECTIONS: *Use your completed graphic organizer to help you summarize Sobel's essay from* Longitude *on the lines below.*

_____

_____

_____

_____

_____

from **Longitude** by Dava Sobel
Vocabulary Builder

Word List

contested   configuration   converge   derived   haphazardly   impervious

A. DIRECTIONS: *Create two different sentences for each of the following words. You may use a different form of the word in your second sentence.*

    Examples: Early sea captains wandered <u>haphazardly</u> across the oceans.

           This <u>haphazard</u> method of exploration nevertheless resulted in many great discoveries.

1. configuration

_____

_____

2. derived

_____

_____

3. impervious

_____

_____

4. converge

_____

_____

5. contested

_____

_____

B. WORD STUDY: The **Latin root *-fig-*** means "to form." Answer the following questions using one of these words that contain the root *-fig-: figment, figurine, reconfigure.*

1. If a child is caught breaking a rule, why might her explanation be a *figment* of her imagination?
2. Why would a rag doll be more appropriate than a *figurine* for a baby's toy?
3. Why might a teacher need to *reconfigure* his classroom before parents come to visit?

"The Spider and the Wasp" by Alexander Petrunkevitch
from Longitude by Dava Sobel

Integrated Language Skills: Grammar

Direct and Indirect Objects

A **direct object** is a noun or pronoun that receives the action of an action verb. You can determine whether a word is a direct object by asking *Whom?* or *What?* after an action verb.

An **indirect object** is used with a direct object and names the person/thing that something is given to or done for. You can tell whether a word is an indirect object by finding the direct object and asking *To or for whom?* or *To or for what?* after the action verb.

Examples: Latonya wore her new <u>dress</u>. (*Dress* is the direct object because it receives the action of the verb *wore*.)

Tami gave <u>Latonya</u> a <u>compliment</u>. (*Latonya* is the indirect object and *compliment* is the direct object.)

A. PRACTICE: *The following sentences are based on "The Spider and the Wasp" or the excerpt from* Longitude. *Circle each indirect object and underline each direct object. One sentence has more than one direct object.*

1. The mother wasp examines a tarantula closely.
2. She paralyzes the spider with venom.
3. The wasp then digs the spider a grave and buries it with her young.
4. Any sailor can determine latitude by looking at the position of the sun.
5. Longitude gave early sailors a much more difficult problem, though.
6. One must know the time in two places at once to determine longitude.

B. Writing Application: *On the lines below, write a paragraph about either "The Spider and the Wasp" or the excerpt from* Longitude. *Be sure to include at least four direct objects and three indirect objects. Circle each indirect object and underline each direct object.*

_____

_____

_____

_____

_____

_____

_____

_____

_____

_____

_____

Name _____ Date _____

from **Longitude** by Dava Sobel
"The Spider and the Wasp" by Alexander Petrunkevitch

Integrated Language Skills: Support for Writing a Business Letter

To help you write your business letter asking King George III for recognition for Harrison's invention, use the following chart to organize your thoughts. Make a list of points and examples to answer the question in each column.

What makes your (Harrison's) clock different from previous clocks?	How does your (Harrison's) clock solve the problem of determining longitude?	What problems have you (Harrison) had trying to get recognition for your invention?

Now, use your notes to write a business letter from Harrison's point of view asking King George III for recognition for solving the problem of determining longitude.

To help you write your business letter requesting funds to do more research on tarantulas and wasps, use the following chart to organize your thoughts. Make a list of points and examples to answer the question in each column.

Why is the topic of scientific interest?	What do we currently know about the topic?	What mysteries could be solved with more research?

Now, use your notes to write your business letter requesting funds to do additional research on tarantulas and wasps.

"**The Sun Parlor**" by Dorothy West
Writing About the Big Question
What kind of knowledge changes our lives?

Big Question Vocabulary

adapt	awareness	empathy	enlighten	evolve
growth	history	ignorance	influence	insight
modified	question	reflect	revise	understanding

A. *Use one or more words from the list above to complete each sentence.*

1. Sometimes it takes years to develop _____ into our actions and to understand why we behaved the way we did.

2. Our self-interest can _____ how we treat others.

3. After the death of a beloved family member, people often _____ on their relationship with that person.

B. *Follow the directions in responding to each of the items below.*

1. List two different times that you acquired important self-knowledge.

_____

_____

2. Choose one piece of knowledge you listed and explain whether it changed your life. Use at least two of the Big Question vocabulary words.

_____

_____

C. *Complete the sentence below. Then, write a short paragraph in which you connect this experience to the big question.*

When you gain insight through your mistreatment of others, you often feel

_____

_____

_____

"The Sun Parlor" by Dorothy West
Literary Analysis: Reflective Essay

A **reflective essay** is a brief nonfiction work in which a writer presents the experiences that shaped or inspired his or her thoughts on a topic. In a reflective essay, a writer draws on an event, a time period, or an idea from his or her own life and experience. The writer weaves a connection between personal experience and a point of general interest, such as a lesson about life. The writer's reflections focus on a specific object, scene, occasion, place, or idea.

Dorothy West shares a personal experience and its meaning in her reflective essay "The Sun Parlor." West's unique perceptions and understanding of her own experience lead her to create a new experience for her readers. It is a writer's individual perspective that makes reflective writing engaging and fresh, even when the topic is a familiar one.

DIRECTIONS: *Refer to "The Sun Parlor" to answer the following questions.*

1. What lesson about life does West wish to share with her readers in "The Sun Parlor"?

   _____

   _____

   _____

2. What event does West say she regrets? Why do you think this event stayed in her mind for so many years?

   _____

   _____

   _____

3. What is unique about the way West shares the events of "The Sun Parlor" with her readers?

   _____

   _____

   _____

4. At the end of the essay, West asks Sis if her mother ever let her play in the sun parlor when West was not there. However, she does not want to hear the answer and states that it is enough for her that Sis listened. Why do you think West feels this way? How would you feel in the same situation?

   _____

   _____

   _____

   _____

"The Sun Parlor" by Dorothy West

Reading: Ask Questions to Analyze Main Ideas and Supporting Details

To fully understand an essay, you must **analyze main ideas and supporting details.** To do this, note each main point the writer makes. Then, identify the ideas or facts that explain or illustrate it. To help you analyze, **ask questions** as you read. Ask yourself what the topic of the passage is, what main point is being made, and which details support the point.

A. DIRECTIONS: *Ask yourself the following questions as you read "The Sun Parlor." Then, record your answers on the lines below each question.*

1. What is the topic of the essay?

_____

_____

2. What is the main point being made?

_____

_____

3. Which details support this point?

_____

_____

_____

_____

_____

B. DIRECTIONS: *On the following lines, summarize "The Sun Parlor." Use your answers to the previous questions to help you write your summary.*

_____

_____

_____

_____

_____

_____

_____

_____

_____

Name _____ Date _____

"**The Sun Parlor**" by Dorothy West
Vocabulary Builder

Word List

cajoling   convalesce   lavished   rejuvenation   subordinate   succinct

A. DIRECTIONS: *Think about the meaning of the italicized word in each item below. Then, answer the question and explain your answer.*

1. If the director of a school play *lavished* praise on his cast and crew after opening night, did the performance go well or did it go poorly?

   _____

   _____

2. Is a coach *subordinate* to his team?

   _____

   _____

3. Would having an argument with your best friend bring a sense of *rejuvenation*?

   _____

   _____

4. Which person would be more likely to experience *cajoling* in her job: an actress or a firefighter?

   _____

   _____

5. If a family member must *convalesce* for a month after being ill, did she have a severe case of the flu or a mild cold?

   _____

   _____

6. If you gave a *succinct* answer to your father, were you speaking for a long time or did you say just a few words?

   _____

   _____

B. WORD STUDY: The **Latin prefix suc-** means "under" or "less or lower than." Answer each of the following questions using one of these words containing *suc-*: *succor, succumb, successor.*

1. Why would a person give *succor* to someone who was hurt?

2. What will you be doing if you *succumb* to the temptation of chocolate cake?

3. Why might the *successor* to the team captain be unsure of herself?

from **In Commemoration: One Million Volumes** by Rudolfo Anaya

Writing About the Big Question

What kind of knowledge changes our lives?

Big Question Vocabulary

adapt	awareness	empathy	enlighten	evolve
growth	history	ignorance	influence	insight
modified	question	reflect	revise	understanding

A. *Use one or more words from the list above to complete each sentence.*

1. We start out as children who listen to stories, but we _____ into adults who read and sometimes write stories.

2. Reading can _____ people about subjects they never imagined.

3. _____ the importance of books is a necessary trait if you love libraries.

4. Thinking about new ideas that you may have discovered in books is one way to combat _____ .

B. *Follow the directions in responding to each of the items below.*

1. List two times when you read something that made a big impact on you.

   _____

   _____

2. Choose one experience you listed and explain whether it changed your life. Use at least two of the Big Question vocabulary words.

   _____

   _____

C. *Complete the sentence below. Then, write a short paragraph in which you connect this experience to the big question.*

For the author, acquiring information means that _____

_____

_____

_____

from In Commemoration: One Million Volumes by Rudolfo A. Anaya
Literary Analysis: Reflective Essay

A **reflective essay** is a brief nonfiction work in which a writer presents the experiences that shaped or inspired his or her thoughts on a topic. In a reflective essay, a writer draws on an event, a time period, or an idea from his or her own life and experience. The writer weaves a connection between personal experience and a point of general interest, such as a lesson about life. The writer's reflections focus on a specific object, scene, occasion, place, or idea.

Rudolfo Anaya shares a personal experience and its meaning in the excerpt from *In Commemoration: One Million Volumes*. Anaya's unique perceptions and understanding of his own experience lead him to create a new experience for his readers. It is a writer's individual perspective that makes reflective writing engaging and fresh, even when the topic is a familiar one.

DIRECTIONS: *Refer to the excerpt from* In Commemoration: One Million Volumes *to answer the following questions.*

1. What lesson about life does Anaya wish to share with his readers?

   _____

   _____

   _____

2. Why are libraries so important to Anaya?

   _____

   _____

   _____

3. What is unique about the way Anaya shares the events of the excerpt from *In Commemoration: One Million Volumes* with his readers?

   _____

   _____

   _____

4. Why does Anaya associate books and libraries with freedom? With what do you associate books and libraries? Why?

   _____

   _____

   _____

   _____

Name _____ Date _____

from **In Commemoration: One Million Volumes** by Rudolfo A. Anaya
Reading: Ask Questions to Analyze Main Ideas and Supporting Details

To fully understand an essay, you must **analyze main ideas and supporting details.** To do this, note each main point the writer makes. Then, identify the ideas or facts that explain or illustrate it. To help you analyze, **ask questions** as you read. Ask yourself what the topic of the passage is, what main point is being made, and which details support the point.

A. DIRECTIONS: *Ask yourself the following questions as you read the excerpt from* In Commemoration: One Million Volumes. *Then record your answers on the lines below each question.*

1. What is the topic of the excerpt?

_____

_____

2. What is the main point being made?

_____

_____

3. Which details support this point?

_____

_____

_____

_____

_____

B. DIRECTIONS: *On the following lines, summarize the passage from* In Commemoration: One Million Volumes. *Use your answers to the previous questions to help you write your summary.*

_____

_____

_____

_____

_____

_____

_____

_____

_____

_____

Name _____ Date _____

from **In Commemoration: One Million Volumes** by Rudolfo A. Anaya

Vocabulary Builder

Word List

dilapidated   enthralls   infinite   inherent   paradox   poignant

A. DIRECTIONS: *Think about the meaning of the italicized word in each item below. Then, answer the question and explain your answer.*

1. Is knowledge of important events in history something that could be *inherent*?

   _____

   _____

2. Would a *dilapidated* courthouse be more or less in need of repair than one that is not dilapidated?

   _____

   _____

3. If a movie *enthralls* the audience, is it likely to make money at the box office?

   _____

   _____

4. Which event would be more *poignant* for those involved: shopping for groceries or graduating from high school?

   _____

   _____

5. Can a library ever have an *infinite* number of books?

   _____

   _____

6. If an answer to a question is a *paradox*, is that answer logical and easy to understand?

   _____

   _____

B. WORD STUDY: The **Greek prefix *para-*** means "beside" or "beyond." Provide an explanation for your answer to each question containing a word with the prefix *para-*.

1. Will a *parasite* choose to live in isolation?

   _____

2. If you *paraphrase* a sentence, are you copying it word for word?

   _____

3. If you wanted to master a science experiment, would you follow or ignore a *paradigm* of that experiment?

   _____

All-in-One Workbook
140

"The Sun Parlor" by Dorothy West
from **In Commemoration: One Million Volumes** by Rudolfo A. Anaya
Integrated Language Skills: Grammar

Subject Complements: Predicate Nominatives and Predicate Adjectives

Predicate nominatives and predicate adjectives are subject complements. They appear after a linking verb and tell something about the subject of the sentence. A **predicate nominative** is a noun or pronoun that appears with a linking verb and renames, identifies, or explains the subject of the sentence. A subject and a predicate nominative are two different words for the same person, place, or thing. The linking verb joins them and equates them. A **predicate adjective** is an adjective that appears with a linking verb and describes the subject of the sentence.

Examples: Dorothy West's special room is her sun <u>parlor</u>. (*Parlor* is a predicate nominative, which renames the subject, *room*.)

Books are <u>fascinating</u> to Rudolfo Anaya. (*Fascinating* is a predicate adjective, which describes the subject, *books*.)

A. PRACTICE: *The following sentences are based on "The Sun Parlor" or the excerpt from* In Commemoration: One Million Volumes. *Underline each predicate nominative or predicate adjective and write* PN *or* PA *on the line before each sentence.*

____ 1. Sis was a young girl who wanted to play in West's sun parlor.

____ 2. West seemed sad and regretful that she did not allow Sis to play in the room.

____ 3. The author and her brothers and sisters were obedient children.

____ 4. Libraries are Anaya's refuge.

____ 5. To Anaya, books are exciting and uplifting.

____ 6. Anaya, a writer, is an intelligent and thoughtful man.

B. Writing Application: *On the lines below, write a paragraph responding to either "The Sun Parlor" or the excerpt from* In Commemoration: One Million Volumes. *Use at least five subject complements in your paragraph. Underline each predicate nominative once and each predicate adjective twice.*

_____

_____

_____

_____

_____

_____

_____

_____

Name _____ Date _____

"The Sun Parlor" by Dorothy West
from **In Commemoration: One Million Volumes** by Rudolfo A. Anaya
Integrated Language Skills: Support for Writing a Memoir

Before writing your memoir, use the graphic organizer below to help you describe a room or building that has been meaningful to you in your life.

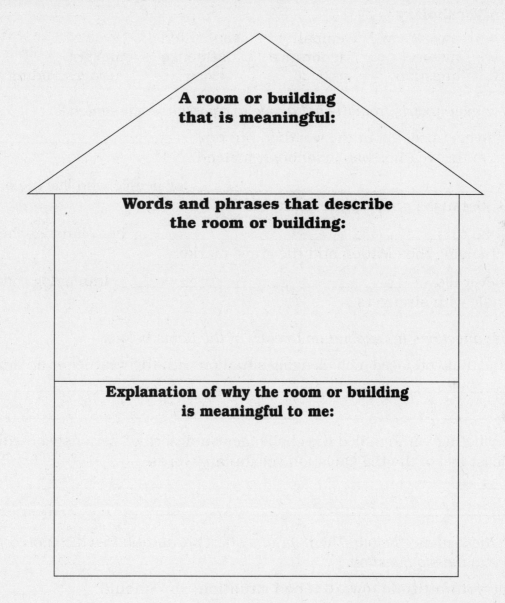

A room or building that is meaningful:

Words and phrases that describe the room or building:

Explanation of why the room or building is meaningful to me:

Now, use your notes to write your memoir about a room or building that has meaning for you.

Name _____ Date _____

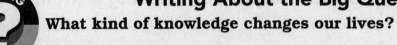

"A Toast to the Oldest Inhabitant: The Weather of New England" by Mark Twain
"The Dog that Bit People" by James Thurber

Writing About the Big Question

What kind of knowledge changes our lives?

Big Question Vocabulary

adapt	awareness	empathy	enlighten	evolve
growth	history	ignorance	influence	insight
modified	question	reflect	revise	understanding

A. *Use one or more words from the list above to complete each sentence.*

1. We used to get upset about the weather, but our _____ response to the weather was to ignore it instead.

2. I have _____ for people who live in cold climates, because I grew up in Alaska.

3. Mother had to _____ her plans for the dog's burial, changing the location and the grave marker.

4. Muggs never did _____ into a dog that was comfortable with strangers.

B. *Follow the directions in responding to each of the items below.*

1. List a time that you faced a challenging situation with the weather or an animal.

   _____

   _____

2. Explain whether you handled the challenge you described seriously or with humor. Use at least two of the Big Question vocabulary words.

   _____

   _____

C. *Complete the sentence below. Then, write a short paragraph in which you connect this experience to the big question.*

To change your attitude toward a bad situation, you should _____

_____

_____

_____

Name _____ Date _____

"A Toast to the Oldest Inhabitant: The Weather of New England" by Mark Twain
"The Dog That Bit People" by James Thurber
Literary Analysis: Humorous Writing

Humorous writing is writing in which people, events, and ideas are presented in unexpected, amusing ways. Techniques for creating humor include the following:

- **Hyperbole** is exaggeration for effect in which a writer describes something as if it were much greater than it is. Describing a creek as a "yawning gorge" is an example of hyperbole.
- A writer uses **understatement** to portray a person, an event, or an idea as if it were much less than it is. Saying that "the avalanche was a minor inconvenience for hikers" is an example of understatement.
- **Satire** is a writer's use of humor to point out the foolishness of a particular type of human behavior. In "The Dog That Bit People," for example, Thurber satirizes the behavior of pet owners who believe their pets can do no wrong.

DIRECTIONS: *Read each of the following passages from "A Toast to the Oldest Inhabitant" and "The Dog That Bit People." Then, identify each passage as an example of hyperbole or understatement, and explain what makes it so.*

"A Toast to the Oldest Inhabitant: The Weather of New England"

1. In the spring I have counted one hundred and thirty-six different kinds of weather inside of four and twenty hours.

   This is an example of _____ because _____

   _____ .

2. You fix up for the drought . . . and ten to one you get drowned. You make up your mind that the earthquake is due . . . and the first thing you know, you get struck by lightning. These are great disappointments. But they can't be helped.

   This is an example of _____ because _____

   _____ .

"The Dog That Bit People"

3. There was a slight advantage to being one of the family, for he didn't bite the family as often as he bit strangers.

   This is an example of _____ because _____

   _____ .

4. Muggs went up the backstairs and down the frontstairs and had me cornered in the living room. I managed to get up onto the mantelpiece above the fireplace, but it gave way and came down with a tremendous crash throwing a large marble clock, several vases, and myself heavily to the floor.

   This is an example of _____ because _____

   _____ .

"A Toast to the Oldest Inhabitant: The Weather of New England" by Mark Twain
"The Dog That Bit People" by James Thurber
Vocabulary Builder

Word List

blemished	choleric	commences	incredulity
indignant	irascible	sumptuous	vagaries

A. DIRECTIONS: *Revise each sentence so that the underlined word is used logically. Be sure to keep the underlined word in your revision.*

Example: The <u>sumptuous</u> meal left the guests hungry.

Answer: The <u>sumptuous</u> meal satisfied everyone.

1. Her perfect day was <u>blemished</u> by a single compliment.

   _____

2. Once the presentation <u>commences</u>, feel free to ask questions.

   _____

3. The <u>vagaries</u> of the weather allow us to plan our outdoor activities in advance.

   _____

4. Jack's mother showed <u>incredulity</u> when he claimed to have cleaned his room in two hours.

   _____

5. The <u>choleric</u> old woman gave the children in her front yard a warm welcome.

   _____

6. Getting a good night's sleep makes me <u>irascible</u> in the morning.

   _____

7. Mia felt <u>indignant</u> after being awarded a part in the play.

   _____

B. DIRECTIONS: *On the line, write the letter of the word that is most nearly similar in meaning to the word in CAPITAL LETTERS.*

____ 1. SUMPTUOUS:
   A. sleepy   B. extravagant   C. rigid   D. conceited

____ 2. INCREDULITY:
   A. awe   B. joyfulness   C. disbelief   D. poverty

____ 3. COMMENCES:
   A. deals   B. enters   C. invites   D. starts

____ 4. BLEMISHED:
   A. smooth   B. damaged   C. cold   D. old

____ 5. VAGARIES:
   A. belief   B. stillness   C. caprice   D. silence

"A Toast to the Oldest Inhabitant: The Weather of New England" by Mark Twain
"The Dog That Bit People" by James Thurber

Integrated Language Skills: Support for Comparing Literary Works

A humorous essay or speech is a nonfiction composition in which the writer presents people, events, and ideas in unexpected, amusing ways. Identify the techniques—hyperbole, understatement, satire—Twain and Thurber use to create humor in their writing. Record these elements, and examples of each, in the chart. As you write, think about how the comic techniques of these writers are different and similar.

"A Toast to the Oldest Inhabitant: The Weather of New England"	
Comic Technique	**Example in Selection**
1.	1.
2.	2.
3.	3.
4.	4.

"A Toast to the Oldest Inhabitant: The Weather of New England"	
Comic Technique	**Example in Selection**
1.	1.
2.	2.
3.	3.
4.	4.

"**Keep Memory Alive**" by Elie Wiesel
Writing About the Big Question
What kind of knowledge changes our lives?

Big Question Vocabulary

adapt	awareness	empathy	enlighten	evolve
growth	history	ignorance	influence	insight
modified	question	reflect	revise	understanding

A. *Use one or more words from the list above to complete each sentence.*

1. Elie Wiesel experienced one of the most painful moments in world _____ .

2. It was impossible to gain _____ into the cruel hearts of those who persecuted him.

3. Claiming _____ about the suffering and mistreatment of others is never a good excuse.

4. Wiesel wants to _____ others to stand up for the rights of the oppressed.

B. *Follow the directions in responding to each of the items below.*

1. List two different times in which you learned about or experienced an unjust situation.

   _____

   _____

2. Write two sentences explaining one of the situations you listed, and describe how it made you feel. Use at least two of the Big Question vocabulary words.

   _____

   _____

C. *Complete the sentence below. Then, write a short paragraph in which you connect this experience to the big question.*

When you learn that people are capable of brutality against others, you can choose to _____ .

_____

_____

_____

Name _____ Date _____

"**Keep Memory Alive**" by Elie Wiesel
Literary Analysis: Persuasive Writing

Persuasive writing is nonfiction intended to convince people to take a particular action or agree with the author's point of view. Persuasive writers present **arguments,** using reason to support their positions. They also use **rhetorical devices,** or patterns of words that create emphasis and stir emotion. Rhetorical devices include the following:

- **Repetition**—the reuse of a key word or idea for emphasis
- **Parallelism**—similar grammatical structures used to express related ideas
- **Slogans and saws**—short, catchy phrases
- **Rhetorical questions**—questions that are intended to have obvious answers and that are asked for effect

Examples of persuasive writing include persuasive essays, speeches, advertisements, political writings, legal arguments, sales brochures, and fund-raising letters.

A. DIRECTIONS: *Answer the following about Elie Wiesel's speech "Keep Memory Alive."*

1. What sentence in Weisel's speech sums up the point with which he wants his listeners to agree?

   _____

   _____

2. List three reasonable, persuasive elements Wiesel uses to support his main point. Identify the type of argument or rhetorical device used in each.

   _____

   _____

   _____

   _____

   _____

   _____

3. Why is this message more powerful coming from Elie Wiesel than from someone else?

   _____

   _____

   _____

4. Why is it important to Wiesel to keep the memory of what happened to him and his people alive?

   _____

   _____

   _____

Name _____ Date _____

"Keep Memory Alive" by Elie Wiesel
Reading: Test the Writer's Logic to Evaluate Persuasive Appeals

When reading persuasive writing, **evaluate the writer's appeals** to decide whether the writer makes a good case for his or her point of view. If a writer calls for a particular action or makes a specific claim, **test the writer's logic.** To do this, consider whether the evidence and reasoning the writer presents supports the point. For example, if a writer claims that fish make better pets than dogs, he or she needs to support this opinion with evidence and reasoning. A good supporting point might be that fish cannot dig up one's yard. An illogical or poor argument might be that mice have a tendency to bite. This argument does not support the point that fish make better pets than dogs.

DIRECTIONS: *First, fill in the main point with which Elie Wiesel wants his audience to agree. Then, list four appeals he uses in his speech and evaluate the logic of each.*

1. What is the main point with which Wiesel wants his audience to agree?

_____

_____

2. List four appeals from "Keep Memory Alive" and test the logic of each.

A. _____

_____

_____

B. _____

_____

_____

C. _____

_____

_____

D. _____

_____

_____

Name _____ Date _____

"**Keep Memory Alive**" by Elie Wiesel
Vocabulary Builder

Word List

accomplices   bewilderment   naïve   presumptuous   profound   transcends

A. DIRECTIONS: *Write a sentence that demonstrates the meaning of each of the vocabulary words.*

1. A situation that might cause *bewilderment:* _____
_____

2. People who are *accomplices:* _____
_____

3. Characteristics of someone who is *naïve:* _____
_____

4. Someone who might make a *profound* statement: _____
_____

5. Feelings a person might have when he or she *transcends* expectations: _____
_____

B. WORD STUDY: The **Latin root -*scend*-** means "climb." Revise each sentence so that the underlined word containing the root -*scend*- is used logically. Be sure not to change the underlined word.

1. We knew that to *ascend* the mountain, we would have to climb down slowly.
_____

2. The mountaineer's *descent* took her higher and higher until she could see across the valley.
_____

3. The ballerina's dance was *transcendent*, and the audience walked out in disappointment.
_____

from **"Nobel Lecture"** by Alexander Solzhenitsyn
Writing About the Big Question

What kind of knowledge changes our lives?

Big Question Vocabulary

adapt	awareness	empathy	enlighten	evolve
growth	history	ignorance	influence	insight
modified	question	reflect	revise	understanding

A. *Use one or more words from the list above to complete each sentence.*

1. Throughout _____ writers have been a uniting force for freedom.

2. Writers often _____ repressive governments and write critically about them.

3. Solzhenitsyn wants to banish lies and _____ the world with the truth.

4. Getting rid of _____ and providing the truth about society is a writer's greatest challenge.

B. *Follow the directions in responding to each of the items below.*

1. List two situations in which you had to tell the truth but did not want to.

   _____

   _____

2. Write two sentences explaining one of the situations you listed, and describe how it made you feel. Use at least two of the Big Question vocabulary words.

   _____

   _____

C. *Complete the sentence below. Then, write a short paragraph in which you connect this experience to the big question.*

Writers who present the truth about society help people _____

_____

_____

_____

from "**Nobel Lecture**" by Alexander Solzhenitsyn

Literary Analysis: Persuasive Writing

Persuasive writing is nonfiction intended to convince people to take a particular action or agree with the author's point of view. Persuasive writers present **arguments,** using reason to support their positions. They also use **rhetorical devices,** or patterns of words that create emphasis and stir emotion. Rhetorical devices include the following:

- **Repetition**—the reuse of a key word or idea for emphasis
- **Parallelism**—similar grammatical structures used to express related ideas
- **Slogans and saws**—short, catchy phrases
- **Rhetorical questions**—questions that are intended to have obvious answers and that are asked for effect

Examples of persuasive writing include persuasive essays, speeches, advertisements, political writings, legal arguments, sales brochures, and fund-raising letters.

A. DIRECTIONS: *Answer the following questions.*

1. What sentence in Solzhenitsyn's speech sums up the point with which he wants his listeners to agree?

   _____

2. List three reasonable, persuasive elements Solzhenitsyn uses to support his main point. Identify the type of argument or rhetorical device used in each.

   _____

   _____

   _____

   _____

3. Why is this message more powerful coming from Alexander Solzhenitsyn than from someone else?

   _____

   _____

4. Why is it important to Solzhenitsyn to establish the idea of "world literature"?

   _____

   _____

B. DIRECTIONS: *In a brief essay, explain whether or not you were persuaded by this speech to agree with Solzhenitsyn. Be very specific about which words, phrases, points, arguments, and rhetorical devices impressed you most or failed to effectively persuade you, and explain why.*

_____

_____

_____

_____

Name _____   Date _____

from **"Nobel Lecture"** by Alexander Solzhenitsyn

Reading: Test the Writer's Logic to Evaluate Persuasive Appeals

When reading persuasive writing, **evaluate the writer's appeals** to decide whether the writer makes a good case for his or her point of view. If a writer calls for a particular action or makes a specific claim, **test the writer's logic.** To do this, consider whether the evidence and reasoning the writer presents supports the point he or she is trying to make. For example, if a writer claims that fish make better pets than dogs, he or she needs to support this opinion with evidence and reasoning. A good supporting point might be that fish cannot dig up one's yard. An illogical or a poor argument might be that mice have a tendency to bite. This argument does not support the point that fish make better pets than dogs.

DIRECTIONS: *First, fill in the main point with which Solzhenitsyn wants his audience to agree. Then, list four appeals he uses in his speech and evaluate the logic of each.*

1. What is the main point with which Solzhenitsyn wants his audience to agree?

   _____

   _____

2. List four appeals from Solzhenitsyn's "Nobel Lecture" and test the logic of each.

   A. _____

   _____

   _____

   _____

   B. _____

   _____

   _____

   _____

   C. _____

   _____

   _____

   _____

   D. _____

   _____

   _____

   _____

Name _____ Date _____

from **"Nobel Lecture"** by Alexander Solzhenitsyn
Vocabulary Builder

Word List

aggregate   condemn   inexorably   jurisdiction   oratory   reciprocity

A. DIRECTIONS: *Write a sentence that demonstrates the meaning of each of the words.*

A situation in which *reciprocity* is usually expected: A person giving a ride to a friend might expect *reciprocity* if he or she ever needs a ride.

1. Something that happens *inexorably*: _____

   _____

2. Things that can be an *aggregate*: _____

   _____

3. Someone who has *jurisdiction*: _____

   _____

4. Something or someone that people can *condemn*: _____

   _____

5. A situation that would involve *oratory*: _____

   _____

B. WORD STUDY: The Latin root -*jur*- means "law" or "right." Answer each of the following questions. Explain your answers.

1. Is a *jury* interested in breaking the law?

   _____

2. If you had an *injury* to your leg, would you go see a doctor or go play a football game?

   _____

3. Would a *juror* report to a courtroom or to a cafeteria?

   _____

Name _____ Date _____

"Keep Memory Alive" by Elie Wiesel
from **"Nobel Lecture"** by Alexander Solzhenitsyn
Integrated Language Skills: Grammar

Degrees of Adverbs

Most adverbs have three different forms to show degrees of comparison—the *positive*, the *comparative*, and the *superlative*. There are different ways to form the comparative and superlative degrees of adverbs. Notice how the forms of the adverbs in the chart change to show degrees of comparison.

Positive	Comparative	Superlative
People fighting injustice want change to come *early*.	Those who speak out can make change occur *earlier* than we think.	The *earliest* time that change can come is when leaders listen to their people.
Solzhenitsyn *firmly* believes in the power of writing to change nations.	Solzhenitsyn believed this fact *more firmly* when people around the world read his work.	Solzhenitsyn probably believed in his work *most firmly* when he witnessed the fall of the Soviet Union.
Wiesel speaks very *well*.	Wiesel speaks *better* than most people.	Wiesel is the *best* speaker I have ever heard.

A. PRACTICE: *The following sentences are based on Wiesel's "Keep Memory Alive" or the excerpt from Solzhenitsyn's "Nobel Lecture." On the line before each sentence, identify the degree of comparison of each italicized adverb or adverb phrase.*

_____ 1. Wiesel speaks *most passionately* about the danger of remaining silent.

_____ 2. Wiesel delivered his acceptance speech *skillfully*.

_____ 3. Solzhenitsyn *strongly* urges his listeners to speak out against violence.

_____ 4. The Soviet Union fell *sooner* than Solzhenitsyn might have expected.

B. Writing Application: *On the following lines, write a paragraph responding to either "Keep Memory Alive" or the excerpt from "Nobel Lecture." Underline the adverbs that have a positive degree of comparison once, underline the adverbs or adverb phrases that are comparative twice, and underline the adverbs or adverb phrases that are superlative three times. Use at least six adverbs that show degrees of comparison.*

_____

_____

_____

_____

_____

Name _____ Date _____

"Keep Memory Alive" by Elie Wiesel
from **"Nobel Lecture"** by Alexander Solzhenitsyn
Integrated Language Skills: Support for Writing a Letter

For your letter to Elie Wiesel or Alexander Solzhenitsyn, use the following graphic organizer to help you take a position on the writer's claim, choose a principle, and plan your logical arguments to support it.

Position	General Principle	Arguments

Now, use your notes to write your letter to Elie Wiesel or Alexander Solzhenitsyn. Remember to use language that is appropriate to your reader. Wiesel and Solzhenitsyn are respected and educated men whom you have not met, so use formal language and avoid slang or jargon.

Now, use your notes to write your letter to Elie Wiesel or Alexander Solzhenitsyn. Remember to use language that is appropriate to your reader. Wiesel and Solzhenitsyn are respected and educated men whom you have not met, so use formal language and avoid slang or jargon.

All-in-One Workbook
© Pearson Education, Inc. All rights reserved.
156

"The American Idea" by Theodore H. White
Writing About the Big Question

What kind of knowledge changes our lives?

Big Question Vocabulary

adapt	awareness	empathy	enlighten	evolve
growth	history	ignorance	influence	insight
modified	question	reflect	revise	understanding

A. *Use one or more words from the list above to complete each sentence.*

1. The Declaration of Independence has served the United States from its _____ as a tiny nation to a global power.

2. The _____ of America is filled with tough, smart people who helped create a successful government.

3. Thomas Jefferson _____ his thoughts enough to please both John Adams and Benjamin Franklin.

4. Although archrivals for much of their lives, Jefferson and Adams did _____ into friends once more as they grew older.

B. *Follow the directions in responding to each of the items below.*

1. List two situations in which a compromise you made produced an important result.

_____

_____

2. Write two sentences explaining one of the situations you listed, and describe the impact it made on your life. Use at least two of the Big Question vocabulary words.

_____

_____

C. *Complete the sentence below. Then, write a short paragraph in which you connect this experience to the big question.*

People who left their countries to live in the United States developed an awareness of _____

_____

_____

_____

Name _____ Date _____

"The American Idea" by Theodore H. White
Literary Analysis: Analytic and Interpretive Essays

In an **analytic essay,** a writer explores a subject by breaking it into parts. In an **interpretive essay,** a writer offers a view of the meaning or significance of an issue of general interest. The author of an interpretive essay introduces an issue and then addresses it, presenting his or her ideas and analysis based on his or her own ideas, values, and beliefs. A single essay may combine features of both types of essay.

Writers of analytic and interpretive essays might use any of the following types of appeals to support their points:

- Appeals to authority, which call on the opinions of experts or other respected people
- Appeals to reason, which call on logic
- Emotional appeals, which tap a reader's fears, sympathy, or pride
- Appeals to shared values, which call on beliefs shared by many about what is good, right, or fair

A. DIRECTIONS: *Fill in the following table with one or more examples of each type of appeal from "The American Idea." If there are no examples of a particular appeal, write NONE.*

Appeals to Authority	
Appeals to Reason	
Emotional Appeals	
Appeals to Shared Values	

B. DIRECTIONS: *On the following lines, write a short essay in which you explain whether "The American Idea" is an analytic essay, an interpretive essay, or both. How do you know?*

_____

_____

_____

_____

_____

Name _____ Date _____

Reading: Distinguish Between Fact and Opinion to Evaluate Writers' Appeals

To **evaluate a writer's appeals,** decide whether the writer makes a good case for his or her point of view. First, **distinguish between fact and opinion** to determine what kind of support a writer should provide. A statement of fact can be proven true or false. A statement of opinion expresses a belief or a viewpoint and should be supported by facts or logical reasoning.

DIRECTIONS: *In the following chart, list ten facts and five opinions White includes in his essay about the American idea. Then, list facts or logical reasons the author gives to support each opinion.*

Facts	
1. _____ _____	6. _____ _____
2. _____ _____	7. _____ _____
3. _____ _____	8. _____ _____
4. _____ _____	9. _____ _____
5. _____ _____	10. _____ _____

Opinions	Support for Opinions
1. _____ _____	1. _____ _____
2. _____ _____	2. _____ _____
3. _____ _____	3. _____ _____
4. _____ _____	4. _____ _____
5. _____ _____	5. _____ _____

"**The American Idea**" by Theodore H. White
Vocabulary Builder

Word List

embodied   emigrants   relentlessly   subversion   successive   universal

A. DIRECTIONS: *Provide an explanation for your answer to each question.*

1. If you were thinking about an animal, would your thoughts be *embodied* by a soft toy that looked like a dog?

   _____

2. Would *emigrants* be packed and ready to travel or settling into a future in their home country?

   _____

3. If the wind blew *relentlessly*, would there be a break when everything was still?

   _____

4. If your school had *universal* hat day, would everyone wear a hat?

   _____

5. If your cousin had three *successive* gray cats, did she have three cats at the same time?

   _____

6. If the dictator was worried about *subversion*, did he feel secure in the loyalty of the citizens?

   _____

B. WORD STUDY: The **Greek prefix em-** means "in." Answer each of the following questions using one of these words containing *em-*: *empathy, emperor, embrace.*

1. Is an *emperor* someone who is in power or who serves those in power?

   _____

2. If someone has *empathy*, does that person disregard the feelings of others?

   _____

3. If you give a person an *embrace*, are you putting your arms around that person or running away from that person?

   _____

"What Makes a Degas a Degas?" by Richard Mühlberger
Writing About the Big Question
What kind of knowledge changes our lives?

Big Question Vocabulary

adapt   awareness   empathy   enlighten   evolve
growth   history   ignorance   influence   insight
modified   question   reflect   revise   understanding

A. *Use one or more words from the list above to complete each sentence.*

1. Painting can help us _____ on the beauty of the world by presenting a new perspective.

2. Degas' _____ of painting, drawing, and photography allowed him to use various techniques in his own work.

3. Degas could _____ his painting style to look as though he had drawn with pastels.

4. An understanding of art _____ allows an artist to learn from past masters.

B. *Follow the directions in responding to each of the items below.*

1. List two encounters you have had with art (a painting, drawing, or sculpture) that made an impact on you.

   _____

   _____

2. Write two sentences explaining one of the experiences you listed, and describe the effect it had on your life. Use at least two of the Big Question vocabulary words.

   _____

   _____

C. *Complete the sentences below. Then, write a short paragraph in which you connect this experience to the big question.*

Understanding how to interpret art is valuable because you gain insight into

_____ .

Artists can influence us by _____

_____

_____

Name _____ Date _____

"**What Makes a Degas a Degas?**" by Richard Mühlberger

Literary Analysis: Analytic and Interpretive Essays

In an **analytic essay,** a writer explores a subject by breaking it into parts. In an **interpretive essay,** a writer offers a view of the meaning or significance of an issue of general interest. The author of an interpretive essay introduces an issue and then addresses it, presenting his or her ideas and analysis based on his or her own ideas, values, and beliefs. A single essay may combine features of both types of essay.

Writers of analytic and interpretive essays might use any of the following types of appeals to support their points:

- Appeals to authority, which call on the opinions of experts or other respected people
- Appeals to reason, which call on logic
- Emotional appeals, which tap a reader's fears, sympathy, or pride
- Appeals to shared values, which call on beliefs shared by many about what is good, right, or fair

A. DIRECTIONS: *Fill in the following table with one or more examples of each type of appeal from "What Makes a Degas a Degas?" If there are no examples of a particular appeal, write NONE.*

Appeals to Authority	
Appeals to Reason	
Emotional Appeals	
Appeals to Shared Values	

B. DIRECTIONS: *On the following lines, write a short essay in which you explain whether "What Makes a Degas a Degas?" is an analytic essay, an interpretive essay, or both. How do you know?*

_____

_____

_____

_____

_____

_____

_____

Name _____ Date _____

"**What Makes a Degas a Degas?**" by Richard Mühlberger
Reading: Distinguish Between Fact and Opinion to Evaluate Writers' Appeals

To **evaluate a writer's appeals,** decide whether the writer makes a good case for his or her point of view. First, **distinguish between fact and opinion** to determine what kind of support a writer should provide. A statement of fact can be proven true or false. A statement of opinion expresses a belief or a viewpoint and should be supported by facts or logical reasoning.

DIRECTIONS: *In the following chart, list ten facts and five opinions Mühlberger includes in his essay about Degas. Then, list facts or logical reasons the author gives to support each opinion.*

Facts	
1. _____ _____	6. _____ _____
2. _____ _____	7. _____ _____
3. _____ _____	8. _____ _____
4. _____ _____	9. _____ _____
5. _____ _____	10. _____ _____

Opinions	Support for Opinions
1. _____ _____	1. _____ _____
2. _____ _____	2. _____ _____
3. _____ _____	3. _____ _____
4. _____ _____	4. _____ _____
5. _____ _____	5. _____ _____

"What Makes a Degas a Degas?" by Richard Mühlberger
Vocabulary Builder

Word List

immaterial   lacquered   recalls   silhouette   simulating   spontaneous

A. DIRECTIONS: *Provide an explanation for your answer to each question.*

1. Does a *lacquered* table feel like rough logs just cut from a tree?

   _____

2. Are your ideas about the school recycling program *immaterial* or concrete?

   _____

3. If your mother *recalls* your first day of kindergarten, is she thinking about the past or trying to forget the past?

   _____

4. Would you submit a *silhouette* of your family if you wanted to show a detailed, colorful representation of their appearance?

   _____

5. If you had to tie bandages because your health class was *simulating* an accident, was anyone actually hurt?

   _____

6. If your class was *spontaneous* and sang to your teacher on her birthday, had you planned that moment for a long time?

   _____

B. WORD STUDY: The **Latin prefix *im-*** means "not" or "without." Answer each of the following questions using one of these words containing *im-*: *immense, immortal, improbable.*

1. If something is *immense*, is it easy to carry in your pocket?

   _____

2. If something is *immortal*, does it have a short lifespan?

   _____

3. When your team registered an *improbable* victory, were people expecting you to win?

   _____

"What Makes a Degas a Degas?" by Richard Mühlberger
"The American Idea" by Theodore H. White

Integrated Language Skills: Grammar

Degrees of Adjectives

Most adjectives have three different forms to show degrees of comparison—the *positive*, the *comparative*, and the *superlative*. The positive is used to describe one item, group, or person. The comparative is used to describe two items, groups, or people. The superlative is used when describing three or more items, groups, or people.

There are different ways to form the comparative and superlative degrees of adjectives. Add *-er*, *more*, or *less* to form the comparative and *-est*, *most*, or *least* to form the superlative of most one- and two-syllable adjectives. Add *more* and *most* or *less* and *least* to adjectives of three or more syllables to form the comparative and superlative.

Impressionist paintings seem *spontaneous*. (Positive)

Impressionist paintings seem *more spontaneous* than other styles. (Comparative)

The Impressionist paintings looked the *most spontaneous* of all the paintings I saw in the art museum. (Superlative)

A. PRACTICE: *The following sentences are based on "What Makes a Degas a Degas?" or "The American Idea." On the line before each sentence, identify the degree of comparison of each underlined adjective or adjective phrase.*

(Comparative) Degas mimicked pastels using oil paints to create a *fresher* look.

_____ 1. Degas's *greatest* thrill as a child was looking at art.

_____ 2. Degas found photography to be *more inspirational* than traditional painting styles.

_____ 3. The *simple* idea of freedom inspired Americans to fight for their own country.

_____ 4. Jefferson believed the American call to freedom was a *universal* promise to the world.

B. Writing Application: *On the following lines, write a paragraph responding to either "What Makes a Degas a Degas?" or "The American Idea." Underline the adjectives that have a positive degree of comparison, underline the adjectives or adjective phrases that are comparative twice, and underline the adjectives or adjective phrases that are superlative three times. Use at least six adjectives that show degrees of comparison.*

_____

_____

_____

_____

_____

_____

_____

"The American Idea" by Theodore H. White
"What Makes a Degas a Degas?" by Richard Mühlberger

Integrated Language Skills: Support for Writing a Critique

For your critique of White's or Mühlberger's essay, use the following graphic organizer to help you identify one of the author's central claims and evaluate the evidence he uses to support it. In the ovals, write facts and opinions the author uses as evidence and jot down ideas about the effectiveness of each.

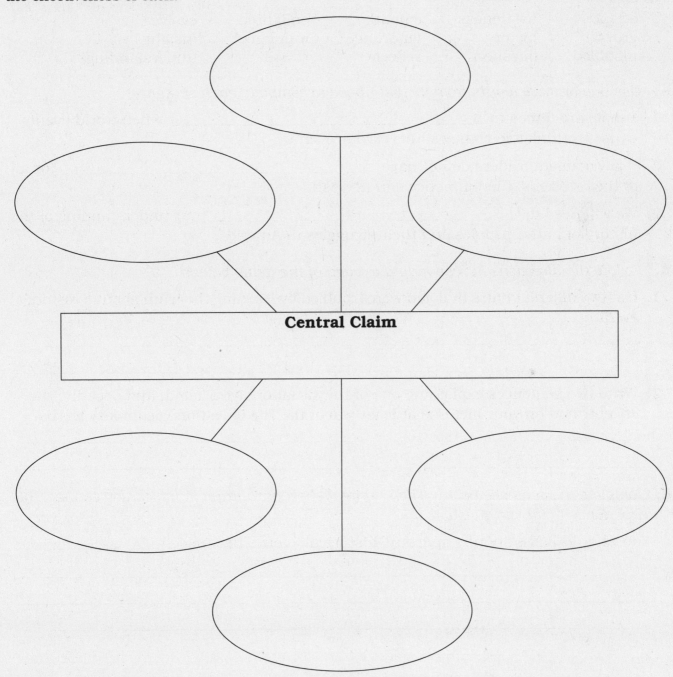

Central Claim

Now, use your notes to write your critique of "The American Idea" or "What Makes a Degas a Degas?"

***from* Desert Exile: The Uprooting of a Japanese-American Family** by Yoshiko Uchida
***from* The Way to Rainy Mountain** by N. Scott Momaday

Writing About the Big Question

What kind of knowledge changes our lives?

Big Question Vocabulary

adapt	awareness	empathy	enlighten	evolve
growth	history	ignorance	influence	insight
modified	question	reflect	revise	understanding

A. *Use one or more words from the list above to complete each sentence.*

1. People are forced to _____ when world events cause unthinkable changes in everyday events.

2. If government leaders do not have _____ for all of their citizens, then injustice can flourish.

3. We will need to _____ our understanding of the history of native peoples and their struggles in America.

B. *Follow the directions in responding to each of the items below.*

1. List two different times that you were troubled by learning the truth about a historical event.

   _____

   _____

2. Write two sentences explaining one of the situations you listed, and describe the effect it had on your life. Use at least two of the Big Question vocabulary words.

   _____

   _____

C. *Complete the sentence below. Then, write a short paragraph in which you connect this experience to the big question.*

   You should learn about important historical events because _____

   _____

   _____

   _____

from **Desert Exile: The Uprooting of a Japanese-American Family** by Yoshiko Uchida
from **The Way to Rainy Mountain** by N. Scott Momaday
Literary Analysis: Author's Purpose

An **author's purpose** is his or her main reason for writing. Common purposes include the following:

- *to inform,* as in a newspaper report
- *to entertain,* as in a mystery story
- *to persuade,* as in an editorial
- *to pay tribute to,* or *commemorate,* as in an obituary

A writer may have more than a single purpose for writing. In these selections, for example, both Momaday and Uchida write to inform readers about a slice of history. However, each author has other, more personal, reasons for writing. These reasons may include to mourn what is gone, to heal old wounds, to expose an injustice, or to better understand themselves.

DIRECTIONS: *Identify Uchida's or Momaday's purpose for including the details in each of the following passages.*

from *Desert Exile*

1. It had rained the day before and the hundreds of people who had trampled on the track had turned it into a miserable mass of slippery mud. _____

_____

2. I wrote to my non-Japanese friends in Berkeley, shamelessly asking them to send us food, and they obliged with large cartons of cookies, nuts, dried fruit, and jams. _____

_____

3. The wonderful news had come like an unexpected gift, but even as we hugged each other in joy, we didn't quite dare believe it until we actually saw him. . . . _____

_____

from *The Way to Rainy Mountain*

4. I like to think of [my grandmother] as a child. When she was born, the Kiowas were living the last great moment of their history. For more than a hundred years they had controlled the open range. . . . _____

_____

5. At the top of the ridge I caught sight of Devil's Tower upthrust against the gray sky as if in the birth of time the core of the earth had broken through its crust and the motion of the world was begun. _____

_____

6. There, where it ought to be, at the end of a long and legendary way, was my grandmother's grave. . . . Looking back once, I saw the mountain and came away. _____

_____

Name _____ Date _____

from Desert Exile: The Uprooting of a Japanese-American Family by Yoshiko Uchida
from The Way to Rainy Mountain by N. Scott Momaday
Vocabulary Builder

Word List

adept   assuage   infirm   nomadic   tenuous   unwieldy

DIRECTIONS: *Find a synonym for each word in the Word List. Use each synonym in a sentence that makes the meaning of the word clear.*

    Example: Word List word: *adept* Synonym: *skilled*
               Sentence: The Kiowa took pride in being *skilled* horsemen.

1. *unwieldy* Synonym: _____
    Sentence: _____

2. *assuage* Synonym: _____
    Sentence: _____

3. *infirm* Synonym: _____
    Sentence: _____

4. *nomadic* Synonym: _____
    Sentence: _____

5. *tenuous* Synonym: _____
    Sentence: _____

B. DIRECTIONS: *Circle the letter of the words that express a relationship most like the relationship of the pair of words in CAPITAL LETTERS.*

1. ADEPT : GYMNAST
    A. unappreciated : ignored
    B. physician : doctor
    C. entertain : audience
    D. knowledgeable : teacher

2. TENUOUS : STRONG
    A. certain : doubtful
    B. satisfied : contented
    C. quickly : hastily
    D. determined : purpose

3. UNWIELDY : UNMANAGEABLE
    A. confusion : chaos
    B. light : heavy
    C. teacher : student
    D. bright : color

4. ASSUAGE : GUILT
    A. bake : cook
    B. minimize : pain
    C. house : home
    D. sympathize : empathize

5. INFIRM : HEALTHY
    A. tall : immeasurable
    B. doctor : patient
    C. medication : pain
    D. fast : slow

6. NOMADIC : WORKERS
    A. cultivated : ploughed
    B. cattle : ranch
    C. permanent : farmers
    D. wandering : traveling

Name _____   Date _____

from **Desert Exile: The Uprooting of a Japanese-American Family** by Yoshiko Uchida
from **The Way to Rainy Mountain** by N. Scott Momaday
Support for Comparing Literary Works

An author's purpose is his or her main reason for writing. A reporter might write to inform people about a news event, while a short-story writer might write to entertain. Use the chart below to compare the authors' main and secondary reasons for writing these selections. Include details to support your ideas.

from *Desert Exile*	
Uchida's main purpose:	
Author's other purpose(s): 1. 2. 3.	**Most powerful details in passage:** 1. 2. 3.

from *The Way to Rainy Mountain*	
Momaday's main purpose:	
Author's other purpose(s): 1. 2. 3.	**Most powerful details in passage:** 1. 2. 3.

Now, use your notes to write a brief statement about the similarities and differences between the authors' purposes in these two selections.

Can't Build, performed by Hydra

Unh . . . GMS . . . HYDRA . . . MCMI . . . We got another one! Brooklyn! Lessons of life, baby! Ha ha . . .

Yo, I'm playin' ball at the park one day, just a quick pick me up game around the way / Now, I'm quite nice off the top, on my block, plus I got hops, I block shots, and then my shot drops, (yeeeah) / That's how we do around here, (yup) / You can ask anybody that you knew around here / If you new around here, then you got schooled, line, line, fence, fence, park rules / Some talk trash and some talk junk, we don't get mad at a foul, man, we not punks, but one kid - he was really obtuse runnin' off at the mouth with the **verbal** abuse, usin' hurtful words just to cause **confusion,** (word? . . .) so we wouldn't understand who was winnin' or losin' / I said, "There's nothin' wrong with **self-expression,** but can you speak your mind without so much aggression / "It's all good, yo," he shot back / "As long as we catch a win, man, we got that" / Nah . . .

If it ain't truth—Nah, I can't build with you

If it ain't right—Nah, I can't build with you

If there's no love—Man, I can't build with you

And if we can't build—Son, I can't chill with you

If there's no truth—Nah, I can't build with you

If there's no proof—Nah, I can't build with you

Actin' uncouth?—Nah, I can't build with you

It ain't all good, I'm just keeping it real with you . . .

Sometimes we get heated on the b-ball court, but it's all sport, at least that's what we all thought / But this guy, was really comin' outta his face / No doubt a disgrace / He was really outta his place / I wanted out of his space / He tried give me a pound, I left him hangin' like Jordan an' he was from outer space – (You ain't fly!)

He couldn't understand my hesitation, I told him what I meant and this was my **explanation:**

Look, my fam only **interact** with facts, we don't communicate with those that are holdin' us back / In fact, we don't answer 'less you show respect, if you want us to **respond,** get your feelings in check, control your **emotions,** keep it in **context** with everything else that came before and what comes next / Take it light, dude, it's just a game we play, this is street-ball, player, not the NBA, and the way you're talkin' is tryin my patience /

You're about to find yourself in complete **isolation** /

In other words all by yourself, and have the rest of this **discourse,** by yourself /

Don't **misinterpret** my **meaning** or definition, Don't get it twisted, we ain't beefin', I'm not dissin' / Listen, I came here to have fun, get my A game on, while there's still some sun /

Continued

Can't Build, *continued*

I'm done talkin', man, it really ain't worth it / Nothing you're saying will serve a positive purpose, so . . .

If it ain't truth – Nah, I can't build with you
If it ain't right – Nah, I can't build with you
If there's no love – Man, I can't build with you
And if we can't build – Son, I can't chill with you
If there's no truth – Nah, I can't build with you
If there's no proof – Nah, I can't build with you
Actin' uncouth? – Nah, I can't build with you
It ain't all good, I'm just keeping it real with you . . .

Look, all I'm sayin' is I don't deal with negativity in MY life. If you can't make the **connection,** relate to the **language** to **convey,** or communicate to you . . .

Then there's nothin' more to talk about.

Song Title: **Can't Build**
Artist / Performed by Hydra
Vocals: Grame "GMS" Sibersky
Lyrics by Grame "GMS" Sibersky
Music composed by Keith Middleton
Produced by Keith Middleton
Technical Production: Mike Pandolfo, Wonderful
Executive Producer: Keith London, Defined Mind

Name _____ Date _____

Unit 4: Poetry
Big Question Vocabulary—1

The Big Question: Does all communication serve a positive purpose?

In your textbook, you learned words that are useful for talking about communication. In our lives, we communicate by speaking, listening, writing, and reading. We can also communicate through body language.

DIRECTIONS: *Review the following definitions of words you can use when talking about communication.*

confusion: perplexity or bewilderment; a lack of clear understanding

connection: an association, a relationship, or an attachment

context: the set of circumstances that surround a particular event or situation

convey: to get an idea across; to communicate or impart

discourse: communication or conversation

A. *Now, for each Big Question vocabulary word, write a synonym, an antonym, and a sentence in which you use the word correctly.*

Word	Synonym	Antonym	Example Sentence
1. confusion			
2. connection			
3. context			
4. convey			
5. discourse			

B. *Write two to three sentences in which you use three or more of the vocabulary words on this page to write a generalization about communication.*

_____

_____

_____

_____

_____

Name _____ Date _____

Unit 4: Poetry
Big Question Vocabulary—2

The Big Question: Does all communication serve a positive purpose?

DIRECTIONS: *Review the following definitions of words you can use when talking about communication.*

emotion: a feeling, such as joy, sorrow, fear, hate, or love

explanation: a statement made to clarify something or make it understandable

interact: to communicate or have an exchange with someone else

isolation: the state of being alone or separated from others

language: the system of words and the rules for using them that people use to communicate with one another in speech and in writing

Now, decide whether each statement below is true or false, based on the meanings of the underlined vocabulary words. Circle T or F, and then explain your answers.

1. One cannot communicate an <u>emotion</u> without words.
   T / F _____
   _____

2. An <u>explanation</u> of how you feel about a situation would help you communicate more effectively with others about it.
   T / F _____
   _____

3. To <u>interact</u> with someone, you must communicate in some way.
   T / F _____
   _____

4. You might feel a sense of <u>isolation</u> if you are the only one in a room to hold a certain opinion and everyone else holds a different opinion.
   T / F _____
   _____

5. People cannot communicate with each if they do not know one another's <u>languages</u>.
   T / F _____
   _____

Name _____ Date _____

Unit 4: Poetry
Big Question Vocabulary—3

The Big Question: Does all communication serve a positive purpose?

DIRECTIONS: *Review the following definitions of words you can use when talking about communication.*

meaning: what is intended to be expressed or indicated

misinterpret: to misunderstand

respond: to reply or answer in words

self-expression: communicating one's thoughts and feelings

verbal: expressed in spoken words

Now, use the word given in parentheses to answer each question.

1. When you write a poem, how do you come up with an idea you care about? **(meaning, self-expression)**

   _____

   _____

2. What usually causes disagreements between friends? **(misinterpret, respond)**

   _____

   _____

3. How can you participate in a classroom discussion? **(respond, verbal)**

   _____

   _____

4. How can a person communicate with a pet? **(meaning, verbal, respond)**

   _____

   _____

5. Do we have to communicate? **(meaning, self-expression)**

   _____

   _____

Name _____ Date _____

Unit 4: Poetry
Applying the Big Question

The Big Question: Does all communication serve a positive purpose?

DIRECTIONS: *Complete the chart below to apply what you have learned about the ways in which communication makes a positive or negative impact on others. One row has been completed for you.*

Example	Message communicated	Who communicates	Purpose of communication	Positive purpose? Explain.	What I learned
From Literature	Men fought and died "In Flanders Fields" during World War I.	Dead soldiers buried in Flanders Fields are the speakers.	The purpose is either to get more men to fight or to criticize war by talking about death.	Yes. The purpose rallies patriotism or tries to save lives.	Communication can be critical but still have a positive purpose.
From Literature					
From Science					
From Social Studies					
From Real Life					

Cornelius Eady
Listening and Viewing

Segment 1: Meet Cornelius Eady
- What did Cornelius Eady come to understand about jazz that changed the way he approached writing? Why might poetry be an effective way in which to convey personal stories?

_____

_____

_____

Segment 2: Poetry
- Why does Cornelius Eady use repetition in his poetry? In your view, what does Cornelius Eady hope to achieve by using repetition and short words in his poems?

_____

_____

_____

Segment 3: The Writing Process
- Why does Cornelius Eady read his poems aloud as he is writing them? How can reading a poem aloud give the reader (or the writer) a different perspective of the poem?

_____

_____

_____

Segment 4: The Rewards of Writing
- What does Cornelius Eady hope readers can learn from his poems? In your opinion, why might it be important to share your stories with others through writing?

_____

_____

_____

Learning About Poetry

There are three main types of poetry: **Narrative** poetry tells a story and has a plot, characters, and a setting. It includes **epics,** long poems about the feats of gods or heroes, and **ballads,** songlike poems with short stanzas and a refrain. **Dramatic** poetry tells a story using a character's own thoughts or spoken statements. **Lyric** poetry expresses the feelings of a single speaker.

Poetic forms include **haiku,** poems of three unrhymed lines of five, seven, and five syllables; **tanka,** poems of five unrhymed lines of five, seven, five, seven, and seven syllables; **free verse,** which has neither a set pattern of rhythm nor rhyme; and **sonnets,** fourteen-line lyric poems with formal patterns of rhyme, rhythm, and line structure.

Poets frequently uses **figurative language** to make comparisons. **Similes** use *like* or *as* to compare unlike things; **metaphors** speak of one thing in terms of another; and **personification** gives human traits to nonhuman things.

Poets also uses **imagery** to create vivid impressions, or **images.** Images are developed using **sensory language,** which relates to the senses of sight, touch, taste, smell, hearing, and movement.

Finally, poets use **sound devices** to achieve a musical quality. They use **rhythm,** the pattern of stressed and unstressed syllables of words in sequence (an ordered pattern of rhythm is **meter**); **rhyme,** the repetition of identical or similar sounds in the last syllables of words; **alliteration,** the repetition of the initial consonant sounds of words; **assonance,** the repetition of vowel sounds in words that are close to each other; and **consonance,** the repetition of consonants in words that are close to each other and contain different vowels.

A. DIRECTIONS: *Read the description of each element of poetry. Then, write its definition. Choose from the terms in boldface type in the preceding passage.*

_____ 1. a comparison that speaks of one thing in terms of another

_____ 2. the pattern of stressed and unstressed syllables in sequence

_____ 3. a long narrative poem about the accomplishments of a hero

_____ 4. a poem without rhyme or a set pattern of rhythm

_____ 5. the repetition of similar sounds in the last syllables of words

_____ 6. nonhuman things described as having human traits

_____ 7. vivid impressions that relate to the senses

_____ 8. a fourteen-line lyric poem

B. DIRECTIONS: *Read this poem. Then, describe the form it takes and the devices it uses.*

The snow fell all night / A blanket bringing no warmth / Winter has arrived.

_____

_____

_____

_____

The Poetry of Cornelius Eady
Model Selection: Poetry

A lyric poem expresses the feelings of a single speaker. Lyric poems often use **figurative language,** writing that departs from the standard meaning of words to express ideas or feelings in new ways. The following are three types of figurative language.

- **similes:** comparisons that use *like* or *as* to compare two essentially unlike things
- **metaphors:** comparisons that speak of one thing in terms of another
- **personification:** comparisons that give human traits to nonhuman things

A. DIRECTIONS: *"The Poetic Interpretation of the Twist" and "The Empty Dance Shoes" are lyric poems in which the poet uses figurative language to express his feelings. Complete the following chart by writing down at least two examples of each kind of figurative language. The examples may come from either one of Eady's poems.*

Simile:
Metaphor:
Personification:

B. DIRECTIONS: *The speaker of "The Poetic Interpretation of the Twist" reveals a great deal about himself and his feelings in the poem. Describe three things you learn about the speaker, and tell how you learn each one.*

_____

_____

_____

_____

_____

_____

Name _____ Date _____

Poetry Collection 1: Alexander Pushkin, Federico García Lorca,
Elizabeth Bishop, and Rudyard Kipling

Writing About the Big Question

Does all communication serve a positive purpose?

Big Question Vocabulary

confusion	connection	context	convey	discourse
emotion	explanation	interact	isolation	language
meaning	misinterpret	respond	self-expression	verbal

A. *Use one or more words from the list above to complete each sentence.*

1. There was much _____ about the assignment, because we did not hear the directions.

2. If you do not write clearly, the _____ of what you are trying to express will be lost.

3. Lyla could explain her ideas well, and this clear _____ made her confident in class.

4. Jay was so upset that his _____ prevented him from explaining what was wrong.

B. *Follow the directions in responding to each of the items below.*

1. List two situations in which you unsuccessfully communicated a piece of information.
   _____.
   _____.

2. Write two sentences explaining one of the experiences you listed. Use at least two of the Big Question vocabulary words.
   _____
   _____

C. *Complete the sentences below. Then, write a short paragraph in which you connect this experience to the big question.*

People, animals, and even things use **language** and non-**verbal** forms of communication to **convey** _____. The purpose of such communication might be to express **emotion** or _____.

Poetry Collection 1: Alexander Pushkin, Federico García Lorca, Elizabeth Bishop,
and Rudyard Kipling

Literary Analysis: Narrative and Lyric Poetry

In poetry, the **speaker** is the voice that says the words of the poem. All poems have a speaker, who is either the poet or a character the poet invents to give the poem a particular voice or point of view.

- In **narrative** poetry, the speaker tells a story in verse.
- In **lyric poetry,** the speaker's thoughts, feelings, and insights create a single, unified impression. Lyric poems include **imagery,** language that appeals to the senses.

DIRECTIONS: *Answer the following questions about the poems in this collection.*

1. "The Bridegroom" begins with these lines:

   For three days Natasha, / The merchant's daughter, / Was missing. The third night, / She ran in, distraught.

   Based on these lines, is "The Bridegroom" a narrative poem or a lyric poem? Explain.

   _____

   _____

2. Identify two examples of imagery in the following lines from "The Guitar." Tell which senses the images appeal to and what feeling the lines create.

   It weeps / For distant things, / Warm southern sands / Desiring white camellias.

   _____

   _____

   _____

3. When the speaker of "The Fish" examines the fish she has caught, she sees five old pieces of fishing line in its jaw, signs that the fish has been hooked before, but got away:

   Like medals with their ribbons / frayed and wavering, / a five-haired beard of wisdom / trailing from his aching jaw.

   What does the speaker's imagery tell you about her feelings toward the fish?

   _____

   _____

4. Read lines 3–6 of "Danny Deever," and then explain how Kipling uses dialogue to tell a story in this poem?

   _____

   _____

   _____

Poetry Collection 1: Alexander Pushkin, Federico García Lorca, Elizabeth Bishop, and Rudyard Kipling

Reading: Read Aloud and Adjust Reading Rate to Read Fluently

Read aloud to appreciate and share the musical qualities of poetry. As you read aloud, **read fluently** and **adjust your reading rate** in the following ways.

- First, read through slowly and carefully. Make sure you understand the poem's complex thoughts and that you can pronounce all the words.
- Use punctuation and group words for meaning. Do not pause at the end of a line unless a punctuation mark indicates that you should.
- Slow down to emphasize an idea or the sounds of words.

The following chart shows how to mark up a poem to help you read it fluently:

Mark the Text	Adjusting Reading Rate
Circle punctuation marks.	Pause.
Underline words or sounds to emphasize.	Slow down.
Bracket phrases or groups of words to read together.	Speed up.

DIRECTIONS: *Write your answers to the following questions.*

1. Copy lines 61–64 of "The Bridegroom" onto a separate sheet of paper and circle all the punctuation marks. Then, answer the questions.

   A. How many complete sentences do the lines contain? _____

   B. After which words should readers pause briefly?

   _____

2. Line 25 of "The Guitar" ends with an exclamation point—"O guitar!" How does this punctuation mark affect the reading of the line?

   _____

   _____

3. Copy lines 7–11 of "The Fish" onto a separate sheet of paper. Then, follow the directions below.

   A. Underline the three adjectives that a reader should emphasize when reading the poem aloud.

   B. Bracket each group of words a reader should say together to make the meaning of the phrase that begins "Here and there . . ." clear.

4. Read aloud the opening lines of "Danny Deever." Then explain the importance that quotation marks and question marks play in reading the poem fluently.

   _____

   _____

   _____

Name _____ Date _____

Poetry Collection 1: Alexander Pushkin, Federico García Lorca, Elizabeth Bishop,
and Rudyard Kipling
Vocabulary Builder

Word List

comrade   foreboding   monotonously   sullen   tumult   venerable

A. DIRECTIONS: *In each item below, think about the meaning of the italicized word and then answer the question.*

1. When might you have a feeling of *foreboding* about taking a test?

    _____

2. How would you feel if a speaker talked *monotonously* about his subject?

    _____

3. How would you treat a *venerable* visitor?

    _____

4. If you were standing near a crowd in a *tumult*, what would you hear?

    _____

5. Would a *sullen* person be lively and fun at a party?

    _____

6. Would a *comrade* be working with you or against you?

    _____

B. WORD STUDY: The **Old English prefix** *fore-* means "before," "in front," "beforehand, ahead of time." Answer the following questions using one of these words that contain the prefix *fore-: forecast, foredoom, forefinger.*

1. Will a *forecast* tell you about yesterday's weather?

    _____

2. If your project has been *foredoomed*, are you expecting a good outcome?

    _____

3. In which position on your hand will you find your *forefinger*?

    _____

Poetry Collection 2: Denise Levertov, William Carlos Williams, Robert Frost, and Naomi Shihab Nye

Writing About the Big Question

Does all communication serve a positive purpose?

Big Question Vocabulary

confusion	connection	context	convey	discourse
emotion	explanation	interact	isolation	language
meaning	misinterpret	respond	self-expression	verbal

A. *Use one or more words from the list above to complete each sentence.*

1. Successful communication depends on being able to _____ your thoughts clearly.

2. She might _____ your meaning if you speak to her using an angry tone of voice.

3. Jill does not _____ well to threats and demands, so ask her nicely to clean her room.

B. *Follow the directions in responding to each of the items below.*

1. Identify two situations in which your communication was successful.

   _____ .

   _____ .

2. Write two sentences explaining one of the experiences you listed. Use at least two of the Big Question vocabulary words.

   _____

   _____

C. *Complete the sentences below. Then, write a short paragraph in which you connect this experience to the big question.*

Communication that seems to begin negatively can actually have a positive **meaning** when _____. Conversely, communication that is uplifting and positive has the ability to lead to **isolation** and sadness when

_____ .

Poetry Collection 2: Denise Levertov, William Carlos Williams, Robert Frost, and Naomi Shihab Nye

Literary Analysis: Narrative and Lyric Poetry

In poetry, the **speaker** is the voice that says the words of the poem. All poems have a speaker, who is either the poet or a character the poet invents to give the poem a particular voice or point of view.

- In **narrative** poetry, the speaker tells a story in verse.
- In **lyric poetry,** the speaker's thoughts, feelings, and insights create a single, unified impression. Lyric poems include **imagery,** language that appeals to the senses.

DIRECTIONS: *Answer the following questions about the poems in this collection.*

1. **A.** Who or what is the speaker in the poem "A Tree Telling of Orpheus"? _____

   B. In a few sentences, summarize the story that the speaker tells in this narrative poem.

   _____

   _____

2. Read the following lines from "Spring and All." What impression of spring does the imagery create?

   They enter the new world naked,
   cold, uncertain of all
   save that they enter.

   _____

   _____

3. Read the following lines from "Mowing." Identify four examples of imagery, and tell to which of the five senses each image appeals.

   Not without feeble-pointed spikes of flowers
   (Pale orchises), and scared a bright green snake.
   The fact is the sweetest dream that labor knows.
   My long scythe whispered and left the hay to make.

   _____

   _____

4. **A.** Who or what is the speaker in the poem "Making a Fist"? _____

   B. Summarize the story that the speaker tells in this narrative poem.

   _____

   _____

   _____

Poetry Collection 2: Denise Levertov, William Carlos Williams, Robert Frost, and Naomi Shihab Nye

Reading: Read Aloud and Adjust Reading Rate to Read Fluently

Read aloud to appreciate and share the musical qualities of poetry. As you read aloud, **read fluently** and **adjust your reading rate** in the following ways.

- First, read through slowly and carefully. Make sure you understand the poem's complex thoughts and that you can pronounce all the words.
- Use punctuation and group words for meaning. Do not pause at the end of a line unless a punctuation mark indicates that you should.
- Slow down to emphasize an idea or the sounds of words.

The following chart shows how to mark up a poem to help you read it fluently:

Mark the Text	Adjusting Reading Rate
Circle punctuation marks.	Pause.
Underline the words or sounds to emphasize.	Slow down.
Bracket phrases or groups of words to read together.	Speed up.

DIRECTIONS: *Write your answers to the following questions.*

1. On a separate sheet of paper, copy lines 80–85 of "A Tree Telling of Orpheus." Circle all the punctuation marks and then answer the questions.

   A. How many complete sentences do the lines contain? _____

   B. After which words should readers pause briefly?

   _____

2. Read lines 16–19 from "Spring and All." Then, follow the directions below.

   A. Underline the five adjectives a reader should emphasize when he or she reads aloud.

   B. Bracket each group of words that should be read together.

3. Read lines 3–6 of "Mowing." Then, answer the questions that follow.

   A. What five types of punctuation does the poet use in these lines?

   _____

   B. Explain how one should adjust reading rate and tone of voice for each punctuation mark.

   _____

   _____

4. Reread "Making a Fist." Explain how a reader should change his or her voice when reading the stanza with quotation marks (lines 7–11).

   _____

   _____

Poetry Collection 2: Denise Levertov, William Carlos Williams, Robert Frost, and Naomi Shihab Nye

Vocabulary Builder

Word List

anguish   clenching   earnest   idle   rejoiced   stark

A. DIRECTIONS: *In each item below, think about the meaning of the italicized word and then write a description that fits the meaning of the word.*

1. Describe a situation in which a person might be *clenching* his or her fists.

   _____

2. Describe a *stark* scene in nature.

   _____

3. Describe something a person might do during idle hours.

   _____

4. Describe a situation in which a person might experience a feeling of *anguish*.

   _____

5. Describe a situation in which people would have *rejoiced*.

   _____

6. Describe how an *earnest* person might behave.

   _____

B. WORD STUDY: The **Latin prefix re-** means "again," "anew," or "back." Answer the following questions using one of these words that contain the prefix *re-: retire, retort, recount.*

1. If you *retire* from a game, are you playing until the last minute?

   _____

2. If you issue a *retort*, are you talking to yourself?

   _____

3. What are family members doing if they *recount* a story about you?

   _____

Poetry Collection 1: Alexander Pushkin, Federico García Lorca, Elizabeth Bishop, Rudyard Kipling
Poetry Collection 2: Denise Levertov, William Carlos Williams, Robert Frost, and Naomi Shihab Nye

Integrated Language Skills: Grammar

Preposition and Object of Preposition

A **preposition** is a word that relates a noun or pronoun that appears with it to another word in the sentence. Common prepositions are *across, against, at, of, on, to, under,* and *with.* The following sentence includes two prepositional phrases. Each preposition is underlined once, and each object is underlined twice.

On the table, there is a scrapbook filled *with* some *letters* and *photographs*.

A. DIRECTIONS: *Draw a circle around each prepositional phrase in the sentences. Then, underline the preposition once and the object, or objects, of the preposition twice.*

1. I bought a birthday gift for Alex.
2. Abraham Lincoln was the President of the United States during the Civil War.
3. Last night there was a ring around the moon.
4. Among my favorite possessions is an antique ring from my grandmother.
5. Did you go to the dance after the game?
6. The girl on the left is my cousin Jenna.
7. The object of the game is guessing the answer to the riddle.
8. Move the table toward the wall.
9. Earth is located between Mars and Venus.
10. Walking with the ball in your hands is against the rules of the game.

B. DIRECTIONS: *Write a paragraph describing your favorite place. Describe the details of the place in spatial order, using prepositions such as* across, above, behind, in front of, near, next to, on, *and* under.

_____

_____

_____

_____

Name _____ Date _____

Poetry Collection 1: Alexander Pushkin, Federico García Lorca, Elizabeth Bishop, and Rudyard Kipling
Poetry Collection 2: Denise Levertov, William Carlos Williams, Robert Frost, and Naomi Shihab Nye

Integrated Language Skills: Support for Writing a Lyric Poem

After you choose a speaker and a subject for your lyric poem, use the following graphic organizer to list imagery that describes the subject.

Subject being described: _____

Speaker in poem: _____

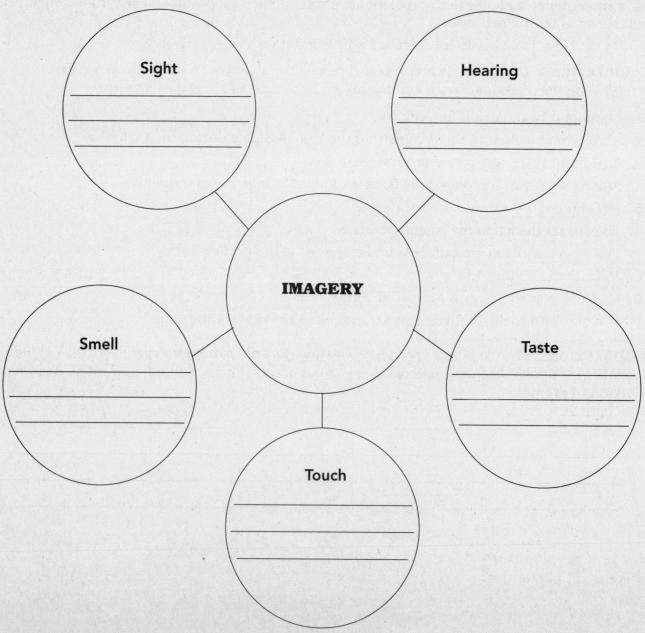

Now, use your notes to write a lyric poem that vividly describes the subject and conveys the speaker's feelings about it.

Name _____ Date _____

Writing About the Big Question

Does all communication serve a positive purpose?

Big Question Vocabulary

confusion	connection	context	convey	discourse
emotion	explanation	interact	isolation	language
meaning	misinterpret	respond	self-expression	verbal

A. *Use one or more words from the list above to complete each sentence.*

1. Communication can help people who live in _____
   reach out to others.

2. _____ communication is necessary when you
   are speaking with group members about a project.

3. A nation's _____ to the rest of the world
   depends on productive communication.

4. The _____ in which communication occurs can
   determine how people interpret the message.

B. *Follow the directions in responding to each of the items below.*

1. List an example in which communication between world leaders could lead to positive results.

   _____.

   _____.

2. Write two sentences explaining your example. Include a negative result that could
   occur if there was no communication. Use at least two Big Question vocabulary
   words.

   _____

   _____

C. *Complete the sentences below. Then, write a short paragraph in which you connect
   this experience to the big question.*

   When people **interact** and **respond** to nature they might feel _____.
   Poets, in particular, might feel a **connection** to nature because _____.

Poetry Collection 3: Ki Tsurayuki, Minamoto no Toshiyori, James Weldon Johnson,
and Dylan Thomas

Literary Analysis: Poetic Form

To unify sounds and ideas in a poem, a poet may follow a **poetic form,** or a defined structure. Each poetic form uses a set number of lines. Some have a unique **meter,** or rhythm, and a unique pattern of **rhymes.** In your textbook, review the traditional poetic forms. Then, complete the exercise.

DIRECTIONS: *Answer the following questions about the poems in this collection.*

1. Both "When I went to visit. . ." and "The clustering clouds. . ." are translations of Japanese poems. Count the syllables in each line of the two poems. Which translation provides a better example of the tanka form? Why?

   _____

   _____

2. Read aloud the first four lines of the poem "My City." Then, answer the following questions.

   When I come down to sleep death's endless night,
       The threshold of the unknown dark to cross,
       What to me then will be the keenest loss,
   When this bright world blurs on my fading sight?

   A. Above each unaccented syllable, draw a ˘. Above each accented syllable, draw a ´.

   B. How many accented and unaccented syllables did you find in each line?

   _____

   C. What is the rhyme scheme of the lines? _____

   D. In what poetic form is "My City" written? _____

3. Read aloud the first two stanzas of "Do Not Go Gentle Into That Good Night." Then, answer the following questions.

   Do not go gentle into that good night,
   Old age should burn and rave at close of day;
   Rage, rage against the dying of the light.

   Though wise men at their end know dark is right,
   Because their words had forked no lightning they
   Do not go gentle into that good night.

   A. How many lines are in each stanza? _____

   B. What is the rhyme scheme of the two stanzas? _____

   C. Which line is repeated? _____

   D. In what poetic form is the poem written? _____

Poetry Collection 3: Ki Tsurayuki, Minamoto no Toshiyori, James Weldon Johnson, and Dylan Thomas

Reading: Preview a Poem to Read Fluently

When you **read fluently,** you read smoothly and with understanding. You place emphasis appropriately and pause where necessary. To increase your fluency when reading a poem, **preview** the work. Look over the text in advance:

- Use footnotes and other text aids to learn unfamiliar words.
- Determine where each sentence in the poem begins and ends. Pause only when the punctuation indicates you should.
- Form a rough idea of the topic and mood of the work. Read the poem with its mood in mind.

DIRECTIONS: *Answer the following questions about the poems in this collection.*

1. Preview the poem "When I went to visit. . . ." What three punctuation marks do you see in the poem?

   _____

2. Preview the poem "The clustering clouds. . . ." How can the punctuation marks help you read the poem smoothly and with understanding?

   _____

3. Preview the poem "My City" and answer the questions.

   A. How many end marks do you find in lines 1–8? _____

   B. How do the end marks in lines 1–8 differ?

   _____

   C. How do these end marks determine the way you should read lines 1–8 for understanding?

   _____

   _____

   D. What end mark is used twice in lines 9–14?

   E. How does the end mark affect how you should read lines 9–14?

   _____

4. Preview the poem "Do Not Go Gentle Into That Good Night." Then, answer the questions.

   A. In stanzas 1–5, how many sentences does each stanza contain? _____

   B. How does the number of sentences in stanzas 1–5 help you read each stanza fluently?

   _____

   C. What word is repeated at the beginning of lines 3, 9, 15, and 19? _____

   D. How does this repetition offer a clue to the overall mood you should convey when reading the poem?

   _____

Poetry Collection 3: Ki Tsurayuki, Minamoto no Toshiyori, James Weldon Johnson, and Dylan Thomas

Vocabulary Builder

Word List

clustering   keenest   lunar   rave   subtile   threshold

A. DIRECTIONS: *Write whether each statement is* true *or* false. *Explain why.*

_____ 1. *Clustering* birds are a common sight in autumn.

_____

_____ 2. A *lunar* eclipse is an eclipse of the sun.

_____

_____ 3. Many homes have chimneys on their *thresholds*.

_____

_____ 4. The animal with the *keenest* eyesight sees the best.

_____

_____ 5. A *subtile* joke has an obvious ending and is easy to understand.

_____

_____ 6. If you *rave* about the election, you are conversing rationally in a quiet voice.

_____

B. WORD STUDY: The **Latin root -lun-** means "moon." Provide an explanation for your answer to each question that includes one of these words containing the root -lun-: *lunacy, lunatic, luna.*

1. Would *lunacy* refer to someone's rational behavior?

_____

2. If a character in a story is the responsible person upon whom everyone depends, is that character likely to be called a *lunatic*?

_____

3. In mythology, is *luna* the goddess of the moon or the sun?

_____

Poetry Collection 4: Priest Jakuren, Ono Komachi,
Theodore Roethke, and William Shakespeare

Writing About the Big Question

Does all communication serve a positive purpose?

Big Question Vocabulary

confusion	connection	context	convey	discourse
emotion	explanation	interact	isolation	language
meaning	misinterpret	respond	self-expression	verbal

A. *Use one or more words from the list above to complete each sentence.*

1. Mary's _____ with others is always civil; her
   language and tone are always appropriate.

2. Joe can _____ positively with his opponents as
   well as with his teammates.

3. Romero's _____ about how he rescued the cat
   was exciting.

4. Julie responded to her brother using negative _____,
   and the words hurt his feelings.

B. *Follow the directions in responding to each of the items below.*

1. List two times when your language made someone feel better.

   _____.

   _____.

2. Write two sentences explaining one of the experiences you listed. Use at least two of
   the Big Question vocabulary words.

   _____

   _____

C. *Complete the sentence below. Then, write a short paragraph in which you connect this
experience to the big question.*

Nature can provide a **context** for thinking in **isolation** about _____,
which can lead to communication about _____.

Name _____ Date _____

Poetry Collection 4: Priest Jakuren, Ono Komachi, Theodore Roethke,
and William Shakespeare

Literary Analysis: Poetic Form

To unify sounds and ideas in a poem, a poet may follow a **poetic form,** or structure, using a set number of lines. Some have a unique **meter,** or rhythm, and a unique pattern of **rhymes.**

Elements	Tanka	Sonnet	Villanelle
Number of lines	5 (may vary in translation, but must be brief)	14: three 4-line *quatrains* + a 2-line *couplet*	19: five 3-line stanzas + one 4-line stanza. Lines 1 and 3 repeat.
Number of syllables/ each line	lines 1, 3 = 5 syllables lines 2, 4, 5 = 7 syllables (may vary in translation)	usually ten syllables per line	Poets may follow different patterns.
Pattern of accents	no set pattern	5 unaccented and 5 accented syllables per line	Poets may follow different patterns.
Rhyme scheme	none	abba, cddc, efef, gg **OR** abab, cdcd, efef, gg	aba, aba, aba, aba, aba, aba
Characteristics	brief; focuses on one idea	ideas in quatrains can answer one another; couplet is a summary	repetition can create chanting effect or suggest intensity

Directions: *Answer the following questions about the poems in this collection.*

1. **A.** How do the translations of the two tanka depart from traditional tanka form?

   _____

   B. Why do you think the translator made these changes in the form?

   _____

2. Read aloud the first two stanzas of "The Waking." Then, answer the questions.

   A. How many lines are in each stanza? _____

   B. What is the rhyme scheme of the two stanzas? _____

   C. Which line is repeated? _____

   D. In what poetic form is the poem written? _____

3. Copy out the first four lines of Shakespeare's Sonnet 18 on a separate sheet of paper. Then, answer the questions.

   A. Above each unaccented syllable, draw a ˘. Above each accented syllable, draw a ´.

   B. How many accented and unaccented syllables did you find in each line?

   _____

   C. What is the rhyme scheme of the lines? _____

All-in-One Workbook
© Pearson Education, Inc. All rights reserved.
195

Poetry Collection 4: Priest Jakuren, Ono Komachi, Theodore Roethke,
and William Shakespeare

Reading: Preview a Poem to Read Fluently

When you **read fluently,** you read smoothly and with understanding. You place emphasis appropriately and pause where necessary. To increase your fluency when reading a poem, **preview** the work. Look over the text in advance:

- Use footnotes and other text aids to learn unfamiliar words.
- Determine where each sentence in the poem begins and ends. Pause only when the punctuation indicates you should.
- Form a rough idea of the topic and mood of the work. Read the poem with its mood in mind.

DIRECTIONS: *Answer the following questions about the poems in this collection.*

1. Preview the poem "One cannot ask loneliness. . . ." What two end marks do you see in the poem? _____

2. Preview the poem "Was it that I went to sleep. . . ." How can the end marks help you read the poem smoothly and with understanding?

   _____

   _____

3. Preview lines 1–6 of "The Waking" and answer the questions.

   A. How many end marks do these lines contain? _____

   B. How does the number of end marks influence how you should read the lines fluently?

   _____

   C. How do the pauses in lines 1–6 help convey the meaning and theme of the poem?

   _____

   _____

   _____

4. In order to read Shakespeare's Sonnet 18 fluently, why is it important to make sure you understand the meanings of the words *temperate* and *eternal* when you preview the poem?

   _____

   _____

   _____

Poetry Collection 4: Priest Jakuren, Ono Komachi, Theodore Roethke,
and William Shakespeare
Vocabulary Builder

Word List

eternal   fate   lease   lowly   steady   temperate

A. DIRECTIONS: *Write whether each statement is* true *or* false. *Explain why.*

_____ 1. Parents can tell their child's *fate* at birth.

_____

_____ 2. Winters in northern Canada are usually *temperate*.

_____

_____ 3. Getting an education is one way that people rise from a *lowly*
position.

_____

_____ 4. An *eternal* mystery is one that can be easily solved.

_____

_____ 5. If you are *steady* on your feet, you rarely trip while climbing the
stairs.

_____

_____ 6. When you have a *lease* on a house, you own it.

_____

B. WORD STUDY: The **Latin root -*temp*-** means "regulate," "moderate," or "time." Provide an
explanation for your answer to each question that includes one of these words containing
the root -*temp*-: *temperance, contemporary, temporary.*

1. If your parents encourage *temperance*, do they want you to be wild and self-indulgent?

_____

2. Is a *contemporary* artist someone who lived in a past era?

_____

3. If your injury is *temporary*, will you feel better in a few days?

_____

Poetry Collection 3: Ki Tsurayuki, Minamoto no Toshiyori, James Weldon Johnson, Dylan Thomas

Poetry Collection 4: Priest Jakuren, Ono Komachi, Theodore Roethke, and William Shakespeare

Integrated Language Skills: Grammar

Direct Objects

A **direct object** is a noun or pronoun that receives the action of a verb. It answers the question *what* or *whom*. Not all action verbs take a direct object. Verbs such as *am, is, are, was,* and *were* are linking verbs. They never take a direct object.

Jen makes **scrapbooks.**
(Jen makes *what?*) (has a direct object)

She spoke to the class about them.
(has an action verb, but no direct object)

Making scrapbooks is her favorite hobby.
(has a linking verb, no direct object)

A. DIRECTIONS: *Underline each direct object in the following sentences. If the sentence does not have a direct object, write* no d.o. *on the line.*

_____ 1. Sean likes very old movies.

_____ 2. He rents DVDs of old comedies.

_____ 3. His favorites are the Marx Brothers.

_____ 4. Sometimes I go to the video store with him.

_____ 5. He invited me to his house to watch a movie yesterday.

B. DIRECTIONS: *Write a paragraph about the kind of books, movies, sports, or crafts that you enjoy. Underline each direct object that you use in your paragraph.*

_____

_____

_____

_____

_____

Poetry Collection 3: Ki Tsurayuki, Minamoto no Toshiyori, James Weldon Johnson, Dylan Thomas

Poetry Collection 4: Priest Jakuren, Ono Komachi, Theodore Roethke, and William Shakespeare

Support for Writing a Tanka

Before drafting your tanka, read the simple example below. Then, draft your own tanka on the blank lines, using only the number of syllables indicated for each line. In your poem, you might want to describe your response to a specific type of weather.

Subject: Lying in bed listening to a storm outside
Mood: Cozy, thankful

Rain beats the windows.	**5 syllables**
Wind howls and sneaks through the cracks.	**7 syllables**
I smile with content.	**5 syllables**
Their fury cannot touch me.	**7 syllables**
I am snug and warm in bed.	**7 syllables**

Subject of Your Poem: _____

Mood You Want to Convey: _____

5 syllables _____

7 syllables _____

5 syllables _____

7 syllables _____

7 syllables _____

Use the space below to jot down ideas for your tanka.

"**Fear**" by Gabriela Mistral
"**The Bean Eaters**" by Gwendolyn Brooks
"**How to React to Familiar Faces**" by Umberto Eco

Writing About the Big Question

Does all communication serve a positive purpose?

Big Question Vocabulary

confusion	connection	context	convey	discourse
emotion	explanation	interact	isolation	language
meaning	misinterpret	respond	self-expression	verbal

A. *Use one or more words from the list above to complete each sentence.*

1. Sometimes we use the strongest _____ when we want to express our deepest passions.

2. Without the proper context, communication can lead to _____ and misunderstandings.

3. We forged a strong _____ with our new classmate by communicating in her native language.

B. *Follow the directions in responding to each of the items below.*

1. List two times when you initiated communication with someone you did not know.

_____.

_____.

2. Write two sentences explaining one of the experiences you listed, describing the outcome of the encounter. Use at least two of the Big Question vocabulary words.

_____

_____

C. *Complete the sentence below. Then, write a short paragraph in which you connect this experience to the big question.*

All communication (does/does not) serve a positive purpose because _____.

Name _____ Date _____

"**Fear**" by Gabriela Mistral
"**The Bean Eaters**" by Gwendolyn Brooks
"**How to React to Familiar Faces**" by Umberto Eco

Literary Analysis: Tone and Mood

Tone and **mood** help create the overall feeling or impression conveyed by a literary work. **Tone** is the author's attitude toward the reader or toward the subject of the work. A literary work's tone can *formal* or *informal, scolding* or *encouraging, humorous* or *serious, matter-of-fact* or *enthusiastic.* **Mood,** or atmosphere, is a general, unified feeling conveyed by the various details of a literary work. The mood of a work may be described as *gloomy* or *joyous, menacing* or *cozy.*

Writers create tone and mood through their choice of words, descriptive details, and images.

A. DIRECTIONS: *Use the chart to compare the tones and moods of these three selections. Describe the tone and mood of each work using vivid and accurate adjectives.*

"Fear" by Gabriela Mistral	"The Bean Eaters" by Gwendolyn Brooks	"How to React to Familiar Faces" by Umberto Eco
Tone:	Tone:	Tone:
Mood:	Mood:	Mood:

Selections by Gabriela Mistral, Gwendolyn Brooks, and Umberto Eco
Vocabulary Builder

Word List

amiably   context   expound   twinges

A. DIRECTIONS: *Complete each sentence with a word from the Word List.*

1. She felt _____ in her hands after gripping the rope for such a long time.
2. Once Reba knew the _____ in which I made my remark, she understood what I meant.
3. Steve responded so _____ to my request to trade books that we became good friends.
4. My father loves to _____ on the rules of football and can talk for hours about the game.

B. DIRECTIONS: *Find a synonym for each word in the Word List. Use each synonym in a sentence that makes the meaning of the word clear.*

    Example: Word: *annoy*
                Synonym: *bother*
                Sentence: Humming in study hall may <u>bother</u> the other students.

1. *amiably*

    Synonym: _____

    Sentence: _____

2. *context*

    Synonym: _____

    Sentence: _____

3. *expound*

    Synonym: _____

    Sentence: _____

4. *twinges*

    Synonym: _____

    Sentence: _____

All-in-One Workbook
202

Selections by Gabriela Mistral, Gwendolyn Brooks, and Umberto Eco
Support for Writing to Compare Literary Works

Before you draft your essay analyzing how each author generates mood, complete the following graphic organizer. Use another sheet of paper if necessary.

	"Fear"	**"The Bean Eaters"**	**"How to React to Familiar Faces"**
Emotional state of . . .	the speaker:	the speaker: the couple:	the speaker:
Details or images related to these emotional states			
The "world" of each selection			
Selection's overall mood			

Now, use your notes to write an essay analyzing the ways in which each author generates a certain mood.

Poetry Collection 5: Yusef Komunyakaa, Eve Merriam, and Emily Dickinson
Writing About the Big Question

Does all communication serve a positive purpose?

Big Question Vocabulary

confusion	connection	context	convey	discourse
emotion	explanation	interact	isolation	language
meaning	misinterpret	respond	self-expression	verbal

A. *Use one or more words from the list above to complete each sentence.*

1. Discovering what you love to do can add _____ to your life and help you fulfill your destiny.

2. We decided to _____ with our new neighbors and discovered that we have much in common.

3. _____ communication works best when you speak clearly.

B. *Follow the directions in responding to each of the items below.*

1. When did you tell someone the truth and make that person feel better? List two occasions.

   _____.

   _____.

2. Write two sentences explaining one of the experiences you listed. Use at least two of the Big Question vocabulary words.

   _____

   _____

C. *Complete the sentences below. Then, write a short paragraph in which you connect this experience to the big question.*

People can make a **connection** to everyday experiences by _____.
Meaning can be found in the ordinary when _____.

All-in-One Workbook
204

Poetry Collection 5: Yusef Komunyakaa, Eve Merriam, and Emily Dickinson
Literary Analysis: Figurative Language

Figurative language is language that is not meant to be taken literally. Poets often use **figures of speech** to convey their ideas in fresh and innovative ways. Figurative language includes these devices:

- A **simile** is a comparison of unlike things using the words *like* or *as.*
- In a **metaphor,** one thing is spoken about as if it were something else.
- In **personification,** an object, animal, or idea is spoken of as if it were human.

Because figurative language is often used to express meaning in concrete pictures, it is an important source of **imagery,** or word-pictures, in poetry.

Read these lines from "The Wind—tapped like a tired Man."

He visited—still flitting— / Then like a timid Man / Again, He tapped—'twas flurriedly—

Notice the use of simile, where the poet uses *like* to compare the wind to a timid man. The poet also personifies the wind.

A. DIRECTIONS: *Complete the following chart by recording two examples of each type of figurative language from the poems.*

Simile		
Metaphor		
Personification		

B. DIRECTIONS: *On the following lines, use each form of figurative language to describe a flower of your choice.*

Flower: _____

Simile: _____

Metaphor: _____

Personification: _____

Poetry Collection 5: Yusef Komunyakaa, Eve Merriam, and Emily Dickinson
Reading: Picture Imagery to Paraphrase Poems

To understand a poem, **paraphrase** it, or restate the meaning of lines in your own words. Begin by **picturing the imagery,** forming clear pictures of the descriptive details in the poem. Then, consider how the lines you will paraphrase are connected with these pictures.

Look at these lines from "Metaphor."

Morning is / a new sheet of paper / for you to write on.

You might picture a "new sheet of paper"—completely blank and empty. This can help you paraphrase the line as, "Morning is the start of a new day, blank and empty for experience to fill."

DIRECTIONS: *In the following chart, describe the image that each quotation creates. Then, restate the line in your own words.*

Quotation	Image	Paraphrase
1. The Sunday afternoon heat / Flared like thin flowered skirts (Komunyakaa)		
2. The bright words and the dark words / are gone (Merriam)		
3. A Rapid—footless Guest— / To offer whom a Chair (Dickinson)		

Poetry Collection 5: Yusef Komunyakaa, Eve Merriam, and Emily Dickinson

Vocabulary Builder

Word List

conjured   countenance   stance   tremulous

A. DIRECTIONS: *On the following lines, write three examples that illustrate each word. For instance, if the word were* ingenious, *you might write* an imaginative inventor, a car that runs on vegetable oil, *or* a solution to an impossible math problem.

1. tremulous

    Example 1: _____

    Example 2: _____

    Example 3: _____

2. countenance

    Example 1: _____

    Example 2: _____

    Example 3: _____

3. stance

    Example 1: _____

    Example 2: _____

    Example 3: _____

4. conjured

    Example 1: _____

    Example 2: _____

    Example 3: _____

B. WORD STUDY: The **Latin suffix -ous** means "characterized by" or "having the quality of." Answer the following questions using one of these words that contain the suffix *ous-:* *tumultuous, joyous, luminous.*

1. Will a *luminous* window be dark?

    _____

2. Will a *joyous* person sulk and complain?

    _____

3. If the meeting was *tumultuous*, did it proceed peacefully?

    _____

Name _____ Date _____

Poetry Collection 6: Edna St. Vincent Millay, Dahlia Ravikovitch, and Emily Dickinson

Writing About the Big Question

 Does all communication serve a positive purpose?

Big Question Vocabulary

confusion	connection	context	convey	discourse
emotion	explanation	interact	isolation	language
meaning	misinterpret	respond	self-expression	verbal

A. *Use one or more words from the list above to complete each sentence.*

1. Accurate and vivid _____ makes written and verbal communication interesting.

2. Jane was overcome with _____ when she heard she won the writing contest.

3. Pablo found it difficult to _____ his true thoughts about the argument with his sister.

4. In the _____ of the team's loss, I can under-stand why Marlene was so upset.

B. *Follow the directions in responding to each of the items below.*

1. List two situations in which communication might cause more problems than solutions.

   _____.

   _____.

2. Write two sentences explaining one of the situations you listed. Use at least two of the Big Question vocabulary words.

   _____

   _____

C. *Complete the sentence below. Then, write a short paragraph in which you connect this experience to the big question.*

Our limitations as humans can lead to **isolation** if _____ or **connection** to others through _____.

Poetry Collection 6: Edna St. Vincent Millay, Dahlia Ravikovitch, and Emily Dickinson
Literary Analysis: Figurative Language

Figurative language is language that is not meant to be taken literally. Poets often use **figures of speech** to convey their ideas in fresh and innovative ways. Figurative language includes these devices:

- A **simile** is a comparison of unlike things using the words *like* or *as.*
- In a **metaphor,** one thing is spoken about as if it were something else.
- In **personification,** an object, animal, or idea is spoken of as if it were human.

Because figurative language is often used to express meaning in concrete pictures, it is an important source of **imagery,** or word-pictures, in poetry.

Read this line from "Pride."

And suddenly the rock has an open wound.

Notice the use of metaphor, in which emotional pain is spoken of as "an open wound." The poet also personifies rocks.

A. DIRECTIONS: *Complete the following chart by recording examples of each type of figurative language from the poems in this grouping. If there are not two examples of a type of figurative language, include only one.*

Simile		
Metaphor		
Personification		

B. DIRECTIONS: *On the following lines, use each form of figurative language to describe an animal of your choice.*

Animal: _____

Simile: _____

Metaphor: _____

Personification: _____

Name _____ Date _____

Poetry Collection 6: Edna St. Vincent Millay, Dahlia Ravikovitch, and Emily Dickinson

Reading: Picture Imagery to Paraphrase Poems

To understand a poem, **paraphrase** it, or restate the meaning of lines in your own words. Begin by **picturing the imagery,** forming clear pictures of the descriptive details in the poem. Then, consider how the lines you will paraphrase are connected with these pictures.

Look at these lines from "Pride."

> And so the moss flourishes, the seaweed / whips around, / the sea pushes through and rolls back—

You might picture waves crashing against a moss-covered rock. This can help you paraphrase the line as, "Rocks, like people, experience weathering over time."

DIRECTIONS: *Describe the image that each quotation in the following chart creates. Then, restate the line in your own words.*

Quotation	Image	Paraphrase
1. But I will not hold the bridle while he cinches the girth. (Millay)		
2. They don't move, so the cracks stay hidden. (Ravikovitch)		
3. The Truth must dazzle gradually (Dickinson)		

All-in-One Workbook
© Pearson Education, Inc. All rights reserved.
210

Name _____ Date _____

Poetry Collection 6: Edna St. Vincent Millay, Dahlia Ravikovitch, and Emily Dickinson
Vocabulary Builder

Word List

circuit   eased   flourishes   haste   infirm   overcome

A. DIRECTIONS: *On the following lines, write two examples that illustrate each word. For instance, if the word were* ingenious, *you might write* an imaginative inventor, a car that runs on vegetable oil, *or* a solution to an impossible math problem.

1. flourishes

   Example 1: _____

   Example 2: _____

2. circuit

   Example 1: _____

   Example 2: _____

3. haste

   Example 1: _____

   Example 2: _____

4. overcome

   Example 1: _____

   Example 2: _____

5. infirm

   Example 1: _____

   Example 2: _____

6. eased

   Example 1: _____

   Example 2: _____

B. WORD STUDY: The **Latin suffix -ary** means "relating to" or "like." Provide an explanation for your answer to each question using one of these words that contain the suffix *ary-*: *imaginary, boundary, missionary.*

1. Is a *boundary* something that goes around a place or through a place?

   _____

2. Does an *imaginary* friend live in your mind or in your house?

   _____

3. If you become a *missionary*, is it likely you will travel often or reside in one place?

   _____

All-in-One Workbook
© Pearson Education, Inc. All rights reserved.
211

Poetry Collection 5: Yusef Komunyakaa, Eve Merriam, and Emily Dickinson
Poetry Collection 6: Edna St. Vincent Millay, Dahlia Ravikovitch, and Emily Dickinson
Integrated Language Skills: Grammar

Prepositional Phrases

A **prepositional phrase** is a phrase that can modify other words by functioning either as an adjective or as an adverb within sentences.

A prepositional phrase that serves as an adjective is termed an *adjective phrase.* It modifies a noun or pronoun and tells *what kind* or *which one.*

Adjective Phrase: The woman *in the blue dress* is a singer.

A prepositional phrase that serves as an adverb is termed an *adverb phrase.* It modifies a verb and tells *where, when, in what way or to what extent.*

Adverb Phrase: Her music group sings *at the folk festival.*

A. PRACTICE: *Underline the prepositional phrase in each of the following sentences. Then, write whether it is used as an* adjective *or* adverb.

_____ 1. The baseball players have their best moments on the ballfield.

_____ 2. The wind is compared to a tired man.

_____ 3. The conscientious objector refuses to give in to Death.

_____ 4. The rocks in the poem represent human feeling.

_____ 5. If you are too honest, the truth can be painful to the listener.

_____ 6. The metaphor in the third verse is striking.

_____ 7. The seal brushes against the rocks and cracks them.

_____ 8. Death flicks his whip at the speaker.

B. Writing Application: *Write four sentences about the poems in these collections. Use a prepositional phrase in each sentence. Underline the prepositional phrases.*

1. _____

2. _____

3. _____

4. _____

Poetry Collection 5: Emily Dickinson, Eve Merriam, Yusef Komunyakaa
Poetry Collection 6: Edna St. Vincent Millay, Dahlia Ravikovitch, and Emily Dickinson

Integrated Language Skills: Support for Writing a Critical Essay

Before you begin writing your critical essay, determine what criteria you will use to evaluate the poems. Fill in the following chart with criteria for evaluating the poems, your evaluation of the poems, and quotations that support your evaluation.

Criteria for Evaluation: _____

_____

	Evaluation	Quotations
"The wind—tapped like a tired Man"		
"Metaphor"		
"Glory"		
"Conscientious Objector"		
"Pride"		
"Tell all the Truth but tell it slant—"		

Now, use your notes to write your critical essay explaining which of these poems you found most effective.

Poetry Collection 7: Langston Hughes, John McCrae, and Carl Sandburg
Writing About the Big Question

 Does all communication serve a positive purpose?

Big Question Vocabulary

confusion	connection	context	convey	discourse
emotion	explanation	interact	isolation	language
meaning	misinterpret	respond	self-expression	verbal

A. *Use one or more words from the list above to complete each sentence.*

1. The _____ generated by the musical concert was so overwhelming, we cried.

2. Dan's gestures were so vague, I was sure we would _____ his message and sit in the wrong place.

3. The professor's formal _____ lasted for an hour and was serious in tone.

4. Lilly's _____ of why the school needs a new library was so convincing that we are ready to plan a fundraiser.

B. *Follow the directions in responding to each of the items below.*

1. List two times when you used a form of communication that was not verbal.

   _____.

   _____.

2. Write two sentences explaining one of the experiences you listed and describe the way in which you communicated. Use at least two of the Big Question vocabulary words.

   _____

   _____

C. *Complete the sentences below. Then, write a short paragraph in which you connect this experience to the big question.*

   Emotion can be powerfully expressed by **language** but also by _____.
   People **respond** to a variety of _____ in the world and in poetry.

Name _____ Date _____

Poetry Collection 7: Langston Hughes, John McCrae, and Carl Sandburg
Literary Analysis: Sound Devices

To spark the music in words, poets use a variety of **sound devices,** or patterns of word-sounds. These include alliteration, assonance, consonance, and onomatopoeia. **Alliteration** is the repetition of consonant sounds at the beginnings of nearby words, as in "silent song." **Assonance** is the repetition of vowel sounds in nearby stressed syllables, as in "deep and dreamless." Unlike rhyming syllables, assonant syllables end in different consonants. **Consonance** is the repetition of consonant sounds at the ends of nearby stressed syllables with different vowel sounds, as in "heat of lightning." **Onomatopoeia** is the use of words to imitate actual sounds, such as *buzz*, *tap*, or *splash*. Sound devices can add to the mood of a poem, imitate the sound of events, or reflect or emphasize a poem's meaning.

Read this line from "Jazz Fantasia."

Drum on your drums, batter on your banjoes, / sob on the long cool winding saxophones.

The *b* in *batter* and *banjoes* is an example of alliteration, the word *drum* is an example of onomatopoeia, and the *ng* sound in *long* and *winding* is an example of consonance. These sound devices help to create a musical sound in the poem.

DIRECTIONS: *Fill in the following chart with at least two examples of each sound device from the poems in this collection.*

Alliteration	Assonance	Consonance	Onomatopoeia

Poetry Collection 7: Langston Hughes, John McCrae, and Carl Sandburg
Reading: Break Down Long Sentences to Paraphrase Poems

To help you understand poetry, **paraphrase** poems, restating the ideas in your own words. First, **break down long sentences** into parts.

- Identify the main actions and who or what performs them.
- Identify details that show when, where, how, or why each action is performed.

Read the following sentence from "Jazz Fantasia."

 Sling your knuckles on the bottoms of the happy / tin pans, let your trombones ooze, and go husha- / husha-hush with the slippery sand-paper.

Who? musicians
Action: play music
Paraphrase: Musicians are playing jazz with tin pans, trombones, and sandpaper.

DIRECTIONS: *Paraphrase the following excerpts from the poems in this collection. Begin by identifying the main actions and who performs them.*

1. Down on Lenox Avenue the other night / By the pale dull pallor of an old gas light / He did a lazy sway. . . . / He did a lazy sway. . . . / To the tune o' those Weary Blues.

   (Hughes)

   Who? _____

   Action: _____

   Paraphrase: _____

   _____

2. Short days ago / We lived, felt dawn, saw sunset glow, / Loved and were loved, and now we lie / In Flanders Fields.

   (McCrae)

   Who? _____

   Action: _____

   Paraphrase: _____

   _____

3. Can the rough stuff . . . now a Mississippi steamboat / pushes up the night river with a hoo-hoo-hoo-oo . . . and / the green lanterns calling to the high soft stars . . . a red / moon rides on the humps of the low river hills . . . go to it, / O jazzmen.

   (Sandburg)

   Who? _____

   Action: _____

   Paraphrase: _____

   _____

Poetry Collection 7: Langston Hughes, John McCrae, and Carl Sandburg
Vocabulary Builder

Word List

ebony   foe   melancholy   pallor

A. DIRECTIONS: *Decide whether each statement below is true or false. Explain your answers.*

1. The *ebony* keys on the piano are the sharps and flats.

   _____

2. A saxophone can create a sound so *melancholy* that people will cry when they hear it.

   _____

3. A musician's *pallor* can show that he has not been outdoors for weeks.

   _____

4. The first person you will call with good news will by your *foe*.

   _____

B. WORD STUDY: The **Latin suffix -or** means "one who takes part in" or "condition, quality, or property of something." Provide an explanation for your answer to each question containing one of these words: *director, actor, competitor.*

1. Would a *director* be the person who controls the artistic production of a film?

   _____

2. Is a *competitor* someone who gives up easily in a contest?

   _____

3. When someone says she is an *actor*, does she avoid performing on a stage?

   _____

Name _____ Date _____

Writing About the Big Question

 Does all communication serve a positive purpose?

Big Question Vocabulary

confusion	connection	context	convey	discourse
emotion	explanation	interact	isolation	language
meaning	misinterpret	respond	self-expression	verbal

A. *Use one or more words from the list above to complete each sentence.*

1. It would be difficult to communicate during a battle because of the _____ and noise on the battlefield.

2. It is important to have confident _____ as long as what we say about ourselves does not intentionally hurt others.

3. Joe thought he should sit in _____ and think about his response before presenting his ideas to the whole group.

B. *Follow the directions in responding to each of the items below.*

1. List three things people can do to ensure their communication with others has positive results.

   _____.

   _____.

2. Choose one idea you listed and write two sentences explaining how that suggestion can lead to positive communication. Use at least two of the Big Question vocabulary words.

   _____

   _____

C. *Complete the sentences below. Then, write a short paragraph in which you connect this experience to the big question.*

Poets create **meaning** using language in various ways, such as _____.
Sometimes readers **respond** to the meaning of the words and other times to the

_____.

Poetry Collection 8: Alfred, Lord Tennyson; Robert Browning; and Jean Toomer
Literary Analysis: Sound Devices

To spark the music in words, poets use a variety of **sound devices,** or patterns of word-sounds. These include alliteration, assonance, consonance, and onomatopoeia. **Alliteration** is the repetition of consonant sounds at the beginnings of nearby words, as in "silent song." **Assonance** is the repetition of vowel sounds in nearby stressed syllables, as in "deep and dreamless." Unlike rhyming syllables, assonant syllables end in different consonants. **Consonance** is the repetition of consonant sounds at the ends of nearby stressed syllables with different vowel sounds, as in "heat of lightning." **Onomatopoeia** is the use of words to imitate actual sounds, such as *buzz, tap,* or *splash.* Sound devices can add to the mood of a poem, imitate the sound of events, or reflect or emphasize a poem's meaning.

Read this line from "Reapers."

And there, a field rat, startled, squealing bleeds

The *s* in *startled* and *squealing* is an example of alliteration; the word *squealing* is an example of onomatopoeia; the long *e* sound in *field, squealing,* and *bleeds* is an example of assonance. These sound devices help to create a grim, rhythmic feel that mimics the movement of the mower.

DIRECTIONS: *Fill in the following chart with at least two examples of each sound device from the poems in this collection.*

Alliteration	Assonance	Consonance	Onomatopoeia

Name _____ Date _____

Reading: Break Down Long Sentences to Paraphrase Poems

To help you understand poetry, **paraphrase** poems, restating the ideas in your own words. First, **break down long sentences** into parts.

- Identify the main actions and who or what performs them.
- Identify details that show when, where, how, or why each action is performed.

Read this sentence from "Reapers."

I see them place the hones / In their hip-pockets as a thing that's done, / And start their silent swinging, one by one.

Who? the reapers
Action: prepare to reap the field
Paraphrase: The reapers put their sharpeners in their pockets and begin to reap the field.

DIRECTIONS: *Paraphrase these excerpts by using the information above.*

1. There hath he lain for ages and will lie / Battening upon huge seaworms in his sleep, / Until the latter fire shall heat the deep; / Then once by man and angels to be seen, / In roaring he shall rise and on the surface die.

   (Tennyson)

   Who? _____

   Action: _____

   Paraphrase: _____

   _____

2. Then a mile of warm sea-scented beach; / Three fields to cross till a farm appears; / A tap at the pane, the quick sharp scratch / And blue spurt of a lighted match, / And a voice less loud, through its joys and fears, / Than the two hearts beating each to each!

   (Browning)

   Who? _____

   Action: _____

   Paraphrase: _____

   _____

3. Black horses drive a mower through the weeds, / And there, a field rat, startled, squealing bleeds. . . .

   (Toomer)

   Who? _____

   Action: _____

   Paraphrase: _____

   _____

Name _____ Date _____

Poetry Collection 8: Alfred, Lord Tennyson; Robert Browning; and Jean Toomer
Vocabulary Builder

Word List

abysmal   millennial   quench   reapers   slumbering

A. DIRECTIONS: *Read the following sentences and fill in each blank with the most appropriate word from the list.* Explain your answer.

1. The _____ boy did not hear his alarm clock ringing.

2. The _____ fears of computer failure in 2000 did not come to pass.

3. We would see the _____ for miles as they moved through the fields of wheat.

4. We could not retrieve our flashlight, because we dropped it down a(n) _____ hole.

5. I was desperate to find water and _____ my thirst.

B. WORD STUDY: The Latin suffix *-ial* means "relating to," "characterized," or "a function of." Answer the following questions using one of these words containing the suffix *-ial: menial, territorial, celestial.*

1. Is a *menial* person a person who has the power and ownership of a household?

_____

2. Would you look up to the sky or down to the ground to see a *celestial* object?

_____

3. Will a *territorial* animal be protective of the area in which it lives?

_____

Poetry Collection 7: Langston Hughes; John McCrae; and Carl Sandburg
Poetry Collection 8: Alfred, Lord Tennyson; Robert Browning; and Jean Toomer

Integrated Language Skills: Grammar

Infinitives

An **infinitive** is a form of the verb that generally appears with the word *to* and acts as a noun, an adjective, or an adverb.

Infinitive as Noun: Last year Ana learned *to drive.* (direct object of *learned*)

Infinitive as Adjective: She had a great desire *to succeed.* (modifies *desire*)

Infinitive as Adverb: I am still unable *to drive.* (modifies *unable*)

An **infinitive phrase** consists of an infinitive along with any modifiers or complements, all acting together as a single part of speech.

Infinitive Phrase Containing a Modifier: He tried *to answer decisively.*

Infinitive Phrase Containing a Complement: No one is really able *to see the future.*

A. PRACTICE: *Underline the infinitive in each of the following sentences and indicate its function. Write* noun, adjective, *or* adverb *before the infinitive.*

_____ 1. Using a steady rhythm, Langston Hughes is able to re-create the feeling of the blues in "Weary Blues."

_____ 2. Carl Sandburg wanted to make his poem sound like the sounds of jazz music.

_____ 3. In "In Flanders Fields," the speakers wish their fight to continue.

_____ 4. To make a poem evocative often requires figurative language.

B. Writing Application: *Follow the directions in parentheses to write four sentences using infinitives and infinitive phrases.*

1. (Use the infinitive to *fight.*)

   _____

2. (Use the infinitive phrase *to play a musical instrument.*)

   _____

3. (Use the infinitive phrase *to sing the blues.*)

   _____

4. (Use the infinitive phrase *to rest in peace.*)

   _____

Poetry Collection 7: Langston Hughes, John McCrae, and Carl Sandburg
Poetry Collection 8: Alfred, Lord Tennyson; Robert Browning; and Jean Toomer

Integrated Language Skills: Support for Writing a Poem

Before you begin to write your poem, fill in the following idea web with details you can include in your poem.

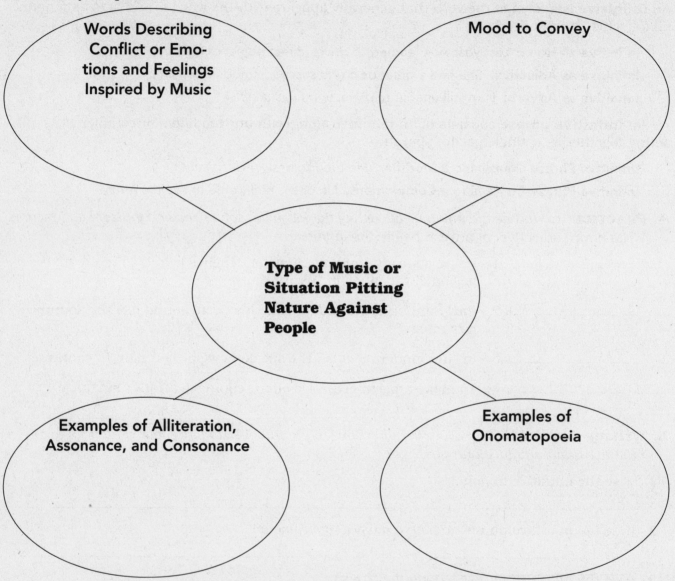

Now, use the details you have collected to write your poem that tells about your favorite kind of music or a collision between nature and the world of people.

Name _____ Date _____

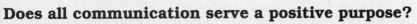

"All" by Bei Dao
"Also All" by Shu Ting
"Hold Fast Your Dreams—and Trust Your Mistakes" by Billy Joel
Writing About the Big Question
Does all communication serve a positive purpose?

Big Question Vocabulary

confusion	connection	context	convey	discourse
emotion	explanation	interact	isolation	language
meaning	misinterpret	respond	self-expression	verbal

A. *Use one or more words from the list above to complete each sentence.*

1. Bill was discouraged by his low score, but he tried to _____ with positive ideas about how he could improve next time.

2. You must be true to your dreams in order to give your life real _____.

3. If we forge a _____ with those around us, we can all help each other in times of need.

4. Dylan chooses to focus on the positive rather than _____ negative thoughts about things he cannot change.

B. *Follow the directions in responding to each of the items below.*

1. List two reasons authors often write about negative topics

   _____

   _____

2. Write two sentences explaining one of the reasons you listed and describe what the author might hope to gain. Use at least two of the Big Question vocabulary words.

   _____

   _____

C. *Complete the sentence below. Then, write a short paragraph in which you connect this experience to the big question.*

Positive communication can inspire others by _____.

"**All**" by Bei Dao
"**Also All**" by Shu Ting
"**Hold Fast Your Dreams—and Trust Your Mistakes**" by Billy Joel

Literary Analysis: Theme

A **theme** is the central idea, message, or insight that the author of a literary work conveys. Some authors present a theme by discussing life's conflicts, challenges, and complications. Writers might use figurative language, such as metaphors, personification, or hyperbole, to help convey a theme.

Each of the authors in this group writes about the meaning of human actions—asking whether our actions add up to something or amount to nothing, whether we should strive for success or strive to find peace in ourselves. Though their general topic is the same, each writer's theme, or insight into that topic, is different. As you read, use a chart like the one shown to note the different insights each author presents.

DIRECTIONS: *As you read, use a chart like the one shown to record the theme each author presents. Describe the techniques the author uses to convey the theme.*

"**All**" by Bei Dao	"**Also All**" by Shu Ting	"**Hold Fast Your Dreams—and Trust Your Mistakes**" by Billy Joel
Theme:	Theme:	Theme:
Techniques that convey theme:	Techniques that convey theme:	Techniques that convey theme:

Selections by Bei Dao, Shu Ting, and Billy Joel
Vocabulary Builder

Word List

idealistic   lamentation   unorthodox   wither

A. DIRECTIONS: *Decide whether each statement is true or false. Explain your answers.*

1. If you water your tomato plants regularly, they will probably *wither*.

   _____

   _____

2. Great *lamentation* often follows a great victory.

   _____

   _____

3. Someone with *unorthodox* behavior follows all the rules and upholds tradition.

   _____

   _____

4. An *idealistic* dream is based in reality and relies on concrete evidence.

   _____

   _____

B. DIRECTIONS: *On the line, write the letter of the word that is most similar in meaning to the word in CAPITAL LETTERS.*

____ 1. WITHER:
    A. shrivel   B. tremble   C. improve   D. endure

____ 2. LAMENTATION:
    A. excitement   B. uncertainty   C. performance   D. weeping

____ 3. UNORTHODOX:
    A. atypical   B. loud   C. conforming   D. angry

____ 4. IDEALISTIC:
    A. happy   B. discontented   C. visionary   D. lost

Name _____ Date _____

Support for Writing to Compare Themes

Before you draft your essay comparing and contrasting the authors' ideas about hope and success, complete the following graphic organizer.

"All"	**"Also All"**
Poet's attitude:	Poet's attitude:
Supporting details:	Supporting details:

Hope and Success

"Hold Fast Your Dreams—and Trust Your Mistakes"

Author's attitude:

Supporting details:

Now, use your notes to write an essay comparing and contrasting the authors' ideas about people's hopes and their pursuit of success.

Man of Love, performed by Queen Godls

Mama said check his **background**

She asked me for his last name

His origins and his lifestyle –

Said his history might be stained

But I questioned if Mama's suspicions

were paranoia or

insight -

Something like intuition

or a plain old

stereotype -

A simplified conception

Based on her first

impression -

A vague idea and sensation (**interpretation**)

That she felt confident making

And she judged the way he talked and his walk

and the clothes he was in

My man reminded her of . . . HIM

But your connections are wrong, mama . . .

I begged my mama, please!

Just get to know him for me

Look deeper and you will see

His true

identity -

Qualities and traits

He's a man of Love not hate

Please don't

anticipate

or expect...

The worst 'cause you don't know him yet

And your conceptions are wrong, mama . . .

Continued

Mama had low

expectations

She said he was from the wrong side of town

And all the bad things she anticipated

Said she knew his type

and he'd just bring me down

But I questioned if mama's precautions

were

prejudice or insight

Something like logic and wisdom

or a

bias and that ain't right!

A preconceived inclination

Like discrimination . . .

But I love this man - He's strong

and he's right for me it's true

please don't lump him in a group or assume he . . .

does not have his own identity -

he's an

individual

And your conceptions are wrong, mama . . .

I begged my mama, Please!

Because he is important (to me, to me)

Fear and biases (oh, yeah)

keep your thoughts

distorted

The facts they have been twisted

and that makes you suspicious

But mama, true

knowledge is . . .

A healthy wisdom

Not just some negative vision, no

He's a man of Love not hate

He will not

manipulate

or con me into makin' (oh no)

unhealthy decisions

But I don't need your permission, mama . . .

He's a man of Love not hate

Your

perspective -

It is tainted

Point of view based on pain and years . . .

of your OWN experience

And I know that you love me, mama . . .

But he's nothing like papa . . .

No, no, no

Pain is **universal** (universal) -

Yeah, everywhere and all the time (all the time)

I know daddy hurt you, (oh yeah . . .)

but mama, this man is mine . . .

_____

Song Title: **Man of Love**
Artist / Performed by Queen GodIs
Lyrics by Queen GodIs
Music composed by Mike Pandolfo, Wonderful
Produced by Mike Pandolfo, Wonderful
Executive Producer: Keith London, Defined Mind

Name _____ Date _____

Unit 5: Drama
Big Question Vocabulary—1

The Big Question: To what extent does experience determine what we perceive?

In your textbook, you learned words that are useful for talking about experience and how it influences our perceptions. The experiences people have affect how they understand literature and see the world around them.

DIRECTIONS: *Review the following definitions of words you can use when talking about experience and perception.*

anticipate: to foresee, predict, or realize beforehand
background: factors that precede or influence a situation or attitude
bias: prejudice, or a tendency to think a certain way
distortion: a false meaning or misrepresentation
expectations: what one thinks will happen

Now, rewrite each sentence by replacing each underlined word or phrase with a vocabulary word from the list above that has a similar meaning.

1. Though I <u>predict</u> we will do extremely well in the competition, I do not want to raise your <u>assumptions</u> too high.

   _____

   _____

2. I have a <u>tendency to think positively</u> about Italian food since my grandmother was Italian.

   _____

   _____

3. Felicia's <u>previous experience</u> is in nursing, so she understands the need for improved health care.

   _____

   _____

4. Marcos's <u>twisting</u> of the facts led Denise to believe that I would not be going to see the play with them because I was avoiding her.

   _____

   _____

Name _____   Date _____

Unit 5: Drama
Big Question Vocabulary—2

The Big Question: To what extent does experience determine what we perceive?

DIRECTIONS: *Review the following definitions of words you can use when talking about experience and perception.*

identity: who or what a person or thing is
impression: the first effect of an experience or perception upon the mind
individual: a person
insight: an understanding of the true nature or underlying truth of a thing
interpretation: an explanation or analysis of the meaning of something

Now, read each sentence and use the context clues and the definitions above to help you rewrite the definition of each underlined word in your own words.

Sentence	Definition in Your Own Words
1. Jacob has a strong sense of his own <u>identity</u> because he has known his entire life what his career would be.	
2. My first <u>impression</u> was that the artist's work was careless, but it is in fact highly detailed and beautiful.	
3. An <u>individual</u> approached from across the parking lot, and it was difficult in the poor light to tell who it was.	
4. Similar past experiences can give us some <u>insight</u> into how other people react to a given situation.	
5. Latonya's <u>interpretation</u> of the meaning of the song's lyrics was completely different from mine.	

Unit 5: Drama
Big Question Vocabulary—3

The Big Question: To what extent does experience determine what we perceive?

DIRECTIONS: *Review the following definitions of words you can use when talking about experience and perception.*

knowledge: understanding; familiarity with facts, truths, or principles

manipulate: to manage or influence skillfully, especially in an unfair manner

perspective: the way one sees the world, as influenced by one's experiences, emotions, and attitudes

stereotype: a simplified and standardized perception of members of a group

universal: applicable in all cases

Now, complete the graphic organizer below by filling in a synonym and an antonym for each vocabulary word.

Synonym	Word	Antonym
	1. knowledge	
	2. manipulate	
	3. perspective	
	4. stereotype	
	5. universal	

Name _____   Date _____

Unit 5: Drama
Applying the Big Question

The Big Question: To what extent does experience determine what we perceive?

DIRECTIONS: *Complete the chart below to apply what you have learned about the extent to which experience determines what we perceive. One row has been completed for you.*

Example	Situation	One Person's Perception	Another Person's Perception	How Each Person's Experience Influenced His or Her Perception
From Literature	In *A Raisin in the Sun,* Walter and Mama disagree about how to use some money they have.	Walter wants to open a store so he can have better opportunities and more self-respect.	Mama wants to buy a house and pay for her daughter's education; she is grateful for the life they have.	Equality and self-respect are Walter's goals; Mama still remembers lynchings and is grateful to have her freedom.
From Literature				
From Science				
From Social Studies				
From Real Life				

Name _____   Date _____

David Henry Hwang
Listening and Viewing

Segment 1: Meet David Henry Hwang
• According to David Henry Hwang, how is writing a play an activity that is sometimes solitary and sometimes social? How might the social part of playwriting influence a playwright when he or she revises a play?

_____

_____

_____

_____

_____

Segment 2: Drama
• What two things must David Henry Hwang keep in mind when writing a play?

_____

_____

_____

_____

_____

Segment 3: The Writing Process
• How can David Henry Hwang's writing process be compared to a road trip? What are the challenges of writing dialogue?

_____

_____

_____

_____

_____

Segment 4: The Rewards of Writing
• According to David Henry Hwang, how do plays create a sense of community? What do you think you could "get out of" watching a dramatic performance?

_____

_____

_____

_____

_____

Learning About Drama

Like fiction, drama features **characters** facing a **conflict,** or struggle, that sparks a sequence of events called the **plot.** Sometimes, a drama includes **parallel plots**—two sets of events that occur at the same time. The conflict reaches a **climax,** or point of greatest intensity, before being solved in the **resolution.** Unlike fiction, drama is a story written to be performed. Actors speak lines of **dialogue,** which are the characters' words.

The elements of drama combine to produce an illusion of reality known as **dramatic effect.** Through this effect, the dramatist explores a **theme,** or central message about life.

Elements of Drama	Types of Drama	Type of Dramatic Speech
Acts and scenes divide the story. The **Script** is the text, including dialogue and stage directions. The **Dialogue** is what the characters say. **Stage directions** are notes that tell how to perform the play. **Sets** are constructions that show where a scene takes place. **Props** are objects that actors use onstage.	**Tragedy** shows the death or downfall of a tragic hero. **Comedy** ends happily after an amusing series of predicaments.	A **Monologue** is a speech in which one character speaks at length. A **Soliloquy** shows a character alone onstage as he or she reveals private thoughts. An **Aside** shows a character as he or she tells private thoughts that are unheard by other characters.

DIRECTIONS: *For each item, tell what dramatic element, type of drama, or type of speech is most clearly involved or most likely to be concerned.*

1. A cup from which a character drinks (element of drama): _____

2. A character describes her secret fears about going to boarding school (type of dramatic speech): _____

3. A play in which characters have a series of misadventures while searching for treasure (type of drama): _____

4. Indicates that characters perform a country dance (element of drama): _____

5. A character makes a rude comment about another character that is heard only by the audience (type of dramatic speech): _____

6. The dungeon in which characters are imprisoned (element of drama): _____

7. An argument between two characters about paying a bill (element of drama): _____

8. A play in which a character insults a god, bringing death to his family and disaster to himself (type of drama): _____

Name _____ Date _____

from **Tibet Through the Red Box** by David Henry Hwang
Model Selection: Drama

A **comedy** is a type of drama that ends happily after an amusing series of predicaments. It often emphasizes human faults and the weaknesses of society. It features the actions of **characters,** the people involved in the events. The characters often face **conflicts,** or struggles that are moved along by the elements of the script. These include **stage directions,** which tell how the work is to be performed and describe **props** and other details, and **dialogue,** the words characters say. Occasionally, a character will give a **monologue,** which is spoken to silent listeners.

A. DIRECTIONS: Tibet Through the Red Box *is a comedy. Use this chart to provide examples of characters, stage directions, props, and dialogue. Describe how each example is important to the action of the play.*

Element	Example	Importance
Characters		
Stage directions		
Props		
Dialogue		

B. DIRECTIONS: *Think about the conflicts that Peter faces in the play. Describe two of these conflicts and explain how they help him develop as a character.*

_____

_____

_____

_____

_____

_____

_____

_____

Antigone, **Prologue–Scene 2,** by Sophocles
Writing About the Big Question

To what extent does experience determine what we perceive?

Big Question Vocabulary

anticipate	background	bias	distortion	expectations
identity	impression	individual	insight	interpretation
knowledge	manipulate	perspective	stereotype	universal

A. *Use one or more words from the list above to complete each sentence.*

1. People who share a common _____ may find it easier to communicate.

2. Because everyone's experiences are different, each person has a unique _____ on important issues.

3. When you _____ something for a long time, it does not always live up to your _____.

B. *Respond to the following item, using full sentences.*

Name an event in your life that has shaped your **identity** and explain why.

_____

_____

C. *Complete the sentences below. Then, write a short paragraph in which you connect the completed sentences to the Big Question.*

Sometimes people want to make their own beliefs appear **universal** because _____

_____

However, the **interpretation** of an action can differ between two people because.

_____

_____

_____

_____

_____

_____

_____

_____

Antigone, **Prologue–Scene 2,** by Sophocles
Literary Analysis: Greek Tragedy—The Protagonist and the Antagonist

Like many Greek tragedies, *Antigone* focuses on a conflict that one character has with an authority figure. In this play, as in other works of literature, the main character, called the **protagonist,** is at the center of the action. The **antagonist** is the character or force that is in conflict with the protagonist. Antigone, the protagonist, is in conflict with Creon, the antagonist, who is both her uncle and the king.

A. DIRECTIONS: *Write your answers to the following questions.*

1. Explain why Antigone is the protagonist of the play.

   _____

   _____

2. What is the nature of the conflict between Creon and Antigone?

   _____

   _____

3. How does Antigone's sense of honor put her in conflict with Creon?

   _____

   _____

4. How does Creon's pride pit him against Antigone?

   _____

   _____

B. DIRECTIONS: *Read the following quotations. Explain how they illustrate the conflict between protagonist and antagonist.*

ISMENE. [*To Antigone*] Go then, if you feel that you must. / You are unwise, / But a loyal friend indeed to those who love you.

CREON. No one values friendship more highly than I; but we must remember that friends made at the risk of wrecking our Ship [the Ship of State] are not real friends at all.

_____

_____

_____

_____

_____

_____

_____

Name _____ Date _____

Antigone, **Prologue–Scene 2**, by Sophocles
Reading: List Events to Summarize

Summarizing is making a short statement of the main events and ideas in a work. When you summarize, retell only the most important ideas and events. As you read *Antigone*, list the events of each scene in order to summarize the action and identify key ideas.

DIRECTIONS: *For the Prologue, Scene 1, and Scene 2, write the most important events in the Events boxes. Then, summarize each group of events in the Scene Summary boxes.*

Prologue—Events

⬇

Prologue—Scene Summary

Scene 1—Events

⬇

Scene 1—Scene Summary

Scene 2—Events

⬇

Scene 2—Scene Summary

Antigone, **Prologue–Scene 2,** by Sophocles
Vocabulary Builder

Word List

brazen   deflects   edict   sated   sententiously   waver

A. DIRECTIONS: *For each of the following items, think about the meaning of the italicized word, and then answer the question.*

1. If you were *sated,* what would you say to someone who offered you a big dinner?

   _____

2. Why would you not want a friend's loyalty to *waver*?

   _____

3. What happens to a ball if someone *deflects* it?

   _____

4. Why would a shy person probably not act in a *brazen* manner?

   _____

5. What is your opinion of someone who speaks *sententiously*?

   _____

6. Why are people not free to ignore an *edict*?

   _____

B. WORD STUDY: *The Latin root -dict- means "speak" or "say." Use what you know about the root -dict- to write a complete sentence in response to each of the following questions.*

1. Does a person's *diction* refer to what the person says or how she or he says it?

   _____

   _____

2. What happens when someone *dictates* a letter?

   _____

   _____

3. How would you describe the leadership of a *dictator*?

   _____

   _____

4. Under what circumstances might someone receive a *benediction*?

   _____

   _____

Antigone, **Prologue–Scene 2**, by Sophocles
Integrated Language Skills: Grammar

Participles and Participial Phrases

A **participle** is a verb form used as an adjective to modify a noun or a pronoun—for example, *a creaking floor* (present participle) or *a fried egg* (past participle). A **participial phrase** consists of a participle and its complements and modifiers. Participial phrases can add details to descriptions—for example, *a dress designed by her aunt*.

A. DIRECTIONS: *In the following sentences, underline the participle. Circle the participial phrase when one appears. Then, identify the noun or the pronoun that is modified.*

1. Jumping, the track star set a new record.

   Noun or pronoun that is modified: _____

2. Roger takes acting lessons after school each Wednesday.

   Noun or pronoun that is modified: _____

3. Encouraged by the crowd, she finished the race.

   Noun or pronoun that is modified: _____

4. Dazed and confused, they stumbled out of the car.

   Noun or pronoun that is modified: _____

5. William Shakespeare, often called "The Bard of Avon," wrote *Hamlet*.

   Noun or pronoun that is modified: _____

B. Writing Application: *Write a brief paragraph about Antigone's conflict with Creon. Use at least three participles or participial phrases in your paragraph.*

_____

_____

_____

_____

_____

_____

_____

_____

_____

_____

Antigone, **Prologue–Scene 2,** by Sophocles
Integrated Language Skills: Support for Writing an Essay

For an essay about the conflict between an individual and a society, use the following graphic organizer. Take notes about the presentation of this theme in the Prologue and in Scenes 1 and 2 of *Antigone.* Write down what each character wants and believes about the central issue of the burial of Polyneices.

WHAT CREON BELIEVES

WHAT ISMENE BELIEVES

BURIAL OF POLYNEICES

WHAT ANTIGONE BELIEVES

WHAT THE CHORUS BELIEVES

Now, use your notes to write an essay about the conflict and the message it conveys. Explain whose position you would support. Give at least two reasons for your opinion.

_____

_____

_____

_____

_____

_____

_____

_____

Name _____ Date _____

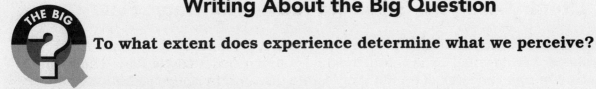

Writing About the Big Question

To what extent does experience determine what we perceive?

Big Question Vocabulary

anticipate	background	bias	distortion	expectations
identity	impression	individual	insight	interpretation
knowledge	manipulate	perspective	stereotype	universal

A. *Use one or more words from the list above to complete each sentence.*

1. Certain experiences are _____ to all human beings.

2. Believing that all boys enjoy sports is an example of a _____.

3. Having prior _____ about a situation that is causing a problem
   may give you _____ into possible solutions.

B. *Respond to the following item, using full sentences.*

It has been said that **knowledge** is power. Describe a situation in which this saying
is or was true for you.

_____

_____

C. *Complete the sentences below. Then, write a short paragraph in which you connect the
completed sentences to the Big Question.*

People may try to use their power to **manipulate** the truth because _____

_____.

Their **bias** against others can color their perception and lead to _____

_____

_____

_____

_____

_____

_____

_____

_____

Antigone, **Scenes 3–5,** by Sophocles
Literary Analysis: Greek Tragedy—The Tragic Flaw

In ancient **Greek tragedy,** a dramatic figure often has a personal characteristic that accounts for his or her downfall. This characteristic is often called a **tragic flaw.** The tragic character is caught up in a series of events that lead to disaster. In *Antigone*, both the protagonist (the main character in conflict with forces or with another character) and the antagonist (the figure in conflict with the main character) have tragic flaws.

DIRECTIONS: *The following are some passages from* Antigone. *Read each passage, going back to its context in the play if necessary, and then identify the tragic flaw and how it reveals itself in each passage.*

1. **CREON.** You consider it right for a man of my years and experience / To go to school to a boy?

   _____

   _____

   _____

   _____

   _____

2. **ANTIGONE.** I have been a stranger here in my own land: / All my life / The blasphemy of my birth has followed me.

   _____

   _____

   _____

   _____

   _____

3. **CREON.** My mind misgives— / The laws of the gods are mighty, and a man must serve them / To the last day of his life!

   _____

   _____

   _____

   _____

   _____

Name _____ Date _____

Antigone, **Scenes 3–5,** by Sophocles
Reading: List Events to Summarize

Summarizing is making a short statement of the main events and ideas in a work. When you summarize, retell only the most important ideas and events. As you read *Antigone,* list the events of each scene in order to summarize the action and identify key ideas.

DIRECTIONS: *For Scene 3, Scene 4, and Scene 5, write the most important events in the Events boxes. Then, summarize each group of events in the Scene Summary boxes.*

Scene 3—Events

⬇

Scene 3—Scene Summary

Scene 4—Events

⬇

Scene 4—Scene Summary

Scene 5—Events

⬇

Scene 5—Scene Summary

Antigone, Scenes 3–5, by Sophocles
Vocabulary Builder

Word List

contempt   deference   lamentation   piety   rash   vile

A. DIRECTIONS: *For each of the following items, write a sentence according to the instructions.*

1. Use *contempt* in a sentence about a brutal dictator.

   _____

   _____

2. Use *lamentation* in a sentence about a national tragedy.

   _____

   _____

3. Use *rash* in a sentence about someone making a decision.

   _____

   _____

4. Use *deference* in a sentence about teachers and students.

   _____

   _____

5. Use *vile* in a sentence about a reality television show.

   _____

   _____

6. Use *piety* in a sentence about someone with a good reputation.

   _____

   _____

B. WORD STUDY: *The Latin root -fer- means "carry, bear, or bring" or "produce." Complete each of the following sentences using a word with the root -fer-.*

1. _____ land produces abundant crops.

2. A _____ can transport passengers from the mainland to an island.

3. Trees and shrubs that have cones are called _____.

Antigone, **Scenes 3–5,** by Sophocles
Integrated Language Skills: Grammar

A **clause** is a group of words that has both a subject and a verb. An **independent clause** can stand by itself as a sentence. A **subordinate clause,** however, cannot stand by itself. There are three types of subordinate clauses: **adjective clauses, adverb clauses,** and **noun clauses.**

Independent clause: Sophocles wrote *Antigone* and other plays.

Adjective Clause: *Antigone* is the first play <u>that we are reading this year</u>. (modifies *play*)

Adverb Clause: <u>As *Antigone* is a tragedy,</u> we do not expect a happy ending. (modifies *expect*)

Noun Clause: <u>Whoever buried Polyneices</u> would be punished. (functions as the subject of the independent clause)

A. DIRECTIONS: *Underline the subordinate clause in each item. Then, write whether it is an as adjective, adverb, or noun clause.*

1. _____ Although the sky was cloudy, the open-air production of *Antigone* would go on.

2. _____ The actors, who had rehearsed for weeks, were eager to begin.

3. _____ Outside on the lawn, the audience wondered if the show would be canceled.

4. _____ They were relieved, however, when the sky began to clear.

5. _____ Whoever saw the show that night enjoyed the production immensely.

B. Writing Application: *Write sentences using the clauses given.*

1. that she sang

   _____

2. wherever the road would take them

   _____

3. who were first to arrive

   _____

4. which will be an advantage

   _____

5. because he had made the finals

   _____

C. Writing Application: *Write a brief paragraph about how the weather will affect your plans for this evening. Underline the subordinate clauses. Use at least two.*

_____

_____

_____

_____

Antigone, **Scenes 3–5,** by Sophocles

Integrated Language Skills: Support for Writing an Essay

Use the graphic organizer to gather ideas for a brief reflective essay about Creon's fate. Take notes about this topic in Scenes 3–5 of *Antigone*. Identify your reasons and any relevant quotations as you answer the following questions.

Question	Reasons	Quotations
Can Creon's fate be considered fair punishment for the decisions he made?		
Was there a single right course of action that Creon should have taken?		
In general, what does Creon's fate suggest about human behavior?		

Now, use your notes to write a brief reflective essay about Creon's fate. Use at least three quotations from the play to support your main points.

_____

_____

_____

_____

_____

_____

_____

Name _____ Date _____

from **An Enemy of the People** by Henrik Ibsen
Writing About the Big Question

To what extent does experience determine what we perceive?

Big Question Vocabulary

anticipate	background	bias	distortion	expectations
identity	impression	individual	insight	interpretation
knowledge	manipulate	perspective	stereotype	universal

A. *Circle the more appropriate word from each pair listed to complete each sentence.*

1. My Italian heritage is an important part of my <u>identity/individual</u>.

2. It was a <u>distortion/stereotype</u> of the truth to say he had a criminal record when he really had only one speeding ticket.

3. Witnessing a selfless act of heroism made a lasting <u>impression/interpretation</u> on me.

B. *Respond to the following items, using full sentences. Use at least one of the Big Question vocabulary words in your response.*

1. Describe a disagreement you have had with someone you know.

   _____

   _____

2. What do you think caused this disagreement?

   _____

   _____

C. *Complete the sentence below. Then, write a short paragraph in which you connect the completed sentence to the Big Question.*

   When making a decision that might be unpopular with others, you should consider your past experiences and then _____.

   _____

   _____

   _____

   _____

   _____

   _____

   _____

Antigone by Sophocles
from **An Enemy of the People** by Henrik Ibsen
Literary Analysis: Universal and Culturally Specific Themes

The **theme** of a literary work is its message. The theme may be **culturally specific,** or it may be **universal.** A **culturally specific theme** reflects the circumstances and beliefs of the writer's culture. A **universal theme** is meaningful to people of all times and places.

A single work may have both a culturally specific theme *and* a universal theme. For example, a Greek epic poem may feature a hero who honors the gods and is therefore rewarded by them. The poem's theme is culturally specific because it reflects the beliefs of the culture: "The gods favor those who honor them." It also expresses a universal theme: "Humility will be rewarded."

DIRECTIONS: *Read each passage below. Then, answer the questions that follow.*

From *Antigone* by Sophocles:

CREON. [Polyneices] made war on his country. Eteocles defended it.

ANTIGONE. Nevertheless, there are honors due all the dead.

CREON. But not the same for the wicked as for the just.

ANTIGONE. Ah, Creon, Creon. / Which of us shall say what the gods hold wicked?

CREON. An enemy is an enemy, even dead.

ANTIGONE. It is my nature to join in love, not hate.

CREON. (*Finally losing patience*) Go join them, then; if you must have your love, / Find it in hell!

From *An Enemy of the People* by Henrik Ibsen:

MAYOR STOCKMANN. . . . As a private person—why, that's another matter. But as a subordinate official at the baths, you're not entitled to express any opinions that contradict your superiors.

DR. STOCKMANN. That's going too far! I, as a doctor, a man of science, aren't entitled to—!

MAYOR STOCKMANN. What's involved here isn't a purely scientific problem. It's a mixture of both technical and economic considerations.

DR. STOCKMANN. I don't care what . . . it is! I want the freedom to express myself on any problem under the sun!

MAYOR STOCKMANN. Anything you like—except for the baths. We forbid you that.

1. A. Underline two phrases in the passage from *Antigone* that reflect the specific culture in which that play takes place.

   B. What culturally specific theme about the gods is suggested in the passage?

   _____

2. A. Underline two phrases in the passage from *An Enemy of the People* that reflect the specific culture in which that play takes place.

   B. What culturally specific theme that relates to modern business or politics is suggested?

   _____

3. What universal theme about duty to self is suggested by *both* passages?

   _____

Name _____ Date _____

Antigone by Sophocles
from **An Enemy of the People** by Henrik Ibsen
Vocabulary Builder

Word List

adamant   exorbitant   impending   impetuosity

A. DIRECTIONS: *Fill in each blank with the correct word from the Word List.*

1. The students had known the research assignment was _____, but they hadn't expected it to come so soon.

2. The students also felt that the requirement of writing a twenty-five-page paper was _____.

3. "I think it is an act of _____ for you to make such an assignment," remarked one student. "Perhaps you should give it a little more thought."

4. Unfortunately, this comment made the teacher even more _____. "Your paper is due on Friday," she replied.

B. DIRECTIONS: *One word in each pair below is from the Word List. Use each pair of words in a sentence that demonstrates the meaning of the vocabulary word.*

1. price; exorbitant

   _____

2. impending; dentist

   _____

3. regret; impetuosity

   _____

4. adamant; flavor

   _____

C. DIRECTIONS: *Circle the letter of the words that express a relationship most like the relationship of the pair of words in CAPITAL LETTERS.*

1. EXORBITANT : REASONABLE ::
   A. alarming : emergency
   B. roundabout : straightforward
   C. comical : humorous
   D. inspire : motivate

2. IMPETUOSITY : RASHNESS ::
   A. revealed : concealed
   B. approve : proposition
   C. rapidly : speedily
   D. confidence : uncertainty

Antigone by Sophocles
from **An Enemy of the People** by Henrik Ibsen
Integrated Language Skills: Support for Writing a Comparative Essay

Before you draft your essay comparing and contrasting the universal themes presented in *Antigone* and *An Enemy of the People,* complete the graphic organizer below.

	Antigone	*An Enemy of the People*
Culturally Specific Elements		
Universal Ideas		
Problem or Conflict		

Now, use your notes to write an essay in which you compare the universal themes expressed in *Antigone* and *An Enemy of the People.*

The Tragedy of Julius Caesar, *Act I,* by William Shakespeare
Writing About the Big Question

To what extent does experience determine what we perceive?

Big Question Vocabulary

anticipate	background	bias	distortion	expectations
identity	impression	individual	insight	interpretation
knowledge	manipulate	perspective	stereotype	universal

A. *Circle the more appropriate word from each pair listed to complete each sentence.*

1. When I saw that the two team leaders disliked each other, I anticipated/manipulated problems with the project.

2. Her insulting remarks revealed her background/bias against politicians.

3. My personal experiences have affected my individual/universal outlook on life.

B. *Respond to the following items, using full sentences.*

1. Describe a time when someone or something differed from your **expectations.**

   _____

   _____

2. Why do you think you expected this person or thing to be different?

   _____

   _____

C. *Complete the sentence below. Then, write a short paragraph in which you connect the completed sentence to the Big Question.*

A person might form an **impression** of someone based on **knowledge** about the person or on _____

_____

_____

_____

_____

_____

_____

_____

All-in-One Workbook
254

Name _____ Date _____

The Tragedy of Julius Caesar, *Act I*, by William Shakespeare
Literary Analysis: Shakespeare's Tragedies

Like other tragedies, **Shakespeare's tragedies** are plays that tell of a reversal of fortune, from good to bad, experienced by a man or woman, usually of noble birth. In Shakespeare's tragedies, the character and actions of the hero, rather than fate, play the strongest role in bringing about the hero's downfall.

Act I of a Shakespearean tragedy typically introduces the main characters, the setting, and the conflict that the hero will confront in the rest of the play. Shakespeare uses dialogue to let us know, in a dramatic way, what is going on as the play begins.

DIRECTIONS: *Answer the following questions to summarize what you learn from Act I of* The Tragedy of Julius Caesar.

1. In Act I, Scene i, lines 33–53, what do you learn about the conflict that has already occurred between Pompey and Caesar?

   _____

   _____

2. In Act I, Scene i, lines 33–75, what do you learn about how Flavius and Marullus feel about Caesar's return?

   _____

   _____

3. What do you learn about Caesar's character from his behavior in the following situations in Act I, Scene ii?

   A. the soothsayer's warning (lines 18–25):

   _____

   B. his description of Cassius (lines 192–214):

   _____

   _____

   C. his reaction to being offered the crown (lines 234–275):

   _____

   _____

4. What do you learn about the characters of Cassius and Brutus in Act I, Scene ii?

   _____

   _____

5. How does the dialogue between Cassius and Brutus in Act I, Scene ii, establish the conflict that will drive the rest of the play?

   _____

   _____

Name _____ Date _____

The Tragedy of Julius Caesar, *Act I*, by William Shakespeare
Reading: Use Text Aids to Read Shakespearean Drama

Shakespeare's plays contain language and references with which most modern readers are not familiar. When reading Shakespearean drama, **use text aids** to help you understand what is going on in the play.

- Review the *dramatis personae*—the cast of characters—at the beginning of the play.
- Read any background information provided about the play.
- As you read the play, consult the marginal notes, called **glosses,** beside the text. These notes define words and explain references. After you consult the glosses, reread the passage to make sure you understand what it means.

DIRECTIONS: *Use the text aids for Act I to help you answer the following questions.*

1. In Act I, Scene i, lines 31–33, the cobbler states his reason for being in the street: "But indeed, sir, we make holiday to see Caesar and to rejoice in his triumph." What sort of triumph is Caesar having?

   _____

2. In lines 65–66 of Act I, Scene i, Flavius tells Marullus to remove decorations from the statues. Marullus questions him in lines 67–68, saying it is the feast of Lupercal. What and when is the feast of Lupercal?

   _____

3. At the opening of Act I, Scene ii, Antony is dressed "for the course," or for a race. Why is a race being held? Why does Caesar tell Antony to touch Calpurnia during the race?

   _____

   _____

   _____

4. What date is the ides of March? _____

5. In lines 55–62 of Act I, Scene ii, Cassius flatters Brutus to persuade him to oppose Caesar. Use the text aids for these lines to express what Cassius says in your own words.

   _____

   _____

   _____

   _____

6. In lines 28–32 of Act I, Scene iii, Casca interprets the strange natural events that have been occurring in Rome since Caesar returned. Use the text aids to express what he says in your own words.

   _____

   _____

   _____

   _____

Name _____ Date _____

Word List

infirmity   portentous   prodigious   replication   servile   spare

A. DIRECTIONS: *For each of the following items, think about the meaning of the italicized word, and then answer the question.*

1. When is a *servile* attitude appropriate?

   _____

   _____

2. What might be a challenge faced by someone who has an *infirmity*?

   _____

   _____

3. When might *replication* of an experiment be useful?

   _____

   _____

4. What is an example of a *prodigious* work of architecture?

   _____

   _____

5. How might the rumbling of a volcano be a *portentous* sign?

   _____

   _____

6. How might a *spare* person change his or her appearance?

   _____

   _____

B. WORD STUDY: *The Latin suffix* -ile *means "having the quality of." Complete each of the following sentences using a word with the suffix* -ile.

1. It's not surprising that babies act _____ .

2. Be careful handling that _____ vase.

3. You must be both strong and _____ to rock climb successfully.

The Tragedy of Julius Caesar, *Act II,* by William Shakespeare
Writing About the Big Question

To what extent does experience determine what we perceive?

Big Question Vocabulary

anticipate	background	bias	distortion	expectations
identity	impression	individual	insight	interpretation
knowledge	manipulate	perspective	stereotype	universal

A. *Circle the more appropriate word from each pair listed to complete each sentence.*

1. Realizing that the main character reminded me of myself affected my <u>distortion/</u> <u>interpretation</u> of the book.

2. Advertisers sometimes try to <u>manipulate/stereotype</u> our feelings with images of cute animals or children.

3. To solve a problem, it sometimes helps to look at it from a new <u>bias/perspective</u>.

B. *Respond to the following item, using full sentences.*

Give an example of a way a person's **background** might shape his or her thinking.

_____

_____

C. *Complete the sentences below. Then, write a short paragraph in which you connect the completed sentences to the Big Question.*

Sometimes, a person's **expectations** of how another person will act are based on

assumptions about _____.

The problem with such assumptions is that _____

_____

_____

_____

_____

_____

_____

_____

The Tragedy of Julius Caesar, *Act II,* by William Shakespeare
Literary Analysis: Blank Verse

The Tragedy of Julius Caesar is written in blank verse. **Blank verse** is a poetic form that has unrhymed lines written in *iambic pentameter.*

- An **iamb** is a *foot* (unit of rhythm) in which an unstressed syllable is followed by a stressed syllable: da-DUH.
- **Pentameter** refers to a rhythmic pattern in which each line has five feet.
- In **iambic pentameter,** the typical line has five iambs, or five stressed syllables each preceded by an unstressed syllable. The symbol [˘] is used to show unstressed syllables. The symbol [´] is used to show stressed syllables.

   Example: You SHALL / con FESS / that YOU / are BOTH / de CEIVED.

In Shakespeare's plays, the characters representing the nobility (who have most of the lines) speak in iambic pentameter. The commoners speak in prose. Sometimes, Shakespeare changes the rhythmic pattern in a line to capture the sound of speech or to add contrast or emphasis.

A. DIRECTIONS: *In the following lines spoken by Artemidorus in Act II, mark the unstressed and stressed syllables, using [˘] and [´]. When you are done, put a [+] in front of each line that is perfect iambic pentameter. Put a [–] in front of each line that is not perfect iambic pentameter.*

_____ Here will I stand till Caesar pass along,

_____ And as a suitor will I give him this.

_____ My heart laments that virtue cannot live

_____ Out of the teeth of emulation.

_____ If thou read this, O Caesar, thou mayest live;

_____ If not, the Fates with traitors do contrive.

(Act II, Scene iii, ll. 8–13)

B. DIRECTIONS: *Answer the following questions about the blank verse in the passage that you have just read.*

1. Which line breaks from iambic pentameter the most? With what words does it break, and why?

   _____

   _____

2. How does the meter of the final line hint that this is the closing line of the speech?

   _____

   _____

Name _____ Date _____

The Tragedy of Julius Caesar, *Act II,* by William Shakespeare
Reading: Paraphrase Shakespearean Drama

Paraphrasing a line or passage from a work means restating its meaning in your own words. To paraphrase when reading Shakespearean drama, follow these steps:

- Look for punctuation that shows where the sentences in the passage end.
- For each sentence, identify the subject and verb and put them into their usual order. You may also need to add helping verbs and use modern verb and pronoun forms.
- Use text aids or a dictionary to help you "translate" unfamiliar words and phrases.

> Between the acting of a dreadful thing
> And the first motion, all the interim is
> Like a phantasma, or a hideous dream.
> (Act II, Scene i, ll. 63–65)

Normal order:	All the interim between the acting of a dreadful thing and the first motion is like a phantasma, or a hideous dream.
Paraphrase (in your own words):	The time between thinking about doing a dreadful deed and doing the deed is like a nightmare.

DIRECTIONS: *Paraphrase the following passages from Act II. Remember that a paraphrase is a restatement of a passage in your own words.*

1. Th' abuse of greatness is when it disjoins
   Remorse from power; and to speak truth of Caesar,
   I have not known when his affections swayed
   More than his reason.

   (Act II, Scene i, ll. 18–21)

   _____

   _____

   _____

2. But it is doubtful yet
   Whether Caesar will come forth today or no;
   For he is superstitious grown of late,
   Quite from the main opinion he held once
   Of fantasy, of dreams, and ceremonies.

   (Act II, Scene i, ll. 193–197)

   _____

   _____

   _____

The Tragedy of Julius Caesar, *Act II*, by William Shakespeare
Vocabulary Builder

Word List

augmented   entreated   imminent   insurrection   resolution   wrathfully

A. DIRECTIONS: *Write a sentence to answer each question based on the meaning of the word in italics.*

1. What is an event that is *imminent* at your school?

   _____

2. How would you feel if your boss *augmented* your paycheck, and why?

   _____

3. Why is *resolution* necessary to achieve success in life?

   _____

4. How would a government respond to an *insurrection*?

   _____

5. If a defense lawyer *entreated* a judge, what might the lawyer want?

   _____

6. Is it helpful to behave *wrathfully* in a frustrating situation? Why or why not?

   _____

B. WORD STUDY: *The Latin prefix* en- *means "in or into," or "make or cause to be," or "put or get on." Use what you know about the prefix* en- *to write a complete sentence in response to each of the following questions.*

1. How might you *encourage* someone to try something new?

   _____

   _____

2. If a landscape is *enveloped* in fog, what does it look like?

   _____

   _____

3. What is a common source of *enchantment* in fairy tales?

   _____

   _____

Name _____ Date _____

The Tragedy of Julius Caesar, *Act III,* by William Shakespeare
Writing About the Big Question

To what extent does experience determine what we perceive?

Big Question Vocabulary

anticipate	background	bias	distortion	expectations
identity	impression	individual	insight	interpretation
knowledge	manipulate	perspective	stereotype	universal

A. *Use one or more words from the list above to complete each sentence.*

1. They say you never get a second chance to make a first _____.

2. I think that TV character is too much of a _____ to be realistic.

3. This class has been so interesting that it's far exceeded my _____.

B. *Respond to the following items, using full sentences.*

1. Describe a time when you changed your mind about someone or something.

   _____

   _____

2. What made you change your opinion?

   _____

   _____

C. *Complete the sentence below. Then, write a short paragraph in which you connect the completed sentence to the Big Question. Use at least two of the Big Question vocabulary words in your response.*

   Sometimes, the same situation can look completely different when _____

   _____

   _____

   _____

   _____

   _____

   _____

   _____

   _____

Name _____ Date _____

The Tragedy of Julius Caesar, *Act III,* by William Shakespeare
Literary Analysis: Dramatic Speeches

In plays, most of the information about characters and events is expressed through **dialogue,** the conversations between or among characters. However, Shakespeare's plays also use the following types of **dramatic speeches** to convey information:

- An **aside** is a remark that a character makes, usually to the audience, which is not heard by other characters on stage. Some asides are spoken to one other character but are not heard by the rest of the characters on stage.
- A **soliloquy** is a long speech in which a character, usually alone on stage, speaks as if to himself or herself, unheard by any other character.
- A **monologue** is a long, uninterrupted speech by one character. It is heard by the other characters on stage.

Soliloquies and asides often reveal a character's true feelings and intentions, which may be different from the feelings and intentions he or she expresses when speaking in dialogue or in monologues.

DIRECTIONS: *On the following chart, identify each speech as* dialogue, monologue, aside, *or* soliloquy. *Paraphrase the feelings expressed in each speech. Then, write* yes *or* no *to indicate whether you think the character is expressing his true feelings in the speech.*

Speech	Type	Paraphrase	True Feelings?
1. Caesar: Act III, Scene i, ll. 58–73			
2. Brutus: Act III, Scene i, ll. 103–110			
3. Antony: Act III, Scene i, ll. 218–222			
4. Cassius, Act III, Scene i, ll. 232–235			
5. Antony: Act III, Scene i, ll. 254–275			

The Tragedy of Julius Caesar, *Act III,* by William Shakespeare
Reading: Analyze the Imagery of Shakespearean Tragedy

To fully appreciate Shakespearean tragedy, you should analyze the **imagery,** or language that appeals to the senses. In Act III, Shakespeare uses many images that focus on violence and the body. Some of these images follow a common pattern:

- wounds that speak
- burying Caesar's body rather than speaking praise of him
- "plucking" a poet's name out of his heart

In each of these images, a reference to words—speech, praise, and names—is coupled with an image of a person's physical body—wounds, a corpse, blood, and the heart. Through this imagery, Shakespeare makes a direct connection between the growing violence in Rome and the disrespect for laws and titles—the words that hold society together.

DIRECTIONS: *Answer the following questions to analyze the imagery in the passages from Act III.*

1. In these lines from Antony's soliloquy, what do Caesar's wounds "beg" him to do?

    Over thy wounds now do I prophesy
    (Which like dumb mouths do ope their ruby lips
    To beg the voice and utterance of my tongue),
    A curse shall light upon the limbs of men;
    Domestic fury and fierce civil strife
    Shall cumber all the parts of Italy. . . .

    (Act III, Scene i, ll. 259–264)

    _____

    _____

    _____

2. According to the following lines from Antony's monologue to the crowd, what would the "tongue in every wound of Caesar's" urge Romans to do?

    I tell you that which you yourselves do know,
    Show you sweet Caesar's wounds, poor poor dumb mouths,
    And bid them speak for me. But were I Brutus,
    And Brutus Antony, there were an Antony
    Would ruffle up your spirits, and put a tongue
    In every wound of Caesar's that should move
    The stones of Rome to rise and mutiny.

    (Act III, Scene ii, ll. 225–231)

    _____

    _____

    _____

The Tragedy of Julius Caesar, *Act III,* by William Shakespeare
Vocabulary Builder

Word List

confounded   discourse   interred   prophesy   spectacle   strife

A. DIRECTIONS: *Decide whether each statement is true or false, and then circle* T *or* F. *Explain your answer based on the meaning of the word in italics.*

T / F   **1.** A person might feel *confounded* while reading a complicated mystery novel.

_____

_____

T / F   **2.** Speakers usually use slang when they *discourse* on a sensitive topic.

_____

_____

T / F   **3.** The Pharaohs of ancient Egypt were *interred* in marvelously decorated tombs.

_____

T / F   **4.** It is often difficult to *prophesy* the outcome of an election.

_____

T / F   **5.** People are usually most reasonable during a period of *strife*.

_____

_____

T / F   **6.** A high-wire act at a circus is intended to be an entertaining *spectacle*.

_____

_____

B. WORD STUDY: *The Latin root* -spect- *means "look at" or "behold." Use what you know about the root* -spect- *to write a complete sentence in response to each of the following questions.*

1. What is one way to show *perspective* in a drawing?

_____

_____

2. What traits might an *introspective* person display?

_____

_____

3. What might an *inspector* at an airport do?

_____

_____

The Tragedy of Julius Caesar, *Act IV,* by William Shakespeare
Writing About the Big Question

To what extent does experience determine what we perceive?

Big Question Vocabulary

anticipate	background	bias	distortion	expectations
identity	impression	individual	insight	interpretation
knowledge	manipulate	perspective	stereotype	universal

A. *Use one or more words from the list above to complete each sentence.*

1. Coming from a working-class _____ gave the mayor

   _____ into certain issues that affect working people.

2. Conflicts with parents are a nearly _____ problem among teens.

3. One thing you will do during your teen years is to establish your

   _____ as an _____,

B. *Respond to the following item, using full sentences.*

Give an example of an event that could give you **insight** into a person's character.

_____

_____

C. *Complete the sentence below. Then, write a short paragraph in which you connect the completed sentence to the Big Question.*

If you are going to entrust someone with an important responsibility, you should

_____

_____

_____

_____

_____

_____

_____

_____

_____

The Tragedy of Julius Caesar, *Act IV*, by William Shakespeare
Literary Analysis: Conflict in Drama

Conflict, the struggle between opposing forces, creates drama. In literature, a conflict may take one of two forms:

- In an **external conflict,** a character struggles with an outside force, such as another character, a group of characters, or a natural force such as the weather.
- In an **internal conflict,** the character struggles with his or her own opposing beliefs, desires, or values.

In Act IV, there are several external conflicts among the main characters in the play. In addition, Brutus continues to feel internal conflicts about his participation in the conspiracy against Caesar.

A. DIRECTIONS: *For each of the following external conflicts, tell what issue the two characters disagree about. Explain the reasons each character gives for his view.*

External Conflicts

1. Antony vs. Octavius: Act IV, Scene i, ll. 12–40

   Issue: _____

   Antony's view/reasons: _____

   _____

   Octavius' view/reasons: _____

   _____

2. Brutus vs. Cassius: Act IV, Scene iii, ll. 7–32

   Issue: _____

   Brutus' view/reasons: _____

   _____

   Cassius' view/reasons: _____

   _____

B. DIRECTIONS: *Describe the internal conflict Brutus may be feeling in each passage.*

Internal Conflict

1. Act IV, Scene ii, ll. 6–27:

   _____

   _____

2. Act IV, Scene iii, ll. 274–289:

   _____

   _____

Name _____ Date _____

The Tragedy of Julius Caesar, *Act IV,* by William Shakespeare
Reading: Read Between the Lines

When reading Shakespearean drama, you need to **read between the lines** to find the deeper meaning of a character's words or actions.

- Keep the larger situation in mind as you read. For instance, early in Act IV, Antony describes Lepidus as "Meet to be sent on errands." Note that Antony has been deciding which of his political rivals will die and which will share power. Between the lines, he is saying, "Fit to run errands—and nothing else."
- Follow **indirect** references. For example, when Lucilius reports on Cassius, Brutus says, "Thou has described / A hot friend cooling." "A hot friend" refers to Cassius, whom Brutus worries is no longer his ally.

DIRECTIONS: *Using your ability to read between the lines and to understand the characters and situations in Act IV, answer the following questions.*

1. **A.** In the opening lines of Act IV, Scene i, Antony, Octavius, and Lepidus discuss which Romans must die. What specific individuals do they mention as being marked for death?

   _____

   B. What does this conversation reveal about the characters of these three men?

   _____

   _____

2. **A.** At the beginning of Act IV, Scene iii, Brutus and Cassius call each other names and argue about who is the better soldier when they should be planning how to defeat Antony. Why do you think they are arguing in such a personal, petty way?

   _____

   _____

   B. What does this argument reveal about Brutus' and Cassius' leadership abilities?

   _____

   _____

3. **A.** Why is Cassius so shocked when he finally hears the news of Portia's death from Brutus? What does Cassius mean when he says, "How scap'd I killing when I cross'd you so?"

   _____

   _____

   _____

   B. In lines 146–191 of Act IV, Scene iii, how does Brutus react to the death of his wife, Portia? What does his reaction reveal about his commitment to the philosophy of Stoicism?

   _____

   _____

   _____

Name _____ Date _____

The Tragedy of Julius Caesar, *Act IV,* by William Shakespeare
Vocabulary Builder

Word Box

  chastisement   condemned   legacies   mirth   presume   rash

A. DIRECTIONS: *Write a sentence to respond to each of the following items.*

1. Describe a *rash* purchasing decision a person might make in a store.

   _____

   _____

2. Describe a situation in which a child might receive *chastisement.*

   _____

   _____

3. Explain what might happen to a *condemned* criminal.

   _____

   _____

4. Describe the kind of document that would list *legacies.*

   _____

   _____

5. Explain why it may be a bad idea to *presume* that someone shares your political views.

   _____

   _____

6. Describe a situation in which a high school student would feel *mirth.*

   _____

   _____

B. WORD STUDY: *The Latin root -sum- means "take" or "use." Complete each of the following sentences using a word with the root -sum-.*

1. Now that we've finished lunch, let's _____ work.

2. Don't _____ he is telling the truth unless he can prove it.

3. I hate to shop so I'm not much of a _____ .

Name _____ Date _____

The Tragedy of Julius Caesar, *Act V*, by William Shakespeare
Writing About the Big Question

To what extent does experience determine what we perceive?

Big Question Vocabulary

anticipate	background	bias	distortion	expectations
identity	impression	individual	insight	interpretation
knowledge	manipulate	perspective	stereotype	universal

A. *Circle the more appropriate word from each pair listed to complete each sentence.*

1. When you need to make a decision, it always helps to have more <u>distortion/knowledge</u> about the situation.

2. People sometimes try to <u>anticipate/manipulate</u> the facts to support their own views.

3. Hearing other people's views changed my <u>bias/interpretation</u> of the issue.

B. *Respond to the following items, using full sentences.*

1. Describe a time when you had to make an important decision.

   _____

   _____

2. What knowledge or other factors did you use to make the decision?

   _____

   _____

C. *Complete the sentences below. Then, write a short paragraph in which you connect the completed sentences to the Big Question.*

Sometimes, we may get a misleading **impression** of the facts because _____

_____.

This can lead to _____

_____

_____

_____

_____

_____

_____

270

The Tragedy of Julius Caesar, *Act V,* by William Shakespeare
Literary Analysis: Shakespeare's Tragic Heroes

Traditionally, a **tragic hero** is a person, usually of noble birth, who suffers a catastrophe. The hero's choices leading to the catastrophe may reflect a personal shortcoming, such as pride, called a **tragic flaw.** While Shakespeare's tragic heroes incorporate these traditional elements, he develops them in new ways:

- He adds complexity to his heroes, who may have opposing desires and who may suffer hesitation and doubt before acting.
- He presents a character's inner turmoil directly to the audience through devices such as the *soliloquy,* a speech in which a character speaks thoughts aloud.
- He often focuses on the choices characters make rather than on fate.
- His characters' problems often result from the difference between the reasons for an action and its outcome.

DIRECTIONS: *Answer the questions to analyze the ways in which Brutus is a tragic hero.*

1. **A.** In Act I, Scene ii, what opposing feelings about Caesar caused inner turmoil for Brutus?

   _____

   B. How did Cassius persuade Brutus to overcome his doubts and participate in the assassination plot? Why was Brutus wrong to have trusted Cassius?

   _____

   _____

   _____

2. **A.** In Act II, Scene i, what reasons did Brutus give for not killing Antony?

   _____

   B. In Act III, Scene i, what decision did Brutus make about Antony?

   _____

   C. How did both of these decisions about Antony help bring catastrophe for Brutus?

   _____

   _____

3. With his dying words, Brutus unknowingly reveals a tragic flaw. Read the following lines. Then, explain why it is a shortcoming to believe that everyone is loyal and "true."

   My heart doth joy that yet in all my life
   I found no man but he was true to me. (Act V, Scene v, ll. 34–35)

   _____

   _____

4. How do Brutus' character traits and decisions in the play mark him as a tragic hero?

   _____

   _____

The Tragedy of Julius Caesar, *Act V,* by William Shakespeare
Reading: Compare and Contrast Characters in Shakespearean Drama

In his plays, Shakespeare often emphasizes the important qualities of one character by presenting another character with contrasting qualities. When reading Shakespearean drama, you can gain understanding by **comparing and contrasting characters.** Look for similarities and differences in the characters' personalities, situations, behavior, and attitudes. Pay special attention to how they respond differently to similar situations or problems.

DIRECTIONS: *On the following chart, describe the different character traits that Brutus and Cassius reveal in Acts I–V of* The Tragedy of Julius Caesar.

	Brutus	**Cassius**
Feelings toward Caesar in Acts I and II		
Feelings toward Antony in Acts II and III		
Attitudes toward corruption and bribery in Act IV		
Reaction to criticism and personal loss in Act IV		
Attitudes toward the coming battle in Act V		

The Tragedy of Julius Caesar, *Act V,* by William Shakespeare
Vocabulary Builder

Word List

demeanor   disconsolate   fawned   meditates   misconstrued   presage

A. DIRECTIONS: *Answer the following questions.*

1. What does the appearance of Caesar's ghost *presage*?

   _____

2. Is Antony correct when he says that the assassins *fawned* over Caesar before killing him? Explain.

   _____

3. How would you describe Brutus' characteristic *demeanor*?

   _____

4. What causes Cassius to become *disconsolate* in Act V?

   _____

5. What event has been *misconstrued* by Cassius in Act V?

   _____

6. Which character in the play *meditates* on the most honorable course of action?

   _____

B. WORD STUDY: *The Latin root -stru- means "pile up" or "build." Use what you know about the root -stru- to write a complete sentence in response to each of the following questions.*

1. What is something a *destructive* child might do?

   _____

   _____

2. What would you do if someone *obstructed* your view in a movie theater?

   _____

   _____

3. What is *constructive* criticism?

   _____

   _____

Name _____ Date _____

The Tragedy of Julius Caesar, *Act V,* by William Shakespeare
Integrated Language Skills: Grammar

Clauses

A **clause** is a group of words that has both a subject and a verb. An **independent clause** can stand by itself as a sentence. A **subordinate clause** cannot stand by itself.

Two types of subordinate clauses are adjective clauses and noun clauses. An **adjective clause** modifies a noun or pronoun. A **noun clause** functions as a subject, a direct object, an indirect object, an object of the preposition, or a predicate noun in a sentence.

Adjective clauses:	The ring *that I lost* was once my grandmother's.
	(modifies *ring*)
	Its purple jewel is an amethyst, *which is my birthstone.*
	(modifies *amethyst*)
Noun clauses:	I hope *that someone finds it soon.* (direct object)
	Whoever finds it will get a reward. (subject)

A. PRACTICE: *Underline the subordinate clause in each sentence. Then, write* adjective *or* noun *to identify its function in the sentence.*

_____ 1. I think that Friday is the best day of the week.

_____ 2. The movie that we saw last night was very exciting.

_____ 3. The star who played the lead role is my favorite actor.

_____ 4. Whoever wants a real treat should order the chocolate pie.

_____ 5. I never miss my favorite TV show, which is on Wednesday night.

B. Writing Application: *Write sentences that include the following groups of words as subordinate clauses. Use the type of clause indicated in parentheses.*

1. who caught the ball (adjective clause)

_____

2. who will win the championship (noun clause)

_____

3. that I saw (adjective clause)

_____

4. whatever you want (noun clause)

_____

Name _____ Date _____

Integrated Language Skills: Support for Writing an Editorial

Editorial: Use the following lines to make notes for an editorial expressing your opinion about Rome's future following Caesar's murder.

1. Describe important events that have occurred in Rome since Act I.

   _____

   _____

2. Explain what issues are involved in these violent events.

   _____

   _____

3. List possible consequences of the war between Antony and the conspirators.

   _____

   _____

   _____

4. Put a [+] next to each desirable consequence and a [–] next to each undesirable consequence. Add a note explaining your decisions.

5. Which consequence do you think is most likely? Why?

   _____

   _____

   Now, use these notes to write your editorial.

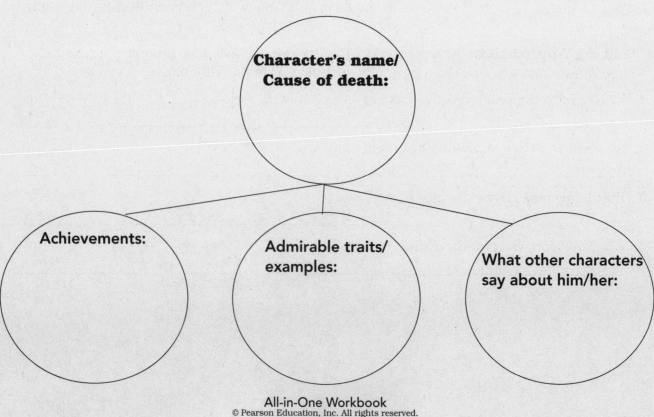

Name _____ Date _____

from **A Raisin in the Sun** by Lorraine Hansberry
The Tragedy of Julius Caesar by William Shakespeare
Writing About the Big Question
To what extent does experience determine what we perceive?

Big Question Vocabulary

anticipate	background	bias	distortion	expectations
identity	impression	individual	insight	interpretation
knowledge	manipulate	perspective	stereotype	universal

A. *Use one or more words from the list above to complete each sentence*

1. Journalists try to be objective and avoid showing any _____ in their writing.

2. I considered it a _____ of the truth to say that I'd had a fight with my friend when it was really just a minor disagreement.

3. Asking yourself whether it will matter twenty years from now can help you put a problem in _____.

B. *Respond to the following item, using full sentences.*

Describe an event that made you feel good about yourself.

_____

_____

C. *Complete the sentence below. Then, write a short paragraph in which you connect the completed sentence to the Big Question.*

To maintain self-respect, you should consider your past experiences and then _____

_____

_____

_____

_____

_____

Name _____ Date _____

from **A Raisin in the Sun** by Lorraine Hansberry
The Tragedy of Julius Caesar by William Shakespeare
Literary Analysis: Character Motivation

A **character's motivation** consists of the feelings and beliefs that guide his or her actions and shape his or her words. To find clues to a character's motivation, ask yourself:

- What does the character say is important to him or her?
- What goals does the character pursue?
- How does the character feel and behave toward other characters?
- What is the character's family and social background?
- Are there any striking similarities or differences between this character and others? If so, what are they?

For example, consider Caesar's speech in *The Tragedy of Julius Caesar,* Act III, Scene i. In that speech, Caesar denies Brutus and Cassius' request that he pardon a banished citizen: "Let me a little show it, even in this—/ That I was constant. Cimber should be banished." From these words, you can tell Caesar is motivated by a stubborn desire to display his power.

DIRECTIONS: *Complete the chart below with clues that show the motivation of Brutus in* The Tragedy of Julius Caesar *and Walter in* A Raisin in the Sun. *Then, use the information in the chart to draw a conclusion about each character's motivation.*

Character	*The Tragedy of Julius Caesar:* Brutus (in Act II, Scene i, lines 112–140)	*A Raisin in the Sun:* Walter
Words or actions that show what the character values		
Goals the character pursues		
Character's attitudes toward other characters		
Character's social or family background		

Brutus' motivation: _____

Walter's motivation: _____

Name _____ Date _____

Vocabulary Builder

Word List

    dignity   looming

A. DIRECTIONS: *Fill in each blank with the correct word from the Word List.*

1. The trail led toward a snow-capped mountain that was _____ in the distance.

2. The proud graduates walked onstage with great _____ to receive their diplomas.

B. DIRECTIONS: *Complete the word map for each Word List Word.*

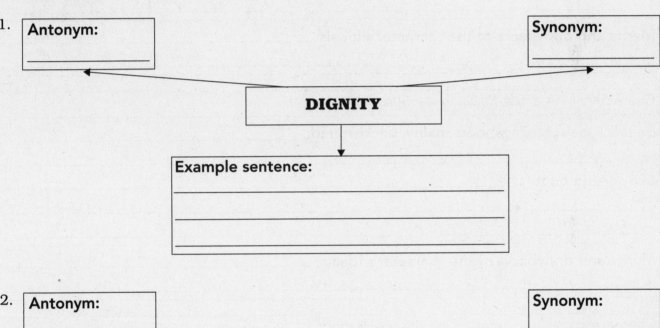

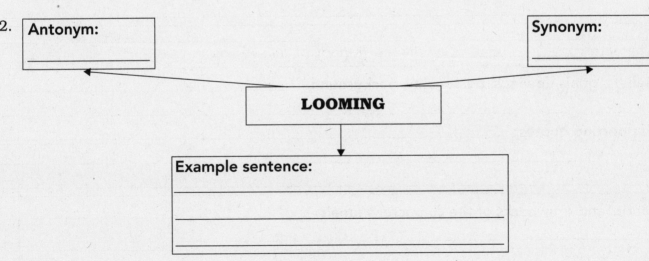

from **A Raisin in the Sun** by Lorraine Hansberry
The Tragedy of Julius Caesar by William Shakespeare

Integrated Language Skills: Support for Writing a Comparative Essay

Before you draft your essay comparing how the characters in these two plays are motivated by their concept of dignity, complete the charts below. For the third chart, choose Brutus, Cassius, or Caesar.

Character: Walter in *A Raisin in the Sun*

Beliefs, goals, feelings, personality, background: _____
_____

Supporting quotes: _____
_____
_____

Merits and drawbacks of the character's ideals: _____
_____

Character: Mama in *A Raisin in the Sun*

Beliefs, goals, feelings, personality, background: _____
_____

Supporting quotes: _____
_____
_____

Merits and drawbacks of the character's ideals: _____
_____

Character: _____ in *The Tragedy of Julius Caesar*

Beliefs, goals, feelings, personality, background: _____
_____

Supporting quotes: _____
_____
_____

Merits and drawbacks of the character's ideals: _____
_____

Now, use your notes to write an essay in which you compare and contrast how these characters are motivated by their ideas about dignity.

Some Kind of Hero, performed by Nina Zeitlin

Anyone can be some kind of hero
If he's **resolute**, determined to be himself
Or is willing to **sacrifice** for someone else
Selflessness is heroism to me

If she wants to be a kind of hero
She must have the **character**
To respect and **honor** herself
Persevering through the toughest of times
With her **inherent** peace of mind

Anyone can be some kind of hero
Anyone that's brave and has the **courage** to be
With honesty and **integrity**
Anyone can be a hero of some kind

He pushes himself, has **determination**
Does his duty, his **responsibility**
Conducts himself like a real man
He controls his own destiny

Faith in her beliefs and **principles**
Is a heroic **attribute**
She's celebrated and **legendary**
A hero
Everyday
She lives life in her own way

Anyone can be some kind of hero
Anyone that has the **courage** to be
Someone with **integrity**
Anyone can be a hero of some kind

Continued

Some kind of hero
Some kind of hero
A hero of some kind
Some kind of hero

Anyone can be some kind of hero
Anyone that has the **courage** to be
Someone with **integrity**
Anyone can be a hero of some kind

Anyone can be some kind of hero
Anyone that has the **courage** to be
Someone with **integrity**
Anyone can be a hero of some kind
A hero of some kind
A hero of some kind

Song Title: **Some Kind of Hero**
Artist / Performed by Nina Zeitlin
Guitar: Josh Green
Bass: Mike Pandolfo
Drums/Percussion: Vlad Gutkovich
Lyrics by Nina Zeitlin
Music composed by Josh Green & Nina Zeitlin
Produced by Mike Pandolfo, Wonderful
Executive Producer: Keith London, Defined Mind

Unit 6: Themes in Literature
Big Question Vocabulary—1

The Big Question: Can anyone be a hero?

In your textbook, you learned words that are useful for talking about heroism. People define heroism in different ways. A hero might be a person who helps others in some exceptional way, a person who has amazing talents or abilities, or a person who sets an outstanding example for others.

DIRECTIONS: *Review the following definitions of words you can use when talking about heroism.*

attributes: positive characteristics

character: one's moral or ethical quality

conduct: personal behavior or way of acting

courage: bravery; the ability to face difficulty or take on challenges

determination: the quality of being resolute or having firmness of purpose

On the lines provided, write an answer to each question. Refer to the meanings of the underlined vocabulary words in your responses.

1. What are some examples of the <u>attributes</u> a star athlete might possess?

   _____

   _____

2. How can you tell if a person has good <u>character</u>?

   _____

   _____

3. How does a person's <u>conduct</u> affect the impressions people form about him or her?

   _____

   _____

4. What is an example that you have observed of a person displaying <u>courage</u>?

   _____

   _____

5. Why might <u>determination</u> be a quality that contributes to heroism?

   _____

   _____

Unit 6: Themes in Literature
Big Question Vocabulary—2

The Big Question: Can anyone be a hero?

DIRECTIONS: *Review the following definitions of words you can use when talking about heroism.*

honor: honesty, fairness, or integrity in one's beliefs and actions

inherent: existing in someone as a permanent and natural element

integrity: the quality of holding to one's principles; honesty

legendary: memorable; worthy of being celebrated in stories

persevere: to persist or keep at something; to continue steadfastly

Create two different sentences for each of the following words. Try to use the word to explain something entirely different in your second sentence.

1. **honor**

   _____

   _____

2. **inherent**

   _____

   _____

3. **integrity**

   _____

   _____

4. **legendary**

   _____

   _____

5. **persevere**

   _____

   _____

Name _____ Date _____

Unit 6: Themes in Literature
Big Question Vocabulary—3

The Big Question: Can anyone be a hero?

DIRECTIONS: *Review the following definitions of words you can use when talking about heroism.*

principles: personal basic truths or guidelines for how to conduct oneself

resolute: firmly resolved or determined; set in one's opinion or approach

responsibility: an obligation or a task that one is committed to performing

sacrifice: to give up or surrender something

selflessness: having little or no concern for oneself; being unselfishg

On the lines below, write a paragraph describing some important characteristics of a hero. You might give examples from your own life or from literature. Use at least three of the Big Question vocabulary words.

_____
_____
_____
_____
_____
_____
_____
_____
_____
_____
_____
_____
_____
_____
_____
_____
_____
_____
_____

Name _____ Date _____

Unit 6: Themes in Literature
Applying the Big Question

The Biq Question: Can anyone be a hero?

DIRECTIONS: *Complete the chart below to apply what you have learned about the different ways in which different types of people can be heroes. One row has been completed for you.*

Example	Identify hero	Does he or she start out as hero?	What characteristics make this person a hero?	What does this hero accomplish?	What I learned
From Literature	Long Arrow from "The Orphan Boy and the Elk Dog"	No, Long Arrow is a poor orphan who cannot hear.	He perseveres and is brave, loyal, and clever.	He discovers and intro-duces horses to his tribe.	Even some-one who is shunned by society can do great things.
From Literature					
From Science					
From Social Studies					
From Real Life					

John Phillip Santos
Listening and Viewing

Segment 1: Meet John Phillip Santos
- How have John Phillip Santos's childhood experiences in San Antonio, Texas, shaped his writing? How do you think John Phillip Santos's contact with writers during his college years helped inspire his future writing career?

_____

_____

_____

_____

Segment 2: Themes in Literature: Heroes and Dreamers
- According to John Phillip Santos, what is a memoir? What do you think you can learn by reading a memoir like John Phillip Santos's book?

_____

_____

_____

_____

Segment 3: The Writing Process
- Why is "gathering" such an important part of John Phillip Santos's writing process? Why do you think John Phillip Santos also gathers information by using a video camera?

_____

_____

_____

_____

Segment 4: The Rewards of Writing
- How has writing helped heal John Phillip Santos's family and also contributed to society?

_____

_____

_____

_____

Learning About Themes in Literature

The **oral tradition** consists of stories and sayings passed on by word of mouth. These stories and sayings explore **universal themes,** or ideas about life shared by many cultures. They may also explore **values,** or model behaviors, cherished by a culture. These stories often use **archetypes,** the characters, situations, images, and symbols that appear in the narratives of many different cultures. The following chart shows some of the oral tradition's **archetypal characters** and the types of stories that often use archetypes.

Types of Stories	Archetypal Characters
Myths: explain the actions of gods and the humans who interact with them	**The Wise and Virtuous King:** a ruler whose reign brings peace and prosperity
Epics: long narrative poems with an epic hero	**The Dreamer:** a character who brings an important gift to society
Folk Tales: stories featuring human or animal heroes	**The Hero:** an unpromising youth who becomes a wise and courageous leader
Fairy Tales: folk tales with fairies or other magical beings	**The Protagonist:** the main character
Parodies: humorous mockeries of archetypal stories	**The Antagonist:** the force opposing the main character

DIRECTIONS: *Label each description with the correct archetypal character name or type of story.*

1. A long poem about a strong woman who defeats a dragon _____

2. A boy who grows up to lead his people to a new land _____

3. A story about how the goddess of beauty turned a woman into a spider

   _____

4. An evil king who fights the hero for a kingdom _____

5. A story about a snake who tricks a fox _____

6. A ruler who takes over a war-torn country and brings it peace _____

7. A girl who finds a magical pearl that will save her homeland _____

8. A funny story about a bumbling hero who creates more problems than he solves

   _____

Name _____   Date _____

from **Places Left Unfinished at the Time of Creation** by John Phillip Santos
Model Selection: Themes in Literature

The **oral tradition** consists of stories and sayings that are passed on by word of mouth. Some writers, such as John Phillip Santos, blend oral traditions with their own stories to create a **personal mythology.**

Storytellers explore **universal themes,** or ideas about life that are shared by many cultures. They may also explore **values,** or model behaviors, cherished by a culture. Some ideas are **shared values,** which are held by many societies. Others are **culturally distinct values,** which are specific to a group. Similarly, **cultural details** relate to the beliefs and customs of a particular group.

A. DIRECTIONS: *Explain what universal theme or value each quotation explores.*

1. These ancestors, living and dead, have asked me the questions they were once asked: Where did our forebears come from and what have we amounted to in this world? Where have we come to in the span of all time, and where are we headed, like an arrow shot long ago into infinite empty space?

   Theme: _____

   _____

2. Even if everything else had been lost—photographs, stories, rumors, and suspicions—if nothing at all from the past remained for us, the land remains, as the original book of the family.

   Value: _____

   _____

B. DIRECTIONS: *Answer the following questions.*

1. In *Places Left Unfinished at the Time of Creation,* John Phillip Santos mentions the Aztec belief of *el Inframundo,* "a mystical limbo dimension," in which all memories are preserved and nothing is lost. Why is this cultural detail important to the narrator as he attempts to connect with his family's past?

   _____

   _____

2. Despite having few written records of his family's past, the narrator acknowledges that he has "always felt connected, oriented, and imparted" by his ancestors. Why?

   _____

   _____

"Prometheus and the First People" Ancient Greek Myth retold by Olivia Coolidge

Writing About the Big Question

Can anyone be a hero?

Big Question Vocabulary

attributes	character	conduct	courage	determination
honor	inherent	integrity	legendary	persevere
principles	resolute	responsibility	sacrifice	selflessness

A. *Use one or more words from the list above to complete each sentence.*

1. We watched Jim give away everything he had to help others, and we praised his _____ and disregard for his own comfort.

2. Heroes have many fine _____, such as courage and strength.

3. Cesar's _____ were so ethical, he even took coins he found on the playground to the school office.

4. Her _____ was appalling, and her teacher sent a note home about her behavior.

B. *Follow the directions in responding to each of the items below.*

1. Identify two characteristics you think are necessary for heroes. Answer in complete sentences.

   _____

   _____

2. Write two sentences explaining one of the characteristics you listed, and describe why you think it is important. Use at least two of the Big Question vocabulary words.

   _____

   _____

C. *Complete the sentences below. Then, write a short paragraph in which you connect this experience to the Big Question.*

When humans act without **honor** and **responsibility**, their behavior can lead to

_____. If they **conduct** themselves with **integrity**, they can become

_____.

"Prometheus and the First People" Ancient Greek Myth retold by Olivia Coolidge
Literary Analysis: Myths

Myths are stories that are part of an oral tradition: Before they were written down, they were told and retold from one generation to the next. Myths reflect the culture of the people who originated and told them.

- Some myths explain a feature of the world by telling of its **origins**—how it came to be. These myths reveal the beliefs of ancient cultures.
- Myths typically include characters with exceptional or fantastic characteristics. These characteristics emphasize qualities that the culture admired or feared.
- Some myths tell of a **quest,** or search, for knowledge or some important object. These myths reveal what was important to a culture.
- Other myths tell of a **transgression,** or the violation of a rule. These myths teach the values of a culture.

DIRECTIONS: *Answer the questions about "Prometheus and the First People."*

1. What does the story of Prometheus describe the origins of?

   _____

2. What transgression did Prometheus commit? How was he punished for it?

   _____

   _____

3. Why is the story of Pandora considered a myth of origins?

   _____

4. What transgression did Pandora commit? What human trait led to Pandora's transgression?

   _____

   _____

5. In what sense is the story of the Great Flood a myth of origins?

   _____

   _____

   _____

Name _____   Date _____

"Prometheus and the First People" Ancient Greek Myth retold by Olivia Coolidge
Reading: Generate Questions to Analyze Cultural Context

Because the myths of a culture have been handed down from generation to generation, they reflect the lives and concerns of the people in a particular culture. To understand a myth, you must understand its cultural context. To **analyze the cultural context** of a myth, first **generate questions** you would like to answer about the people who told it. Then, as you read, note details in the myth that help you answer your questions.

DIRECTIONS: *Before you read "Prometheus and the First People," look at the categories in the following chart. For each category, think of a question you would like to answer about the ancient Greeks. Then, as you read the myth, write down details that can help you answer the questions.*

Category	Question	Relevant Details from Myth
place where they lived		
means of survival		
personal qualities		
customs		

"Prometheus and the First People" Greek Myth retold by Olivia Coolidge
Vocabulary Builder

Word List

counsel   disembarked   endure   heedless   inhabit   toil

A. DIRECTIONS: *Decide whether each statement below is true or false. Circle T or F. Then, explain your answer using the meaning of the word in italics.*

1. After a day of *toil*, a person is likely to be exhausted.

   T / F _____

   _____

2. A *heedless* person considers all the possible consequences before acting.

   T / F _____

   _____

3. A person with legal problems needs to seek *counsel* from a lawyer.

   T / F _____

   _____

4. A cruise begins once all the passengers have *disembarked*.

   T / F _____

   _____

5. If birds *inhabit* that tree, they build their nests in it.

   T / F _____

   _____

6. When you *endure* the summer heat, you become ill when you go out into the high temperatures.

   T / F _____

   _____

B. WORD STUDY: The *Latin root -dur-* means "hard" or "to last." Answer the following questions using one of these words that contain the root *-dur-: endurance, durable, during.*

1. If you enter an *endurance* race, will it be a short, easy event?

   _____

2. Your new shoes are *durable*, so will you have them for a long time?

   _____

3. If you eat *during* the movie, are you eating an hour before the movie begins?

   _____

"The Orphan Boy and the Elk Dog" Native American Myth (Blackfeet)

Writing About the Big Question

Can anyone be a hero?

Big Question Vocabulary

attributes	character	conduct	courage	determination
honor	inherent	integrity	legendary	persevere
principles	resolute	responsibility	sacrifice	selflessness

A. *Use one or more words from the list above to complete each sentence.*

1. Honesty and loyalty are her two strongest traits, which makes us think her _____ is beyond reproach.

2. It was John's _____ to collect all of the balls after practice and put them away.

3. Mia's _____ good will naturally led her to help others first before thinking of herself.

4. If you want to improve your math grade, you must _____ with the extra homework.

B. *Follow the directions in responding to each of the items below.*

1. Being **resolute** is often the first step toward being a hero. List two situations in which your **determination** helped someone. Use complete sentences.

_____

_____

2. Write two sentences explaining one of the situations you listed, and describe how you felt. Use at least two of the Big Question vocabulary words.

_____

_____

C. *Complete the sentence below. Then, write a short paragraph in which you connect this experience to the Big Question.*

To **persevere** in times of hardship shows great **character** and reveals **attributes** that suggest _____.

Name _____ Date _____

"The Orphan Boy and the Elk Dog" Native American Myth (Blackfeet)
Literary Analysis: Myths

Myths are stories that are part of an oral tradition: Before they were written down, they were told and retold from one generation to the next. Myths reflect the culture of the people who originated and told them.

- Some myths explain a feature of the world by telling of its **origins**—how it came to be. These myths reveal the beliefs of ancient cultures.
- Myths typically include characters with exceptional or fantastic characteristics. These characteristics emphasize qualities that the culture admired or feared.
- Some myths tell of a **quest,** or search, for knowledge or some important object. These myths reveal what was important to a culture.
- Other myths tell of a **transgression,** or the violation of a rule. These myths teach the values of a culture.

DIRECTIONS: *Answer the questions about the myth "The Orphan Boy and the Elk Dog."*

1. What does "The Orphan Boy and the Elk Dog" describe the origins of?

_____

2. How does Long Arrow prepare for his quest?

_____

_____

3. What personal qualities does Long Arrow need to succeed on his quest?

_____

_____

4. Once he arrives at the Great One's lodge, what task must Long Arrow complete before he can be given a herd of Elk Dogs?

_____

_____

5. What special gifts does the old spirit chief give to Long Arrow besides the Elk Dogs?

_____

_____

Name _____ Date _____

Reading: Generate Questions to Analyze Cultural Context

Because the myths of a culture have been handed down from generation to generation, they reflect the lives and concerns of the people in a particular culture. To understand a myth, you must understand its cultural context. To **analyze the cultural context** of a myth, first **generate questions** you would like to answer about the people who told it. Then, as you read, note details in the myth that help answer your questions.

DIRECTIONS: *Before you read the "The Orphan Boy and the Elk Dog," look at the categories in the following chart. For each category, think of a question you would like to answer about the Blackfeet. Then, as you read the myth, write down details that can help you answer the questions.*

Category	Question	Relevant Details from Myth
place where they lived		
means of survival		
personal qualities		
customs		

"The Orphan Boy and the Elk Dog" Native American (Blackfeet)
Vocabulary Builder

Word List

emanating   humble   refuse   relish   stifle   surpassed

A. DIRECTIONS: *Decide whether each statement below is true or false. Circle T or F. Then, explain your answer using the meaning of the word in italics.*

1. Most people would perform a boring job with *relish*.

   T / F _____

   _____

2. The person who holds a world record has *surpassed* all other competitors.

   T / F _____

   _____

3. When a lamp is working, you can see light *emanating* from it.

   T / F _____

   _____

4. By encouraging a child's natural talents, parents can *stifle* the child's creativity.

   T / F _____

   _____

5. If you have a bag of *refuse*, you will throw it away.

   T / F _____

   _____

6. A person who is *humble* will boast about her accomplishments.

   T / F _____

   _____

B. WORD STUDY: The *Latin root -fus-* means "to pour." Answer the following questions using one of these words that contain the root *-fus-: infuse, profusely, effusive.*

1. If the coach gives an uplifting speech to the team, will it *infuse* the players with confidence?

   _____

2. If you thanked someone *profusely*, would that person feel slighted?

   _____

3. What might you do if you encountered someone with *effusive* laughter?

   _____

Name _____ Date _____

"Prometheus and the First People" Ancient Greek Myth retold by Olivia Coolidge
"The Orphan Boy and the Elk Dog" Native American Myth (Blackfeet)
Integrated Language Skills: Grammar

Simple and Compound Sentences

A **clause** is a group of words with a subject and a verb. A **simple sentence** is an independent clause that is a complete thought. A **compound sentence** contains two or more independent clauses linked by a semicolon or by a coordinating conjunction (such as *and, but, or, for, nor, so,* or *yet*). In the following examples, subjects are underlined once and verbs are underlined twice.

Simple: Myths are the oldest stories in the world.

Compound: Some myths describe solemn events, but others feature humorous episodes.

A. PRACTICE: *Identify each sentence as* simple *or* compound.

_____ 1. A good storyteller can hold the attention of an audience.

_____ 2. Tone of voice and pacing are important tools of storytellers.

_____ 3. In a good story, the characters come alive, and the suspense builds.

_____ 4. Listeners love plot twists; a humorous twist is especially welcome.

_____ 5. Some stories are realistic, but others are magical and fantastic.

_____ 6. Some of today's stand-up comedians are good storytellers.

_____ 7. We learn about life from stories; that fact will never change.

B. Writing Application: *Write a paragraph comparing and contrasting two famous people or two people whom you know. Use both simple sentences and compound sentences in your paragraph.*

_____

_____

_____

_____

Name _____ Date _____

"Prometheus and the First People" Ancient Greek Myth retold by Olivia Coolidge
"The Orphan Boy and the Elk Dog" Native American Myth (Blackfeet)
Integrated Language Skills: Support for Writing a Myth

Use the following sentence starters to help your group begin writing sentences for a myth. If you are writing about how some aspect of human life, such as gossip, entered the world, use set A. If you are writing about the origin of something in your everyday world, such as television, use set B. Everyone should finish with sentence starters 5–8. Take turns completing the sentences.

A. Topic: _____

Sentence 1: Long ago, before people learned to _____, no one ever_____
_____.

Sentence 2: Back then, a _____ named _____ lived _____
_____.

Sentence 3: _____ was a good person, but he/she had one big weakness:
_____.

Sentence 4: This weakness got him/her into trouble one day when_____
_____.

B. Topic: _____

SENTENCE 1: In the olden days, before there were _____, people needed to
_____.

SENTENCE 2: Back then, a young _____ named _____ lived
_____.

SENTENCE 3: Most people thought he/she was _____ and
_____.

SENTENCE 4: No one suspected that _____ was actually
_____.

SENTENCE 5:

_____

_____

SENTENCE 6:

_____

_____

SENTENCE 7:

_____

_____

SENTENCE 8:

_____

_____

Continue taking turns until your myth is complete. Then, make any needed revisions, and present your myth to the class.

from **"Sundiata: An Epic of Old Mali"** by D. T. Niane
Writing About the Big Question

Can anyone be a hero?

Big Question Vocabulary

attributes	character	conduct	courage	determination
honor	inherent	integrity	legendary	persevere
principles	resolute	responsibility	sacrifice	selflessness

A. *Use one or more words from the list above to complete each sentence.*

1. If you show _____ and no fear when you encounter danger, people will call you a hero.

2. Stories about _____ heroes who lived long ago are filled with knights and kings.

3. Dan's _____ prevented him from taking advantage of his opponent's injury.

4. If you concentrate, work hard, and show _____, you can solve many problems.

B. *Follow the directions in responding to each of the items below.*

1. List two times you saw someone do something you thought was heroic. Use complete sentences.

   _____

   _____

2. Write two sentences explaining one of the situations you listed, and describe what happened. Use at least two of the Big Question vocabulary words.

   _____

   _____

C. *In the excerpt from Sundiata: An Epic of Old Mail, a young man's determination allows him to overcome his infirmary and regain his famiy's honor. Complete the sentence below. Then, write a short paragraph in which you connect this experience to the Big Question.*

   Showing determination and courage in the face of adversity is heroic because

   _____

   _____

   _____

   _____

from **Sundiata: An Epic of Old Mali** by D. T. Niane
Literary Analysis: Epic and Epic Hero

An **epic** is an extended narrative poem about the deeds of heroes. The typical **epic hero** is a warrior, and his character may be based on a historic or a legendary figure. In a number of epics, the hero strives to win immortality or undying fame through great deeds, especially in combat. The typical hero has the following characteristics:

- He has the virtues of a warrior, such as strength, courage, and perseverance.
- He defends his own honor and the honor of his family.
- He acts ethically, fighting evil and striving for justice.
- He may be marked out by the gods or by fate, and he may therefore benefit from special blessings or suffer from special burdens.

DIRECTIONS: *Answer the following questions to analyze Mari Djata as an epic hero.*

1. What position does Mari Djata have in Mali society?

   _____

2. What special burdens does Mari Djata suffer from as a child?

   _____

   _____

3. What special fate has been predicted for Mari Djata as the son of Sogolon?

   _____

   _____

4. What injustice occurs after the death of King Naré Maghan?

   _____

   _____

5. What humiliation finally motivates Mari Djata to defend his family's honor and achieve justice?

   _____

   _____

6. How does Mari Djata demonstrate his great strength at the end of the selection?

   _____

   _____

Name _____ Date _____

from **Sundiata: An Epic of Old Mali** by D. T. Niane
Reading: Acquire Background Knowledge
to Analyze Cultural Context

To understand an epic, **analyze cultural context,** or determine how the epic reflects the culture in which it was composed. You can **acquire background knowledge** about the cultural context in a number of ways:

- Read introductory sections, footnotes, and other text aids that provide background information.
- Draw conclusions from the details in the selection.

DIRECTIONS: *Answer the following questions to analyze the cultural context of* Sundiata.

1. In the background information before the selection, what do you learn about the cultural setting of this epic?

   _____

   _____

   _____

2. Why is the background information about jinns and soothsayers, given in the footnotes, important to understanding the cultural context of *Sundiata*?

   _____

   _____

   _____

3. Why is the king's presentation of a griot to Mari Djata an important moment in *Sundiata*? How does the background information about griots help you understand the significance of this gift in Mali culture?

   _____

   _____

   _____

4. How does the photo of a baobab tree help you appreciate Mari Djata's amazing feat at the end of the selection?

   _____

   _____

Name _____   Date _____

from **Sundiata: An Epic of Old Mali** by D. T. Niane
Vocabulary Builder

Word List

affront   derisively   efface   estranged   fathom   innuendo

A. DIRECTIONS: *Answer the following questions to show your understanding of the words in italics.*

1. Would you prefer to have someone accuse you directly of wrongdoing or to have him or her use *innuendo*? Explain your answer.

   _____

   _____

2. What is a subject you find difficult to *fathom*? Explain your answer.

   _____

   _____

3. What can you do to help friends who have become *estranged*?

   _____

   _____

4. How might someone feel after experiencing an *affront*? Explain your answer.

   _____

   _____

5. How might someone sound if he were speaking *derisively* to someone? Explain your answer.

   _____

   _____

6. If you try to *efface* the memory of the party, will you reflect on the event for a long time? Explain your answer.

   _____

   _____

B. WORD STUDY: The Latin suffix *-ive* means "of," "belonging to," or "quality of." Provide an explanation for your answer to each question, using one of these words that contain the suffix *-ive: permissive, combative, persuasive.*

1. Does a *permissive* parent let her children do anything they want to do?

   _____

2. If you are *combative*, do you always try to find the most peaceful solution first?

   _____

3. Do you want your *persuasive* speech to change people's minds toward your opinion?

   _____

"Rama's Initiation" *from* **The Ramayana** by R. K. Narayan
Writing About the Big Question
Can anyone be a hero?

Big Question Vocabulary

attributes	character	conduct	courage	determination
honor	inherent	integrity	legendary	persevere
principles	resolute	responsibility	sacrifice	selflessness

A. *Use one or more words from the list above to complete each sentence.*

1. Sophia pushed, pulled, took a deep breath, and with great _____, she dislodged the toy from the tree.

2. She was _____ about inviting everyone to the party, and no one could make her change her mind.

3. I considered it a big _____ to give my sister the last piece of cake.

B. *Follow the directions in responding to each of the items below.*

1. List two people or groups of people who might not be thought of as heroes but whom you consider heroic. Answer in complete sentences.

   _____

   _____

2. Write two sentences describing one of the people you listed, and explain how you feel about him or her. Use at least two of the Big Question vocabulary words.

   _____

   _____

C. *in "Rama's Initiation," a young boy discovers the importance of bravery and strength as he becomes a hero in the fight against evil. Complete the sentence below. Then, write a short paragraph in which you connect this experience to the Big Question.*

Being able to sacrifice something important to you for the greater good can be considered heroic because _____

_____

_____

_____

_____

_____

"Rama's Initiation" *from the* **Ramayana** by R. K. Narayan
Literary Analysis: Epic and Epic Hero

An **epic** is an extended narrative poem about the deeds of heroes. The typical **epic hero** is a warrior, and his character may be based on a historic or a legendary figure. In a number of epics, the hero strives to win immortality or undying fame through great deeds, especially in combat. The typical hero has the following characteristics:

- He has the virtues of a warrior, such as strength, courage, and perseverance.
- He defends his own honor and the honor of his family.
- He acts ethically, fighting evil and striving for justice.
- He may be marked out by the gods or by fate, and he may therefore benefit from special blessings or suffer from special burdens.

DIRECTIONS: *Answer the following questions to analyze Rama as an epic hero.*

1. What position does Rama have in the society of ancient India?

    _____

2. How does the request of the sage Viswamithra suggest that Rama has been chosen by fate for a special destiny?

    _____

    _____

    _____

3. How does Rama prove himself a hero in his battle against evil?

    _____

    _____

4. How does Rama's hesitation before the battle show that he is an ethical hero?

    _____

    _____

5. Why is the appearance of the gods at the end of the selection significant?

    _____

    _____

    _____

"Rama's Initiation" *from the* **Ramayana** by R. K. Narayan
Reading: Acquire Background Knowledge
to Analyze Cultural Context

To understand an epic, **analyze cultural context,** or determine how the epic reflects the culture in which it was composed. You can **acquire background knowledge** about the cultural context in a number of ways:

- Read introductory sections, footnotes, and other text aids that provide background information.
- Draw conclusions from the details in the selection.

DIRECTIONS: *Answer the following questions to analyze the cultural context of the* Ramayana.

1. How does the background information given in the introduction help you understand the character traits that define a Hindu epic hero?

   _____

   _____

   _____

2. What does Rama's mission reveal about Hindu concepts of good and evil? Use the footnotes in the text to help you answer this question.

   _____

   _____

   _____

3. In the selection, what does the passage about *mantras* reveal about Indian culture? Use the footnotes in the text to help you answer this question.

   _____

   _____

   _____

4. What does the story of how Thataka became a demon suggest about the Hindu perception of the relationship between gods and people?

   _____

   _____

   _____

"Rama's Initiation" *from the* **Ramayana** by R. K. Narayan
Vocabulary Builder

Word List

adversaries   decrepitude   esoteric   exuberance   renounced   secular

A. DIRECTIONS: *Answer the following questions to show your understanding of the words in italics.*

1. Is a person of great *decrepitude* likely to have an active lifestyle? Explain your answer.
   _____

2. Describe someone who has *esoteric* knowledge.
   _____

3. Is a church a *secular* institution? Explain your answer.
   _____

4. If someone has *renounced* his support of a candidate, is he going to vote for that person? Explain your answer.
   _____

5. Does her *exuberance* indicate that she is sad about the results of the test? Explain your answer.
   _____

6. Should we be surprised if our *adversaries* try to defeat us? Explain your answer.
   _____

B. WORD STUDY: The Latin suffix *-tude* means "condition of" or "quality of." Provide an explanation for your answer to each question using one of these words that contain the suffix *-tude*: *multitude, solitude, fortitude.*

1. Is a *multitude* of people a small group?
   _____

2. If you like *solitude*, do you enjoy reading alone?
   _____

3. If you have strong inner *fortitude*, do you give up easily in a difficult situation?
   _____

from **Sundiata: An Epic of Old Mali** by D. T. Niane
"Rama's Initiation" *from the* **Ramayana** by R. K. Narayan

Integrated Language Skills: Grammar

Complex and Compound-Complex Sentences

An **independent clause** contains a subject and a verb and can stand alone as a complete sentence. A **subordinate clause** has a subject and a verb, but it cannot stand alone as a complete sentence. A **complex sentence** contains one independent clause and one or more subordinate clauses. A **compound-complex sentence** contains at least one subordinate clause and at least two independent clauses. In the following examples, the independent clauses are underlined once and the subordinate clauses are underlined twice.

Complex: When the monster Grendel threatens a Danish king, Beowulf comes to challenge the beast that no one else can defeat.

Compound-Complex: After Beowulf has killed the monster, the king holds a great feast, but Grendel's mother comes that night to avenge her son's death.

A. PRACTICE: *Identify each of the following sentences as* complex *or* compound-complex. *Underline each independent clause once and each subordinate clause twice.*

_____ 1. The *Iliad* is an epic poem that is based on events from the Trojan War.

_____ 2. Although it is attributed to the poet Homer, the epic actually evolved over centuries of oral tradition, and no one can trace its exact history.

_____ 3. The *Odyssey* describes the adventures of the hero Odysseus, who struggles to reach his home after the Trojan War.

_____ 4. One story that everyone knows from the *Odyssey* is the tale of the Trojan Horse.

_____ 5. The Trojans foolishly accept the huge wooden horse that the Greeks offer them, but hidden inside the horse are Greek soldiers who eventually defeat the Trojans.

B. Writing Application: *Rewrite the following paragraph using both complex and compound-complex sentences. You may keep some simple and compound sentences to achieve sentence variety in the paragraph.*

A culture chooses heroes. The heroes have values. The values are important in that culture. In epics, heroes fight for justice. They also defeat evil enemies. The enemies threaten the heroes' culture. It is interesting to compare and contrast epics from different cultures. Some elements of epics are universal. Others vary from culture to culture.

_____

_____

_____

_____

_____

Name _____ Date _____

from **Sundiata: An Epic of Old Mali** by D. T. Niane
"Rama's Initiation" *from the* **Ramayana** by R. K. Narayan
Integrated Language Skills:
Support for Writing a Newspaper Report

Use the following chart to make notes for your newspaper report about events that occur at the end of the selection from *Sundiata* or the *Ramayana*.

HEADLINE:
WHAT HAPPENED: Who: What: Where: When: Why: How:
QUOTATIONS FROM PEOPLE WHO WERE THERE:
YOUR CLOSING COMMENTS:

Now, use your notes to write a newspaper report of events at the end of the selection.

Name _____ Date _____

Writing About the Big Question

Can anyone be a hero?

Big Question Vocabulary

attributes	character	conduct	courage	determination
honor	inherent	integrity	legendary	persevere
principles	resolute	responsibility	sacrifice	selflessness

A. *Use one or more words from the list above to complete each sentence.*

1. Maintaining your _____ means maintaining your honesty and sincerity during times of hardship.

2. It is my _____ to walk and feed the dog each day.

3. Her most engaging _____ are her friendliness, sincerity, and loyalty.

4. My mother shows _____ when she puts our needs before her own.

B. *Follow the directions in responding to each of the items below.*

1. List two different times when you behaved heroically. Answer in complete sentences.

   _____

   _____

2. Write two sentences describing one of the experiences you listed, and explain how you felt. Use at least two of the Big Question vocabulary words.

   _____

   _____

C. *Complete the sentence below. Then, write a short paragraph in which you connect this experience to the Big Question.*

A hero is a person who _____

_____

_____

_____

_____.

Name _____ Date _____

"**Cupid and Psyche**" retold by Sally Benson

"**Ashputtle**" by Jakob and Wilhelm Grimm

Literary Analysis: Archetypal Narrative Patterns

Archetypal narrative patterns are basic storytelling patterns found in the stories of cultures around the world. These patterns are often found in stories that have been passed along orally, such as fairy tales and myths. Common archetypal patterns include the following:

- a test, quest, or task that a character must complete
- characters, events, or objects that come in threes
- greedy, cruel, or jealous relatives
- a hero who triumphs through cleverness or virtue
- a supernatural guide or helper
- a just end that rewards good or punishes evil

DIRECTIONS: *Complete the following chart by listing examples of each archetypal pattern in "Cupid and Psyche" and "Ashputtle."*

	"Cupid and Psyche"	"Ashputtle"
Test or Task		
Characters, Events, or Objects That Come in Threes		
Cruel or Jealous Relatives		
Hero Who Triumphs		
Supernatural Helpers or Guides		

Name _____ Date _____

"Cupid and Psyche" retold by Sally Benson
"Ashputtle" by Jakob and Wilhelm Grimm
Vocabulary Builder

Word List

adulation   allay   diligence   jeered   nimbly   plague

A. DIRECTIONS: *Decide whether each statement below is true or false. Circle* T *or* F. *Then, explain your answer.*

1. Athletes who show poor sportsmanship deserve their fans' *adulation.*

   T / F _____

   _____

2. Meeting a goal requires both focus and *diligence.*

   T / F _____

   _____

3. Riding in a hot air balloon may help *allay* a fear of heights.

   T / F _____

   _____

4. It would not surprise you to hear that a student's parents *jeered* when she won a spelling bee.

   T / F _____

   _____

5. To *plague* a person with criticism will help him or her improve.

   T / F _____

   _____

6. A hiker who leaps *nimbly* across a stream is likely to fall.

   T / F _____

   _____

B. DIRECTIONS: *On the line, write the letter of the word that is most similar in meaning to the word in CAPITAL LETTERS.*

____ 1. ALLAY: **A.** create   **B.** strengthen   **C.** forget   **D.** relieve

____ 2. JEERED: **A.** mocked   **B.** transported   **C.** celebrated   **D.** sobbed

____ 3. PLAGUE: **A.** depress   **B.** torment   **C.** defeat   **D.** pretend

____ 4. NIMBLY: **A.** gleefully   **B.** hesitantly   **C.** gracefully   **D.** timidly

"**Cupid and Psyche**" retold by Sally Benson
"**Ashputtle**" by Jakob and Wilhelm Grimm
Support for Writing to Compare Literary Works

Before you draft your essay comparing the use of archetypal patterns in each story, complete the notecards below.

How are the archetypal patterns in each story similar and different?

Similar:

Different:

What lesson does each story convey using archetypal patterns?

"Cupid and Psyche":

"Ashputtle":

How do archetypal patterns affect my appreciation of the story?

"Cupid and Psyche":

"Ashputtle":

Now, use your notes to write an essay in which you compare and contrast the use of archetypal narrative patterns in the two stories.

"**Arthur Becomes King of Britain**" *from* **The Once and Future King** by T. H. White
Writing About the Big Question

Can anyone be a hero?

Big Question Vocabulary

attributes	character	conduct	courage	determination
honor	inherent	integrity	legendary	persevere
principles	resolute	responsibility	sacrifice	selflessness

A. *Use one or more words from the list above to complete each sentence.*

1. You might lose all your money, but if you have a good _____, you are truly rich.

2. It takes much _____ to stand up for what you believe in when your ideas are unpopular.

3. The knight was noble and his _____ had earned him the highest respect.

4. If you _____ and stick with the study plan, you will improve your test scores.

B. *Follow the directions in responding to each of the items below.*

1. List two different times you wanted to act heroically but did not. Respond in complete sentences.

   _____

   _____

2. Write two sentences describing one of the experiences you listed, and explain how you felt. Use at least two of the Big Question vocabulary words.

   _____

   _____

C. *Complete the sentence below. Then, write a short paragraph in which you connect this experience to the Big Question.*

Maintaining one's **integrity** and trying to **persevere** against tremendous odds shows that a person is _____

_____

_____

_____

_____.

"Arthur Becomes King of Britain" *from* **The Once and Future King** by T. H. White
Literary Analysis: Legends

Legends are popular stories about the past that have been handed down for generations. Most legends have some basis in historical fact, which may be lost through centuries of retelling. Legends focus on the life and adventures of **legendary heroes,** or characters who are human yet "larger than life." Legends also show a deep concern with right and wrong, honorable actions, and national pride. Legends help shape a people's cultural identity and reflect the values of a community or nation.

A. DIRECTIONS: *Answer the following questions on the lines provided.*

1. How do you know that "Arthur Becomes King of Britain" is part of a legend?

   _____

   _____

2. How is the character of Wart legendary? How is he ordinary? Why do you think the author chose to show Wart as both?

   _____

   _____

   _____

   _____

3. What qualities do you think the author would say makes a person a hero? Why?

   _____

   _____

4. How do you think the legend of King Arthur and Camelot has influenced the culture and values of the United States? Give examples to support your answer.

   _____

   _____

   _____

   _____

B. DIRECTIONS: *In a brief essay, name and describe your personal hero. What makes this person a hero in your mind? Would your hero qualify to be a legendary hero? Why or why not?*

   _____

   _____

   _____

   _____

   _____

   _____

"Arthur Becomes King of Britain" *from* **The Once and Future King** by T. H. White

Reading: Identify Details to Compare and Contrast Worldviews

A **worldview** is the set of values and beliefs held by a culture that is expressed in its literature. To fully understand a retelling of a legend, **compare and contrast** the worldviews it presents. Find similarities and differences between two different cultures—that of the original story and that of the person who retells the story. To do this, **identify details** that reveal characters' beliefs and their reasons for acting or feeling as they do. In addition, identify details that suggest the writer's attitudes. Then, **draw conclusions** from these details about the values and basic beliefs of the characters, as well as those of the writer.

A. DIRECTIONS: *Fill in the Venn diagram to help compare and contrast the worldviews of the characters in "Arthur Becomes King of England" with those of the author. Use details in the story to help make educated guesses about the worldviews of the author and the characters, as well as their reasons for acting or feeling as they do.*

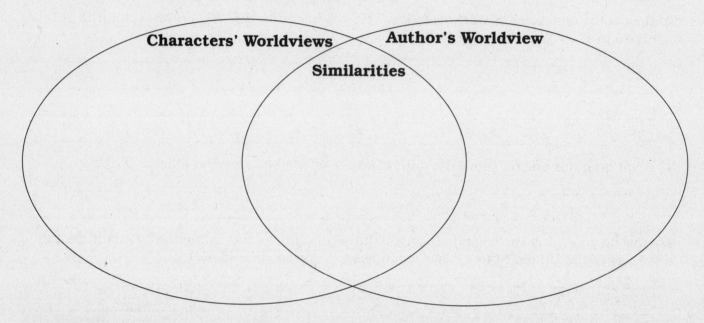

Characters' Worldviews

Author's Worldview

Similarities

B. DIRECTIONS: *Use the Venn diagram to help write a brief essay comparing and contrasting the values and beliefs of the characters' culture in the original story with those of the author. Continue writing on a separate sheet of paper, if necessary.*

_____

_____

_____

_____

_____

_____

_____

_____

"Arthur Becomes King of Britain" *from* **The Once and Future King** by T. H. White
Vocabulary Builder

Word List

desolate   petulantly   skeptically   stickler   sumptuous   surmise

A. DIRECTIONS: *Write at least one synonym, at least one antonym, and an example sentence for each word. Synonyms and antonyms can be words or phrases.*

Word	Synonym	Antonym	Example Sentence
1. stickler			
2. petulantly			
3. surmise			
4. skeptically			
5. sumptuous			
6. desolate			

B. WORD STUDY: The Latin suffix *-ate* means "characterized by" or "associated with." Answer the following questions using one of these words that contain the suffix *-ate*: *desperate, immoderate, regulate.*

1. Is a *desperate* person characterized by laughter, smiling, and optimism?

   _____

2. Is your *immoderate* response a quiet and reserved reaction?

   _____

3. If you *regulate* how much water you use in the shower, are you managing what you consume?

   _____

All-in-One Workbook
316

"**Morte d'Arthur**" by Alfred, Lord Tennyson
Writing About the Big Question

Can anyone be a hero?

Big Question Vocabulary

attributes	character	conduct	courage	determination
honor	inherent	integrity	legendary	persevere
principles	resolute	responsibility	sacrifice	selflessness

A. *Use one or more words from the list above to complete each sentence.*

1. If your _____ is good in class, you will earn praise for listening and being respectful.

2. Marla's _____ skill at soccer was revealed when she played brilliantly with no practice.

3. I admire Jake's patience and kindness, _____ that make him a valued friend.

4. We made a poster stating the school's _____: Show Respect, Listen to Learn, and Stay Healthy.

B. *Follow the directions in responding to each of the items below.*

1. List two traits that you would expect to find in a king who is the leader of a group of knights. Answer in complete sentences.

_____

_____

2. Write two sentences describing one of those traits. Use at least two of the Big Question vocabulary words.

_____

_____

C. *Complete the sentence below. Then, write a short paragraph in which you connect this experience to the Big Question.*

A reader can more easily identify with a **legendary** hero who displays **attributes** such as _____

_____

_____

_____

_____ .

Name _____ Date _____

"**Morte d'Arthur**" by Alfred, Lord Tennyson
Literary Analysis: Legends

Legends are popular stories about the past that have been handed down for generations. Most legends have some basis in historical fact, which may be lost through centuries of retelling. Legends focus on the life and adventures of **legendary heroes,** or characters who are human yet "larger than life." Legends also show a deep concern with right and wrong, honorable actions, and national pride. Legends help shape a people's cultural identity and reflect the values of a community or nation.

A. DIRECTIONS: *Answer the following questions on the lines provided.*

1. How do you know that "Morte d'Arthur" is part of a legend?

   _____

   _____

2. How is the character of Arthur legendary? How is he ordinary? Why do you think the author chose to show Arthur as more legendary than ordinary?

   _____

   _____

   _____

   _____

3. What qualities do you think the author would say makes a person a hero? Why?

   _____

   _____

4. How do you think the legend of King Arthur and Camelot has influenced the culture and values of the United States? Give examples to support your answer.

   _____

   _____

   _____

   _____

B. DIRECTIONS: *In a brief essay, name and describe your personal hero. What makes this person a hero in your mind? Would your hero qualify to be a legendary hero? Why or why not?*

_____

_____

_____

_____

_____

_____

Name _____   Date _____

Reading: Identify Details to Compare and Contrast Worldviews

A **worldview** is the set of values and beliefs held by a culture. A worldview is expressed in the culture's literature. To fully understand a retelling of a legend, **compare and contrast** the worldviews it presents. Find similarities and differences between two different cultures—that of the original story and that of the person who retells the story. To do this, **identify details** that reveal characters' beliefs and their reasons for acting or feeling as they do. In addition, identify details that suggest the writer's attitudes. Then, **draw conclusions** from these details about the values and basic beliefs of the characters as well as those of the writer.

A. DIRECTIONS: *Fill in the Venn diagram to help you compare and contrast the worldviews of the characters in "Morte d'Arthur" (Arthur and Sir Bedivere) within those of the narrator (Everard Hall). Use details in the story to help you make educated guesses about the worldviews of the narrator (and his friends) and of the characters, as well as their reasons for acting or feeling as they do.*

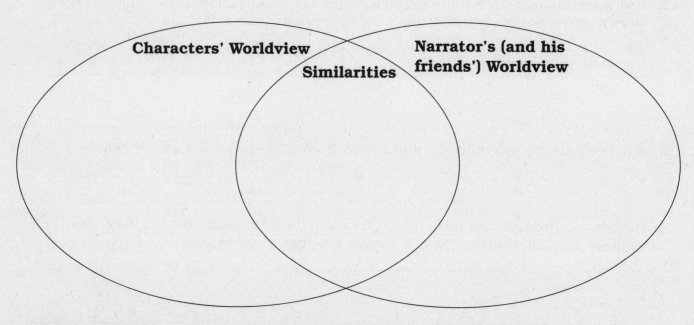

B. DIRECTIONS: *Use your Venn diagram to help you write a brief essay comparing and contrasting the values and beliefs of the characters' culture in the original story with those of the narrator, who represents the worldview of a much later time period.*

_____

_____

_____

_____

_____

_____

Name _____   Date _____

"**Morte d'Arthur**" by Alfred, Lord Tennyson
Vocabulary Builder

Word List

bore   brandished   disparagement   languid   reverence   wistfully

A. DIRECTIONS: *Write at least one synonym, at least one antonym, and an example sentence for each word. Synonyms and antonyms can be words or phrases.*

Word	Synonym	Antonym	Example Sentence
1. disparagement			
2. brandished			
3. languid			
4. bore			
5. reverence			
6. wistfully			

B. WORD STUDY: The Latin suffix *-ment* means "a state of," "act," "product," or "a means of." Answer the following questions using one of these words that contain the suffix *-ment: embarrassment, entertainment, contentment.*

1. Are you eager to show off what you have done if you show *embarrassment*?

   _____

2. If James provides *entertainment* at the party, will he present a show intended to amuse you?

   _____

3. If people find *contentment*, are they dissatisfied and unhappy with their lives?

   _____

"Morte d'Arthur" by Alfred, Lord Tennyson
"Arthur Becomes King of Britain" *from* **The Once and Future King** by T. H. White
Integrated Language Skills: Grammar

Using Commas Correctly

Use commas to separate three or more words, phrases, or clauses in a series.

> Sir Ector, Sir Kay, and Wart each try to pull the sword from the stone.

Use a comma before the coordinating conjunction (*and*, *but*, *or*, *nor*, *for*, *so*, and *yet*) that links two independent clauses in a compound sentence.

> Wart is the only one who can pull the sword out of the stone, so Sir Ector and Sir Kay kneel to their new king.

Use commas to set off introductory, parenthetical, and nonessential words, phrases, and clauses.

> Sir Bedivere, who is the last of Arthur's knights, carries his king to a mystical barge that will carry him to the afterlife.

A. PRACTICE: *Each sentence contains one or more comma errors. Correct the errors by inserting or deleting commas as necessary.*

1. King Pellinore, who loves attention tells his friends, about King Uther's death.
2. After Sir Ector, kneels to Wart he asks if Wart will make Sir Kay his seneschal.
3. Arthur, is dying of a terrible head wound but he faces his death bravely.
4. Because Arthur's reign was a time of knights chivalry and great deeds Sir Bedivere is very upset about the loss of King Arthur and Camelot.
5. Sir Bedivere sadly carries Arthur, to the lake where a mystical barge, is waiting to take Arthur to the afterlife.

B. Writing Application: *Write a paragraph about either "Arthur Becomes King of Britain" or "Morte d'Arthur." Use commas between items in a series, before the coordinating conjunction linking two independent clauses, and to set off introductory or parenthetical words, phrases, or clauses. Circle each comma that you use.*

_____

_____

_____

_____

_____

_____

_____

_____

Name _____ Date _____

"Morte d'Arthur" by Alfred, Lord Tennyson

"Arthur Becomes King of Britain" *from* **The Once and Future King** by T. H. White

Integrated Language Skills: Support for Writing a Script for a Television News Report

Use this graphic organizer to help you write a brief script for a television news report about Wart becoming king of England or the death of King Arthur. Refer to the story "Arthur Becomes King of England" or the poem "Morte d'Arthur" to help you answer the questions *Who? What? Where? When? Why?* and *How?*

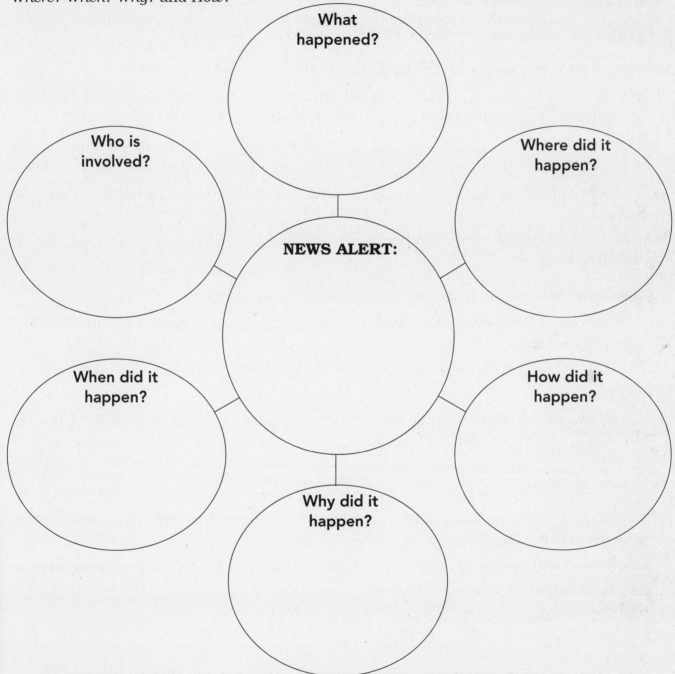

On a separate page, use your notes to outline and draft the script for your television news report about Wart becoming king of England or the death of King Arthur.

All-in-One Workbook

Name _____ Date _____

from **A Connecticut Yankee in King Arthur's Court** by Mark Twain
Writing About the Big Question

Can anyone be a hero?

Big Question Vocabulary

attributes	character	conduct	courage	determination
honor	inherent	integrity	legendary	persevere
principles	resolute	responsibility	sacrifice	selflessness

A. *Use one or more words from the list above to complete each sentence.*

1. If you are _____ about changing your study habits, you must follow your new schedule regardless of what others want you do to.

2. Dan handled the _____ of caring for the horses so well that he got a horse of his own.

3. The story of the _____ knight who slays dragons has been told for ages.

4. She always put the needs of others before her own, and her _____ was inspiring.

B. *Follow the directions in responding to each of the items below.*

1. List two ways in which a world leader could be considered a hero. Respond in complete sentences.

   _____

   _____

2. Write two sentences describing one of the situations you listed. Use at least two of the Big Question vocabulary words.

   _____

   _____

C. *Complete the sentence below. Then, write a short paragraph in which you connect this experience to the Big Question.*

When faced with seemingly insurmountable obstacles, a person with **determination** can unintentionally become a hero by _____

   _____

   _____

   _____

   _____.

Name _____ Date _____

from **A Connecticut Yankee in King Arthur's Court** by Mark Twain
Literary Analysis: Parody

A **parody** is a humorous work that imitates the style or ideas of other works in an exaggerated or a ridiculous way. Parody is a popular form of humor in television and music as well as literature. For example, many sketch comedy shows make use of parody by making fun of newscasts, political speeches, other television shows, well-known personalities, and so on. In music, artists such as "Weird Al" Yankovic substitute humorous lyrics for the real ones in popular music.

In literature, some authors choose to bring a comic element into their stories by imitating other writers or literary styles in humorous or exaggerated ways. Such is the case with Mark Twain's classic *A Connecticut Yankee in King Arthur's Court*, in which Twain mocks the style, story, and characters of the original Arthurian legends.

A. DIRECTIONS: *Fill in the Venn diagram by identifying characteristics of a traditional legendary hero and characteristics of Twain's hero Hank. In the overlapping section, write the characteristics that Hank shares with traditional heroes.*

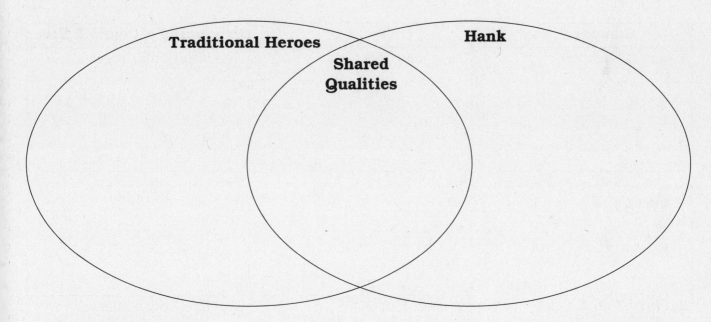

B. DIRECTIONS: *Using the information from your Venn diagram, explain in what ways Hank is a parody of a traditional literary hero and in what ways he is a genuine hero. Then, explain why you think Twain chose to portray Hank this way.*

_____

_____

_____

_____

_____

_____

_____

Name _____ Date _____

from **A Connecticut Yankee in King Arthur's Court** by Mark Twain
Reading: Compare and Contrast to Understand Worldviews

A serious work of literature reflects the writer's **worldview,** or basic beliefs and values. In a parody of the work, another writer may portray this worldview as an illusion, or a set of false beliefs.

When Mark Twain wrote his story of an unwilling time traveler, he knew that his readers would consider his work in the light of what they already knew—their own worldview as well as their understanding of the worldview of Arthurian legend. In fact, Twain depended upon readers making such comparisons for much of the comedy of the novel.

As you read this selection from *A Connecticut Yankee*, look for scenes in which you can **compare and contrast** the world in the book to the world you know.

DIRECTIONS: *Use this chart to help compare and contrast worldviews within and outside the story. List qualities of the topic in the first column to compare or contrast to the topic in the second column. In the third column, write how or why the comparison or contrast is comic.*

Compare . . .	To . . .	Producing a Comic Effect
1. Hank's Reactions	Clarence's Reactions	Describe Comic Effect
2. The Crowd's Belief About the Eclipse	Reality	Describe Comic Effect
3. Era of King Arthur	Modern Era	Describe Comic Effect
4. Merlin	Hank	Describe Comic Effect

Name _____ Date _____

from **A Connecticut Yankee in King Arthur's Court** by Mark Twain
Vocabulary Builder

Word List

calamity   conspicuous   contrive   multitudes   plight   rudiments

A. DIRECTIONS: *Write one example of people or things that demonstrate the meaning of each Word List word, following the example below.*

RUDIMENTS
* simple cooking tasks, such as boiling an egg

1. CALAMITY

   _____

2. MULTITUDES

   _____

3. PLIGHT

   _____

4. CONTRIVE

   _____

5. CONSPICUOUS

   _____

B. WORD STUDY: The Latin prefix *multi-* means "many" or "much." Answer the following questions using one of these words that contain the prefix *multi-: multiple, multicultural, multilingual.*

1. When we joined *multiple* clubs, did we limit ourselves to just one?

   _____

2. If your history project is *multicultural*, are you studying a single culture?

   _____

3. Are *multilingual* people comfortable speaking many languages?

   _____

from **Don Quixote** by Miguel de Cervantes
Writing About the Big Question

Can anyone be a hero?

Big Question Vocabulary

attributes	character	conduct	courage	determination
honor	inherent	integrity	legendary	persevere
principles	resolute	responsibility	sacrifice	selflessness

A. *Use one or more words from the list above to complete each sentence.*

1. Her most appealing _____ are her ability to make everyone feel at ease and her good sense of humor.

2. The _____ coach attended the game and received a special award to honor his illustrious career.

3. Those who serve in the military are willing to _____ their lives for our country.

B. *Follow the directions in responding to each of the items below.*

1. Which two characteristics of a hero would you most like to have? Respond in complete sentences.

   _____

   _____

2. Write two sentences describing one of the characteristics you listed, and explain why it is appealing to you. Use at least two of the Big Question vocabulary words.

   _____

   _____

C. *Complete the sentences below. Then, write a short paragraph in which you connect this experience to the Big Question.*

Someone dreaming about being a **legendary** hero might imagine that _____

_____.

However, the most useful **attributes** for a hero might really be _____

_____

_____

_____

_____.

Name _____ Date _____

from **Don Quixote** by Miguel de Cervantes
Literary Analysis: Parody

A **parody** is a humorous work that imitates the style or ideas of other works in an exaggerated or a ridiculous way. Parody is a popular form of humor in television and music as well as literature. For example, many sketch comedy shows make use of parody by making fun of newscasts, political speeches, other television shows, well-known personalities, and so on. In music, artists such as "Weird Al" Yankovic substitute humorous lyrics for the real ones in popular music.

In literature, some authors choose to bring a comic element into their stories by imitating other writers or literary styles in humorous or exaggerated ways. Such is the case with Miguel de Cervantes's classic *Don Quixote*, in which the author mocks the style of medieval romances.

DIRECTIONS: *Rewrite each of the following passages in simple, straightforward language. Use a dictionary and a thesaurus as necessary to help you rewrite the passages.*

1. But there were none [books of chivalry] he liked so well as those written by the famous Feliciano de Silva, for their lucidity of style and complicated conceits were as pearls in his sight. . . .

   _____

   _____

   _____

   _____

   _____

2. He fancied that it was right . . . that he should make a knight-errant of himself, roaming the world over in full armor and on horseback in quest of adventures.

   _____

   _____

   _____

   _____

3. Those are giants, and if you are afraid, away with you out of here and betake yourself to prayer, while I engage them in fierce and unequal combat.

   _____

   _____

   _____

   _____

   _____

All-in-One Workbook
328

Name _____   Date _____

from **Don Quixote** by Miguel de Cervantes

Reading: Compare and Contrast to Understand Worldviews

A serious work of literature reflects the writer's **worldview,** or basic beliefs and values. In a parody of the work, another writer may portray this worldview as an illusion, or a set of false beliefs.

When Miguel de Cervantes wrote his story of a comical knight, he knew that his readers would consider his work in the light of what they already knew—their own worldview as well as their understanding of the worldview of medieval chivalry. In fact, Cervantes depended upon readers making such comparisons for much of the comedy of the novel.

As you read this selection from *Don Quixote,* look for scenes in which you can **compare and contrast** the world in the book to the world you know. For example, Quixote's best efforts at equipping himself as a knight become comic as the old man comes up with a cardboard helmet, rusty armor, and a broken-down nag for a steed.

DIRECTIONS: *Use this chart to help you compare and contrast worldviews within and outside the story. List qualities of the topic in the first column to compare or contrast to the topic in the second column. In the third column, write how or why the comparison or contrast is comic.*

Compare . . .	To . . .	Producing What Kind of Comic Effect?
1. Sancho Panza	Don Quixote	Describe Comic Effect
2. Quixote's Vision	Reality	Describe Comic Effect
3. Era of Knighthood	Modern Era	Describe Comic Effect
4. Narrator's Language	Plain Speech	Describe Comic Effect

Name _____ Date _____

from **Don Quixote** by Miguel de Cervantes
Vocabulary Builder

Word List

affable   extolled   ingenuity   lucidity   sonorous   veracious

A. DIRECTIONS: *Write one example of people or things that demonstrate the meaning of each Word List word, following the example below.*

LUCIDITY
• a teacher explaining a new concept very clearly to a class

1. SONOROUS
_____

2. EXTOLLED
_____

3. AFFABLE
_____

4. INGENUITY
_____

5. VERACIOUS
_____

B. WORD STUDY: The Latin prefix *ex-* means "out, beyond, from, out of, forth." Answer the following questions using one of these words that contain the prefix *ex-*: *export, expelled, extract.*

1. If you *export* a product, are you sending it away?
_____
_____

2. Will a child who gets *expelled* from school go home or to class?
_____
_____

3. If your dentist is going to *extract* a tooth, will that tooth remain in your mouth?
_____
_____

from **A Connecticut Yankee in King Arthur's Court** by Mark Twain
from **Don Quixote** by Miguel de Cervantes
Integrated Language Skills: Grammar

Using Semicolons

Use a semicolon to join independent clauses not already joined by a coordinating conjunction (*and, but, or, nor, for, so,* and *yet*).

> Don Quixote read countless books about knights and chivalry; he decided he wanted to become a knight himself.

Use semicolons to separate items in a series that already contain commas.

> Characters in *A Connecticut Yankee in King Arthur's Court* include Hank, an unwilling time traveler; Clarence, one of Arthur's subjects; King Arthur, the legendary hero; and Merlin, the king's magician.

A. PRACTICE: *Use a semicolon to combine each pair of sentences.*

1. Sancho Panza is Don Quixote's squire. Sancho follows Don Quixote because it amuses him to do so.

   _____

   _____

2. Don Quixote believes Sancho is a simple-minded peasant. In truth, Sancho has far more common sense than Don Quixote.

   _____

   _____

3. Hank is in King Arthur's dungeon. Hank is to be burned at the stake the next day.

   _____

4. Hank convinces the king and his court that he is a powerful magician. Hank pretends to cause a total eclipse of the sun.

   _____

   _____

B. Writing Application: *Write a paragraph responding to either* Don Quixote *or* A Connecticut Yankee. *Use at least three semicolons to either combine independent clauses or to separate items in a series that already contain commas. Circle each semicolon that you use.*

_____

_____

_____

_____

_____

_____

_____

from **A Connecticut Yankee in King Arthur's Court** by Mark Twain
from **Don Quixote** by Miguel de Cervantes
Integrated Language Skills: Support for Writing a Parody

Use the following graphic organizer to help create a situation and basic plot for your parody in which a twenty-first-century time traveler finds him- or herself in King Arthur's world, or Don Quixote takes on a twenty-first-century challenge. For the major events of the story, be sure to show both the reality of what is happening and the illusion in the characters' minds. Then, on a separate page, write a first draft of your parody.

Introduction: What is the situation the time traveler or Don Quixote faces?

REALITY	ILLUSION

Rising Action: What are some events that lead up to the big event?

REALITY	ILLUSION

Climax and Resolution: What is the big event, and how is it resolved?

REALITY	ILLUSION

Falling Action and Ending: What events help wrap things up?

REALITY	ILLUSION

"Damon and Python" retold by William F. Russell
"Two Friends" by Guy de Maupassant
Writing About the Big Question

 Can anyone be a hero?

Big Question Vocabulary

attributes	character	conduct	courage	determination
honor	inherent	integrity	legendary	persevere
principles	resolute	responsibility	sacrifice	selflessness

A. *Use one or more words from the list above to complete each sentence.*

1. The soldiers showed great _____ when they climbed the hill during the battle.

2. We _____ those who served in the military on Veterans Day.

3. Her _____ was so strong that she kept trying and finally cooked a perfect meal.

4. Jeff's _____ good nature allowed him to see the humor in many situations.

B. *Follow the directions in responding to each of the items below.*

1. Think about heroic characters or people you have read or heard about throughout history. List two of them. Answer in complete sentences.

   _____

   _____

2. Write two sentences describing one of the people on your list, explaining why you think he or she is a hero. Use at least two of the Big Question vocabulary words.

   _____

C. *Complete the sentence below. Then, write a short paragraph in which you connect this experience to the Big Question.*

   A hero is a person who _____

   _____

   _____

   _____

   _____

   _____ .

"Damon and Pythias" retold by William F. Russell
"Two Friends" by Guy de Maupassant
Literary Analysis: Theme and Worldview

The **theme** of a literary work is the central message or insight that it conveys. Many themes are **universal,** or found in the literature of different times and places. For example, the danger of greed is a universal theme. At the same time, a particular writer's expression of a theme will reflect a specific **worldview**—the basic beliefs and values that shape the writer's experience and outlook.

DIRECTIONS: *Read each of the passages below. Then, answer the questions that follow.*

"Damon and Pythias"

Pythias, breathless and exhausted, rushed headlong through the crowd and flung himself into the arms of his beloved friend, sobbing with relief that he had, by the grace of the gods, arrived in time to save Damon's life.

This final exhibition of devoted love and faithfulness was more than even the stony heart of Dionysius, the tyrant, could resist. As the throng of spectators melted into tears at the companions' embrace, the king approached the pair and declared that Pythias was hereby pardoned and his death sentence canceled.

"Two Friends"

"Quick, the password? Your friend won't know. I'll pretend to relent."

Morissot answered not a word.

The Prussian drew M. Sauvage aside and put the same question.

M. Sauvage did not answer.

They stood side by side again.

And the officer began to give commands. The soldiers raised their rifles. . . .

They shook hands, trembling from head to foot with a shudder which they could not control. The officer shouted, "Fire!"

The twelve shots rang out together.

1. What universal theme or idea about friendship is expressed in both passages?

   _____

   _____

2. A. Which passage depicts the world as just? _____

   B. With this worldview in mind, what theme about friendship does the passage express?

   _____

   _____

3. A. Which passage depicts the world as unjust? _____

   B. With this worldview in mind, what theme about friendship does the passage express?

   _____

   _____

"Damon and Pythias" retold by William F. Russell
"Two Friends" by Guy de Maupassant
Vocabulary Builder

Word List

ardent   dire   impediments   jauntiness   relent   serenity

A. DIRECTIONS: *Create two different sentences for each of the following words. You may use a different form of the vocabulary word in your second sentence.*

Example: Plant-eating pests are *impediments* to maintaining a healthy garden.
Frequent snack breaks may *impede* one's progress when studying.

1. ardent

   A. _____

   B. _____

2. relent

   A. _____

   B. _____

3. serenity

   A. _____

   B. _____

4. jauntiness

   A. _____

   B. _____

5. dire

   A. _____

   B. _____

B. DIRECTIONS: *On the line, write the letter of the word that is most nearly* opposite *in meaning to the word in CAPITAL LETTERS.*

_____ 1. ARDENT:

     A. indifferent   B. generous   C. confused   D. confident

_____ 2. JAUNTINESS:

     A. carelessness   B. restlessness   C. seriousness   D. fearlessness

_____ 3. DIRE:

     A. uncertain   B. indistinct   C. bothersome   D. inconsequential

_____ 4. SERENITY:

     A. panic   B. hesitation   C. ignorance   D. meaninglessness

_____ 5. IMPEDIMENTS:

     A. facillitators   B. solutions   C. activities   D. rewards

_____ 6. RELENT:

     A. rebuild   B. gather   C. persist   D. tighten

"Damon and Pythias" retold by William F. Russell
"Two Friends" by Guy de Maupassant
Support for Writing to Compare Literary Works

Before you draft your essay evaluating the themes and worldviews reflected in "Damon and Pythias" and "Two Friends," record your notes in the following chart.

Which story presents friendship more realistically?

Quotations or examples:

Which story does a better job of teaching a clear, inspiring lesson?

Quotations or examples:

Which story does a better job of showing the forces opposing friendship?

Quotations or examples:

Which worldview is closer to your own perspective? How so?

Now, use your notes to write an essay in which you evaluate the themes and worldviews presented in the two stories.

Tips for Improving Your Reading Fluency

You've probably heard the expression "Practice makes perfect." Through your own experiences, you know that practice improves all types of skills. If you play a guitar, you know that practicing has made you a better player. The same is true for sports, for crafts, and for reading. The following tips will help you to practice skills that will lead to reading **fluency**—the ability to read easily, smoothly, and expressively.

Choose your practice materials carefully.

Make reading fun! Make a list of subjects that interest you. Then, search for reading materials—books, magazines, newspapers, reliable Web sites. As you learn more about your interests, you will also be practicing your reading skills.

Choose your practice space and time carefully.

Help your concentration skills. Find a quiet, comfortable place to read—away from the television and other distractions. Get in the habit of treating yourself to an hour of pleasure reading every day—apart from homework and other tasks. Reading about interesting topics in a quiet, comfortable place will provide both pleasure and relaxation.

Practice prereading strategies.

A movie preview gives viewers a good idea about what the movie will be about. Before you read, create your own preview of what you plan to read. Look at pictures and captions, subheads, and diagrams. As you scan, look for unfamiliar words. Find out what those words mean before you start reading.

Use punctuation marks.

Think of punctuation marks as stop signs. For example, the period at the end of a sentence signals the end of a complete thought. From time to time in your reading, stop at that stop sign. Reread the sentence. Summarize the complete thought in your own words.

Read aloud.

Use your voice and your ears as well as your eyes. Read phrases and sentences expressively. Pause at commas and periods. Show emphasis in your voice when you come to an exclamation point. Let your voice naturally rise at the end of a question. If possible, record your reading. Then listen to the recording, noting your pacing and expression.

Pause to ask questions.

Stop reading after a short amount of time (for example, five minutes) or at the end of a meaty paragraph. Look away from the text. Ask yourself questions—What are the main ideas? What message does the author want me to get? What might happen next? If the answers seem unclear, reread—either silently or aloud. Find the answers!

Use what you know.

As you read an informational article, think about what you already know about the topic. Use your knowledge and ideas as background information. Doing so will help you to understand new ideas. As you read fiction or a personal narrative, think about your own experiences. If you have been in a situation that is similar to that of a fictional character, you will be better able to understand his or her feelings, actions, and goals.

Talk about it.

Ask a friend or family member to read what you have read. Take turns reading aloud together, listening to both content and expression. Then discuss what you read. Share, compare, and contrast your ideas. Doing so will reinforce your knowledge of the content of what you read, and may provide new and interesting perspectives about the topic.

Name _____ Date _____

Reading Fluency Assessment Passage 1

Are you interested in discovering information about your ancestors? Perhaps you'd find out that you're descended from royalty, a military hero, or a famous artist. Alternatively, you'll probably discover that like the majority of us, you are descended from honest, hard-working "ordinary" people without fame or fortune. Many people are[50] curious about their family's history, considering it an identity treasure hunt.

As an amateur genealogist, you should follow some fundamental steps for unlocking family history. Begin by creating a chart containing everything you already know, such as birthdates of your immediate family members; then continue on, including the names and[100] birthdates of your grandparents as well. Then, once you have documented everything you know, begin asking questions.

If possible, interview your eldest family members, because they will have the most information to share. Prior to each interview, think about what information you hope to gain, listing specific fact-finding questions. Gather[150] photographs to spark your relative's memories and inspire further discussion. Be certain to bring along a notepad and pencil; better yet, bring an audio or video recorder.

During the interview, don't be discouraged if your relative begins to share memories that are not specifically related to your questions. Listen intently,[200] because many people have uncovered cherished family stories simply by letting memories flow naturally.

After conducting your interviews, track down family documents, including birth certificates, marriage licenses, and death certificates. Make sure to store them in a safe place, and make notes regarding important events and dates.

Once you have[250] recorded your initial research, broaden your search to include libraries, governmental records, and genealogical websites. You are sure to be surprised by what you uncover during your "identity treasure hunt!"[280]

Check Your Understanding

1. When doing genealogical research, most people discover that they have famous ancestors.

   True / False? Explain:

   _____

2. During an interview, why is it important not to interrupt someone who begins to share memories that are not directly related to your questions?

   _____

   _____

1090L

Name _____ Date _____

Reading Fluency Assessment Passage 2

Do you believe we live in the only possible universe? Several science fiction writers suggest that there could be many other existing worlds, often called "parallel" or "alternate" universes.

Some writers create alternate universes that are comically upside-down. Rules that are valid in our world are nonsense in these strange[50] worlds. A famous example is Lewis Carroll's *Alice's Adventures in Wonderland*, where, after falling down a rabbit hole, Alice is beset by weird characters and events. Characters in Wonderland are constantly contradicting the logic of our world. For example, at a trial, the Queen of Hearts demands that the jury[100] announce the sentence before the verdict.

Other science fiction writers create alternate universes more somber in tone. In the trilogy *His Dark Materials*, Philip Pullman describes how characters learn to move in and out of a number of parallel worlds. In one of the worlds, every character's soul has a[150] visible, animal form. So, think about what might happen in another world. What new identity would your soul inhabit—perhaps a rhinoceros, an alligator, a friendly horse, or a puppy?

Some writers use the word *multiverse* to describe all the universes that exist. There may or may not be an[200] intelligent life form overseeing what happens in every universe, guiding events and actions. Often, writers suggest that interactions between universes can have hazardous results, leading to severe problems.

Another kind of alternate universe is a fictional past, in which writers create an intriguing past for our planet. For[250] example, a writer might describe a time when flying rabbits populated the earth. Another writer might invent a medieval world in which electricity was discovered. Although events like this are fictional, they could be absolutely accurate in an alternate universe similar to ours![283]

1100L

Check Your Understanding

1. An alternative universe is one in which things occur in ways that are different from what we are accustomed to on Earth.

True / False? Explain:

_____

2. In a different universe in which you had an animal identity, which animal would you be? Explain.

_____

_____

_____

Reading Fluency Assessment Passage 3

Preparing for the Young Inventors' Forum, Jennifer didn't want to reveal her invention to anyone. She felt anxious as she dragged her computer files into innocent-looking folders, trying desperately to be certain that her notes were secure. Jennifer promised herself that she would relax at the end of this challenging[50] day, because finally she would make her work public.

Jennifer was part of an elite group of high-school students gathered from across the country to take part in a special science program focused on inventions. Her high-school colleagues in the Young Inventors' Forum had worked on what might be called[100] "everyday" innovations. For example, Roberta worked on improving the durability of old-fashioned linoleum floors. Gregory worked on easy-to-wear water packs for quenching athletes' thirst. Rebecca and Manuel worked together on various innovations in athletic shoes.

Jennifer had decided to base her project on inventions that could truly help the world.[150] To that end, she was trying to figure out a better way to store radioactive waste. She knew all about the by-products of nuclear energy, and she also knew that it could be definitely dangerous to keep high-level waste stored in containers that were currently available.

Jennifer had come up[200] with a solution, but she worried that it wouldn't be accepted. Who would believe that a high-school student could solve a problem that had vexed scientists for decades? Jennifer was ready to present her work, but she feared that someone would get into her files and take credit for her[250] ideas. Roberta and Gregory thought she was being silly, but they pledged to help her secure her files. With their help, Jennifer stayed as calm as she could as the day of the Young Inventors' Forum dawned.[287]

1110L

Check Your Understanding

1. The primary goal of all students at the Young Inventors' Forum was to solve the problem of radioactive waste.

True / False? Explain:

_____

2. If you were Jennifer's friend, what would you do to help her stay calm as she waited for the judges' decision? Explain why your idea would be helpful.

_____

_____

_____

Reading Fluency Assessment Passage 4

The phoenix is a fictional bird that was featured in the myths of many ancient cultures, including Egypt, Greece, Rome, Persia, and China. Like the dragon and other mythical beasts, the phoenix appears frequently on ancient temples and shrines. According to legend, the bird lived for 1,400 years, after which[50] it became tired and old. When it came time for the phoenix to die, the bird created a nest of dried-up wood and sweet-smelling spices. Then it set the nest on fire and was consumed in the flames. As the fire illuminated the surrounding area with brightness, a miracle occurred: [100] A new phoenix mysteriously rose from the flames. After that, like clockwork every 1,400 years, a phoenix would die and be reborn in flames.

Scholars are faced with many perplexing questions regarding the meaning of this mythical bird. Did ancient people consider the phoenix a frightening creature, like a dragon[150]? Most experts believe instead that the phoenix was an ancient symbol of eternal life, and they interpret the story of its rebirth as soothing rather than troubling. Other experts suggest that the phoenix myth is one that ancient people might have used to explain the passage of a day. Like[200] a day, the phoenix begins with the rising sun and dies in a blazing sunset, to be reborn at the next sunrise. The experts point out that the bird's wings, which are usually portrayed as red and gold, suggest the rising sun.

The legend of the phoenix, which is more[250] than a thousand years old, has had surprising staying power, in many different cultures. In our own country, the myth is the basis for the name given to Phoenix, the capital city of Arizona. Like the fabulous bird, this city blazes with light—from the hot southwestern sun.[298]

1110L

Check Your Understanding

1. The phoenix was never a real bird.
True / False? Explain:

_____

2. Summarize the relationship that some scholars see between the cycle of the phoenix and the passage of a day.

_____

_____

_____

Reading Fluency Assessment Passage 5

When Roberto and his crew began to work on the new apartment building, the bare lot looked barren and empty. As bulldozers began to level and dig, however, the crew discovered an extraordinary amount of wildlife. They were surprised that so many communities of living things could exist in the[50] shadow of a neighboring skyscraper. Naturally, there were insects, spiders, and worms, but in networks of elaborate underground tunnels there were also moles and at least one family of groundhogs. On overhead telephone wires, pigeons seemed to be keeping surveillance on the project.

One evening at dusk, Roberto spied a[100] parade of rats as they scurried by the construction trailer, apparently looking for dinner. While the rest of the animals might head to another lot, Roberto knew that these unauthorized tenants would be hard to remove. The next day he tried to enlist help from his crew to set humane[150] traps and relocate the rodents to open fields outside the city. When, instead, they threatened to just poison the rats and be done with it, Roberto became infuriated.

"Think about how this will be transformed," Roberto said to the crew. "Instead of tiny animals and weeds, this place will be[200] swarming with people. I'm not sure that's an improvement."

"What do you think will happen to all these living things?" asked William, one of the carpenters. Roberto predicted that the pigeons would stay nearby, and, unless the developers hired an exterminator, the rats would also stay put. The crew had[250] to agree that it was amazing to consider all of the life that existed in a city that, at first glance, seemed to be only for humans.[277]

1120L

Check Your Understanding

1. Roberto and his crew were clearing the lot to build a city park.

True / False? Explain:

_____

2. What appreciation do you think the construction crew gained from their discovery of all the animals? Explain.

_____

_____

Name _____ Date _____

Reading Fluency Assessment Passage 6

Rome is a city that is famously overrun by cats. These animals are not like the domestic housecats living in homes throughout the United States; instead, they are often feral, or wild. They live outdoors, among the ruins of ancient Rome. It is not uncommon to see several cats sunning[50] themselves on the crumbling marble pillars of the Roman Forum. Many people—residents, tourists, and even waiters in restaurants—leave food for the cats. They are also very resourceful, and hunt on their own for mice, lizards, and pigeons.

Some people love to see these cats and are reluctant to[100] remove them from their urban homes. In fact, cats living in three of Rome's historic sites have been named part of Rome's "bio-heritage" by the city council. At these sites, there are cat sanctuaries where volunteers regularly stop by to feed and care for the felines.

Other people, however, feel[150] that the population of stray cats is a burden to the city. They worry that these scruffy animals might spread disease, and they see little distinction between the cats and common pests like rats and other rodents.

Despite the strong feelings of the anti-cat contingent, cats in Italy are supposed[200] to be protected by laws; therefore, the cats cannot be euthanized if they are healthy. Furthermore, because of the huge population of Rome's feral cats, officials have often found it futile to try to control their numbers. Nonetheless, veterinarians at the sanctuaries have begun to spay and neuter the cats[250] so that the population won't continue to grow, and they also encourage people to adopt healthy young kittens. Eventually, they hope to make the famous feral cats of Rome as healthy and well cared for as they deserve to be.[290]

1120L

Check Your Understanding

1. All cats that are *feral* are
   a. Roman.
   b. wild.
   c. house pets.
   d. diseased.

2. Explain why people have mixed feelings about the cats of Rome.

   _____
   _____
   _____

Reading Fluency Assessment Passage 7

About five hundred years ago, Spanish explorers brought the first horses to North America. These horses, considered at the time to be the finest horses in the world, were called Spanish Mustangs. They would become extremely important to several Native American groups, especially the Blackfeet.

The Blackfeet lived on the[50] broad Plains that stretched across the North American continent. They were extremely dependent on buffalo, elk, and deer, which they hunted on foot, often following herds of game for miles before making a kill. Each slaughtered animal provided meat, and its hide provided material for clothing and tipis, shelters that[100] the Blackfeet took with them on their hunting excursions.

When the Blackfeet obtained Spanish Mustangs, they soon discovered that these incredible animals could enable them to move faster during their hunts; they could drag wooden frames containing tipis and slaughtered carcasses; and they helped the Blackfeet defend themselves against their[150] enemies with more confidence, strength, and speed.

In the nineteenth century, when buffalo became scarce and European Americans began moving westward, the Blackfeet, like many Native American groups, had to change their ways. After the United States government claimed their lands, the Blackfeet moved to reservations. Their beloved horses were[200] taken away in order to prevent the Blackfeet from straying back to their lands.

Today, Spanish Mustangs live again with the Blackfeet. In 1994, Robert Blackbull, a Blackfoot teacher, received a Mustang stallion as a gift; he later bought six mares, and he now has a herd of more than[250] a hundred horses on the reservation. Blackbull has established the Blackfeet Buffalo Horse Coalition, an organization that uses these powerful horses to connect Blackfeet youth to the culture of their ancestors. Robert Blackbull calls his Spanish Mustangs "the pride of the past, and the hope of the future."[298]

1150L

Check Your Understanding

1. The Spanish Mustangs helped the Blackfeet

   a. hunt more rapidly.

   b. defend against enemies.

   c. haul supplies and portable shelters.

   d. all of the above.

2. What benefits and terrible problems did the Blackfeet get from European and American settlers?

   _____

   _____

Reading Fluency Assessment Passage 8

The origin of the term *Yankee* has been the subject of considerable and lasting debate for several years. Some historians believe that the word comes from the Dutch name *Janke* (YAHN-kay), while others suggest that it comes from the Dutch nickname *Jan Kaas* (YAHN KAHS),which was first used to describe[50] Dutch pirates in the Caribbean Sea.

Regardless of its origin, people began to use the term *Yankee* to describe people of North America. At first, it was an insulting term. Prior to the American Revolution, British General James Wolfe used it to express malice toward the American colonists. However, the[100] term eventually took on a more positive meaning.

Mark Twain defined a Yankee as a resident of New England, particularly someone who is clever enough to find solutions to difficult problems. A Yankee also came to mean someone who is extremely thrifty, wasting nothing and using every resource wisely.

The[150] phrase *Yankee ingenuity* describes the ability to contrive an effective solution with whatever resources are available. For example, suppose a farmer made the distressing discovery that his dog knocked over an old shed. The farmer might turn this difficult situation into an advantage by using the wood from the[200] shed to build a new doghouse.

No matter how impressive or clever the solution or invention is, a good Yankee never boasts. This lack of bragging might make it appear that a Yankee does things meekly. However, a Yankee has a strong sense of pride hiding under the outer appearance[250] of modesty. Still, a Yankee often does things with an air of solemnity, as though each action is grave and important. To counter this serious side, most Yankees have a dry sense of humor.[284]

1160L

Check Your Understanding

1. Which of these characteristics does *not* apply to the traditional image of a "Yankee"?

   a. thriftiness

   b. dry humor

   c. pride

   d. modesty

2. What message did the author intend to send by using the example of the farmer, the shed, and the doghouse?

   _____

   _____

All-in-One Workbook: Reading Fluency Assessment
346

Reading Fluency Assessment Passage 9

One afternoon, Alan takes a bike ride that brings him to an old cemetery in the woods. When he walks through the gates, he's surprised by how far the cemetery extends, like a neighborhood that consists of headstones rather than homes. Toward the front of the cemetery, he sees giant[50] stone monuments that tower above him, and he pauses to gaze at a huge marble angel with its wings spread fully, every feather revealed.

As he walks further into the cemetery, Alan enters a wide expanse of World War II graves. This section is far less fancy than the first[100] one. It contains just row after row of ordinary stones inscribed with name, military rank, date of birth, date of death. These dull, official stones that seem to have been mass-produced in a factory make Alan think about how many soldiers must have died in the war and how little[150] we know about them now. He wonders what his own headstone will say, or his father's. Most of the people Alan knows will never be able to afford fancy headstones. They have more important things to pay for, like rent and groceries. But Alan figures that as long as people[200] are happy they have no cause for complaint, even if they can't afford extras like fancy headstones.

Alan notices a very old headstone that has started to lean toward the ground. It's so worn by age that he can't decipher its inscription. He worries that eventually the stone will crumble[250] into nothing, so he bends down to pull it back into its proper upright position. But then he decides that maybe it belongs the way it is, leaning. Perhaps he shouldn't interfere, trying to alter the past. He heads back to his bicycle without disturbing anything else.[297]

1170L

Check Your Understanding

1. Alan feels that the soldiers' headstones are more beautiful than the huge stone monuments.

   a. True
   b. False

3. Why is Alan not concerned about having a fancy headstone on his own grave?

   _____

   _____

Reading Fluency Assessment Passage 10

Among the most dreadful catastrophes in European history was the outbreak of a disease called bubonic plague, or black death. Between the years 1347 and 1352, the plague killed about 25 million Europeans, or one out of every three people.

In times of plague, a church bell rang to announce[50] a person's death. Understanding that can help readers appreciate the line by the poet John Donne, "Ask not for whom the bell tolls, it tolls for thee." In other words, the bell that rings to announce one man's death will soon be ringing for another's.

Historians believe that the first[100] major outbreak of bubonic plague occurred in China during the 1330s. At the time, China had most of the world's busiest trading ports. Bubonic plague is spread by fleas, which infect the rats on which they live. Because rats can survive on ships, they can roam almost anywhere in the[150] world. The rats that brought bubonic plague to Europe came in the holds of merchant ships sailing from China.

Plague is a bacterial infection. It spread rapidly throughout Europe, probably due to flea bites and the infected clothing of victims. Symptoms include swelling of the lymph nodes, high fever, and[200] rose-colored blotches on the skin that eventually turn black. There was no known treatment or cure during the Middle Ages. Therefore, people naturally grew desperate when the first symptoms appeared. However, the rose-colored blotches that sufferers took so seriously gave rise to a nursery rhyme sung as a jest, "Ring[250] Around the Rosy."

Bubonic plague is rare in modern times. It can be prevented by controlling fleas on pets and other animals, and, if symptoms are recognized early enough, it can be successfully treated with antibiotics.[286]

1180L

Check Your Understanding

1. In the Middle Ages, bubonic plague

    a. was treated with herbs.
    b. was treated with antibiotics.
    c. was spread by flea bites.
    d. was a serious virus.

2. Faced with this terrible, fast-spreading disease, why might people have made up the jest, "Ring Around the Rosy"?

    _____
    _____
    _____

Reading Fluency Assessment Passage 11

The career of the writer James Thurber is almost inseparable from the famous magazine *The New Yorker*, which published so much of his work. The relationship began in 1930, when the magazine printed one of Thurber's comic drawings. At *The New Yorker*, Thurber found a perfect home for his particular[50] brand of comedy. Perhaps his crowning achievement there was the famous short story "The Secret Life of Walter Mitty." It was first published in *The New Yorker* in 1939.

Many critics feel that "The Secret Life of Walter Mitty" is a perfect example of Thurber's humor. Walter Mitty is a[100] mild-mannered husband who is prone to daydreams and is always at the mercy of his far more practical, rather annoying wife. Their day-to-day existence is full of disagreements based on their different personalities. One day, Walter drives his wife to an appointment to get her hair done. Then he proceeds[150] to do a series of errands that she has ordered him to do. Along the way, he leaves the dull reality of his humdrum life and escapes into a series of fantastic daydreams of a more dramatic and adventurous life. Instead of a henpecked husband, he imagines himself as a[200] fearless pilot, a skilled surgeon, and several other extremely vital men. Many years after appearing in *The New Yorker*, this very funny story was made into a popular movie starring comedian Danny Kaye.

Thurber went on to publish many more cartoons and stories. To many people, his funniest story of[250] all is "The Night the Bed Fell." This story, as well as "The Secret Life of Walter Mitty" and countless others by Thurber, can be found in many anthologies of short stories.[282]

1190L

Check Your Understanding

1. *The New Yorker* published James Thurber's

   a. stories and cartoons

   b. dramas and essays

   c. stories and columns

   d. letters and stories

2. What do you think led Walter Mitty to enjoy his daydreams? Explain, using details from the passage.

   _____

   _____

   _____

Reading Fluency Assessment Passage 12

After Thanksgiving dinner, Gerald spent some time with his grandfather, looking at his collection of World War II souvenirs.

"You probably won't recognize me in this picture," his grandfather said, handing him an old, framed black and white photograph of himself as a young soldier. In the picture, he was[50] still in his twenties, with a full head of dark hair and a face as handsome as that of a movie actor. He leaned into the frame, one hand on his friend's shoulder, as if he had just lurched into the picture at the last second, stumbling into place right[100] before it was taken.

He had been a lieutenant, he told Gerald, serving in the military under a general named Peterson. General Peterson disliked having his picture taken, and so Gerald's grandfather had no photographs to share, but he did tell Gerald a brief story about him. Once, the general[150] came down with pneumonia, a kind of lung infection, but even from his hospital bed he continued to issue orders. "It didn't slow him down a bit," said Gerald's grandfather. "He just turned his bed into an office and had us all working in his hospital room." One day, for[200] a joke, Gerald's grandfather brought the general a get-well present: a megaphone so that he could shout orders instead of merely speaking them.

As funny as the story was, Gerald knew that his grandfather had done more than just joke around during the war. Among other photographs and documents, he[250] found two official letters, citations congratulating his grandfather for his valiant conduct in battle. They commended him for his bravery in rescuing a fellow soldier while under enemy fire.[279]

1200L

Check Your Understanding

1. Gerald's grandfather served as a lieutenant in the Korean War.

   True / False? Explain:

   _____

2. Based on the events and descriptions in this passage, describe what type of person Gerald's grandfather was as a young soldier.

   _____

   _____

Name _____ Date _____

Screening Test

Directions: Read the following passage. Then answer the questions. On the answer sheet, fill in the bubble for the answer that you think is correct.

> For more than three weeks now the weather had held perfectly, but on our first night at the advance base, as if by malignant prearrangement of Nature, we had our first taste of the supernatural fury of a high Himalayan storm. It began with great streamers of lightning that flashed about the mountain like a halo; then heavily through the weird glaze, snow began to fall. The wind howled about the tents with hurricane frenzy, and the wild flapping of the canvas dinned in our ears like machine-gun fire.

1 According to the passage, what happened immediately after the streamers of lightning?
A A halo appeared.
B Heavy rain began.
C Snow fell.
D The canvas flapped.

2 What was the author's purpose in writing this passage?
F to analyze
G to inform
H to persuade
J to give directions

Directions: Read the following questions. On the answer sheet, fill in the bubble for the answer that you think is correct.

3 What is the meaning of the suffix -hood in the word childhood?
A toward a certain direction
B a process or function
C a state or condition
D made of

4 Which is the best definition of the word inappropriate?
F not suitable
G fitting well
H unfriendly
J unlike

Directions: Read the following sentences, and use context clues to figure out the meaning of each underlined word. On the answer sheet, fill in the bubble for the answer that you think is correct.

5 The quiet teenager often spent his time alone, his melancholy disposition evident in his fits of depression and frequent dark moods.
A happy-go-lucky
B sad and dejected
C angry and bitter
D soft-spoken and cowardly

6 The wound was treated with antiseptic.
F germ-laden solution
G prejudice
H infection-preventing substance
J scorn

351

Directions: Read the following questions. On the answer sheet, fill in the bubble for the answer that you think is correct.

7 "Why don't you forget about baseball and learn something nice like knitting?"

What is the connotation of the word <u>knitting</u>?

A a hobby
B an old-fashioned activity
C a craft related to sewing
D a suitable way to spend time

8 "He thought it was strange that she had never heard of baseball."

What is the denotation of the word <u>baseball</u> in this sentence?

F an unpopular sport
G a winter sport
H a difficult sport
J a popular sport

9 "He was the principal person at the event."

Which *best* defines the word <u>principal</u> in this sentence?

A the head of a school
B most intelligent
C most important
D possessing morals

10 "The subject of our discussion is not his favorite."

Which *best* defines the word <u>subject</u> in this sentence?

F length
G topic
H mathematics
J end

Directions: Read the following passages. Then answer the questions. On the answer sheet, fill in the bubble for the answer that you think is correct.

1   The day my son Laurie started kindergarten, he renounced corduroy overalls with bibs and began wearing blue jeans with a belt; I watched him go off the first morning with the older girl next door, seeing clearly that an era of my life was ended, my sweet-voiced nursery-school tot replaced by a long-trousered, swaggering character who forgot to stop at the corner and wave goodbye to me.

2   He came home the same way, the front door slamming open, his cap on the floor, and the voice suddenly become raucous shouting, "Isn't anybody *here*?"

3   At lunch he spoke insolently to his father, spilled his baby sister's milk, and remarked that his teacher said we were not to take the name of the Lord in vain.

11 Which statement *best* expresses the main idea of the passage?

A Laurie has changed from a sweet tot into a rude schoolboy.

B Laurie and his family have a close relationship

C Laurie is a typical child expressing his independence.

D All children must separate from their parents at some point.

12 Which detail from the passage does *not* support the main idea of the passage?

F Laurie does not wave goodbye.

G Laurie flings the door open and shouts.

H Laurie goes to school with his neighbor.

J Laurie speaks insolently to his father.

13 According to the passage, how does Laurie's mother feel about sending her son to kindergarten?

A She is happy.

B She is nostalgic.

C She is relieved.

D She is depressed.

My mother was trustworthy in all matters concerning our care. Grandma was trustworthy in a quite different way. She meant exactly what she said, always. If you borrowed her scissors, you returned them. In like case, my mother would wail ineffectually, "Why does everyone borrow my scissors and never put them back where they were found?" Father would then mutter an idle threat. But Grandma never threatened. She never raised her voice. She simply commanded respect and obedience by her complete expectation that she would be obeyed. And she never gave silly orders or said things like, "Do this because Grandma says so," or "Because Grandma wants you to do it." She simply said, "Do it," and I knew from her tone that it was necessary.

14 According to the passage, how does Grandma compare with the narrator's parents?

F She never minded when people borrowed her things.

G She was answered in a sweet, respectful way.

H She was more trustworthy than the narrator's parents.

J She didn't wail or make threats.

15 Which statement below *most* effectively paraphrases this passage?

A Grandma commanded respect because she was direct and even-tempered.

B The narrator loved her grandmother.

C Grandma was more trustworthy than the narrator's mother.

D The narrator always obeyed her grandmother.

1   Fiona Farmer was seven years old. Her mother was forty-six, her father was fifty-five, her nurse was sixty-one, and her grandmother and grandfather with whom they were spending the summer has reached such altitudes of age that no one remembered what they were. From these great heights Fiona was loved and directed.

2   She wore her hair as her mother had worn it in 1914, braided tight and tied back in a pretzel loop with big stiff ribbons. In winter she was the only girl at school to wear a flannel petticoat and underwear with sleeves. Her mother read to her all the books from her own girlhood: *Rebecca of Sunnybrook Farm*, and *The Five Little Peppers*, and *Under the Lilacs*. Her grandmother read to Fiona all the books she had loved as a child: Mace's *Fairy Tales*, and *The Princess and the Curdie*. . . . She was a pensive child with large eyes and rather elderly manners; all her play was quiet, accompanied at times by nothing noisier than a low continuous murmuring.

16 What can you conclude from reading this passage?
F Fiona is being raised as her mother was.
G Fiona is confused.
H Fiona enjoys school.
J Fiona is pretty.

17 Which statement *best* describes how Fiona compares with other little girls her age?
A Fiona always seems to be alone.
B Fiona has no friends with which to play.
C Fiona has older parents.
D Fiona lives in an isolated, old-fashioned world.

1   At ten o'clock the house began to die.

2   The wind blew. A falling tree bough crashed through the kitchen window. Cleaning solvent, bottled, shattered over the stove. The room was ablaze in an instant!

3   "Fire!" screamed a voice. The house lights flashed, water pumps shot water from the ceilings. But the solvent spread on the linoleum, licking, eating, under the kitchen door, while the voices took it up in a chorus: "Fire, fire, fire!"

4   The house tried to save itself. Doors sprang tightly shut, but the windows were broken by the heat and the wind blew and sucked upon the fire.

18 How does this passage compare with a newspaper article that might be written about the same fire?
F The passage contains many facts.
G The passage is more mysterious and poetic.
H The passage quotes people, just as the article would.
J The passage is easy to understand.

19 According to the passage, what happens just *after* the tree bough crashed through the kitchen window?
A A voice screamed, "Fire!"
B The bottle of cleaning solvent shattered.
C The solvent ate the linoleum.
D The clock struck ten.

One night in the last week in August, when the big campfire party is held, it was very dark and the moon looked smoky. I couldn't help myself: I *had* to tell the story of the red caterpillar that was going to prowl through each tent and bite off everyone's toes. Willie's lip started to tremble so I switched the story to something cheerful. George must not have noticed Willie and the other kids looking nervously at each other because he started a story with "The evil monsters in the woods love when city kids come to camp." He went into great detail describing how the monsters go about eating the hearts of children on the first night they are away from their parents. Willie trembled and trembled until he finally started rolling around in the grass and screaming. All the kids went crazy and scattered behind rocks, almost kicking the fire completely out as they dashed deep into the darkness, yelling bloody murder.

20 What causes Willie to roll around and scream?

  F The other kids scare him when they kick out the fire.

  G He doesn't want to hear a cheerful story.

  H George drops him when he throws him into the air.

  J George tells stories about monsters.

21 What effect does the narrator's story have on George?

  A George is spellbound and eager to hear the ending.

  B George gets excited and tells a scary story.

  C George tells a cheerful story to calm Willie.

  D George encourages the kids to tell some stories.

22 Which of these events happens *first* in the passage?

  F The children look at each other nervously.

  G Willie's lips start to tremble.

  H The narrator makes the caterpillar story more cheerful.

  J George takes over the storytelling duty.

We walked down the path to the wellhouse, attracted by the fragrance of the honeysuckle with which it was covered. Someone was drawing water, and my teacher placed my hand under the spout. As the cool stream gushed over my hand, she spelled into the other the word *water*, first slowly, then rapidly. I stood still, my whole attention fixed upon the motions of her fingers. Suddenly I felt a misty consciousness as of something forgotten—the thrill of returning thought; and somehow the mystery of language was revealed to me. I knew then that "w-a-t-e-r" meant that wonderful, cool something that was flowing over my hand. That living word awakened my soul, gave it light, hope, joy, set it free! There were barriers still, it is true, but barriers that in time could be swept away.

23 Which of the following is the *best* paraphrase of the last sentence of the passage?
  A There are barriers in every facet of life.
  B The narrator is happy.
  C The narrator knows that all barriers can be overcome.
  D There were barriers still, it is true, but barriers that in time could be swept away.

24 What conclusion can you *most* reasonably draw about the narrator?
  F Water is cooler and more refreshing than she ever thought.
  G She understands the real meaning of water now.
  H She once knew about water, but she forgot it somehow.
  J Her teacher is the only person who can teach her new things.

Directions: Each question below consists of a related pair of words, followed by four pairs of words or terms. Select the pair that best expresses a relationship similar to that expressed in the original pair, and then mark that choice on the bubble sheet.

25 NUCLEUS : CELL ::
  A insulation : cold
  B words : manuscript
  C Africa : world
  D sun : solar system

26 MAGIC : TRICKS ::
  F leaf : green
  G frog : fish
  H bouquet : flowers
  J lock : key

Practice Test 1

Directions: *Suppose that you are part of a small group of tenth graders who will travel to City Hall two days from now to make a speech before the mayor and city council. The topic of your speech is why the city should allow high school students to ride public buses for free at any time of day or night. Answer the following questions that follow.*

1. How will you ensure that all of the preparation for your speech is completed on time?
   A. Have one person write the speech and another deliver it.
   B. Have everyone research, write, and deliver a speech independently.
   C. Divide the work, and hold frequent meetings to share information.
   D. Ask the best student to do all of the work.

2. During an oral presentation to your classmates, which of the following is the <u>best</u> way to determine the interest level of the audience?
   F. Stop your presentation and ask them directly for feedback.
   G. Have them fill out a survey on your performance as they listen.
   H. Ensure that what he or she presents will support the main idea of the speech.
   J. Maintain eye contact with them and note any restless or other signs of confusion or boredom.

3. When dividing the speaking duties, what should you do?
   A. Let the person who did the most work do all of the talking.
   B. Make sure that each person speaks during the presentation.
   C. Let the person who is the best speaker do almost all of the talking.
   D. Have each person decide whether he or she wants to speak during the presentation.

4. Which of the following pairs of words describes the <u>most</u> appropriate vocabulary and tone for your speech?
   F. casual and funny   H. forceful and emotional
   G. vague and cold   J. formal and professional

Answer the following questions.

5. Which of the following sentences reveals a bias in the writer?
   A. My sedan gets better gas mileage than my friend's truck.
   B. The deer population has grown dramatically in the last decade.
   C. She believed that a balanced diet was the key to everything good in her life.
   D. New England is the loveliest region in the country.

6. Which of the following is the <u>most</u> reliable source to use for a research report on the life of a contemporary musician?
   F. a videotape of an appearance by the musician on a television talk show
   G. an article about the musician in a fan magazine
   H. an authorized biography of the musician
   J. a two-paragraph entry about the musician on an informational Web site

Read the following passages. Then answer the questions that follow.

Milestones

Ernie had lived in this town all of his life and had never before met Dolores. He was thirty-three years old, and for thirty-one of those years he had lived at home with his mother in a small, dark house on the edge of town near Beckwith's Orchards. Ernie had been a beautiful baby, with a shock of shining black hair and large blue eyes and a round, wise face. But as he had grown, it had become clearer and clearer that though he was indeed a perfectly beautiful child, his mind had not developed with the same perfection. Ernie would not be able to speak in sentences until he was six years old. He would not be able to count the apples in a bowl until he was eight. By the time he was ten, he could sing a simple song. At age twelve, he understood what a joke was. And when he was twenty, something he saw on television made him cry.

7. Which of the following is the best way to rewrite the following section from the passage above?

   By the time he was ten. He could sing a simple song.

   A. By the time, he was ten he could sing a simple song.
   B. By the time he was ten; he could sing a simple song.
   C. By the time he was ten, he could sing a simple song.
   D. Correct as is

8. Which statement best expresses the main idea of the passage above?

   F. Ernie has always lived in the same town.
   G. Ernie developed differently from other children his age.
   H. Ernie was a sensitive and beautiful child.
   J. Ernie likes jokes and television as most other children do.

House of Caring

By 1955 Shishu Bhavan was opened.

Shishu was a building not far from the Mother House on Lower Circular Road. It was unpainted, with crayoned drawings and words splashed across the walls. But Mother Teresa was glad to get it.

As soon as they had cleaned it, Mother Teresa and the sisters went out to the streets and the garbage dumps to pick up the abandoned babies and children.

Some of the babies were less than a day old. Many of them who were brought into Shishu lived only for an hour or so. They were just too small or just too sick to survive. But those who died were clean and they had been held and loved by the sisters.

9. What is the author's primary purpose in this selection?

   A. To persuade others to do more and share in the project
   B. To arouse a patriotic feeling
   C. To bring comfort to people who cared about these babies
   D. To tell about the amazing work of these women

10. Why do you think Mother Teresa and the sisters help the babies?
    F. They are being paid.
    G. They appreciate the value of every individual life.
    H. They need to do something with the building they have cleaned up.
    J. They have been ordered to.

Read the following poems. Then answer the questions that follow.

Untitled by Bashō

Lightning flashes
Then drops into darkness
A heron in flight screeches

11. Which of the following literary devices is used in the line *Then drops into darkness*?
    A. theme
    B. alliteration
    C. assonance
    D. rhyme

"The Taxi" by Amy Lowell

When I go away from you
The world beats dead
Like a slackened drum.
I call out for you against the jutted stars
5   And shout into the ridges of the wind.
Streets coming fast,
One after the other,
Wedge you away from me,
And the lamps of the city prick my eyes
10   So that I can no longer see your face.
Why should I leave you,
To wound myself upon the sharp edges of the night?

12. What is the main idea of this poem?
    F. The speaker is sad because she is leaving.
    G. The speaker enjoys the fast taxi ride.
    H. The speaker is upset that someone has left her.
    I. The speaker is excited about leaving.

13. Based on the context of the poem, what is the meaning of the lines "The world beats dead/ like a slackened drum"?
    A. The world is lifeless when the speaker is not with her friend.
    B. The speaker's friend is a drummer, but no longer plays.
    C. The speaker's drum is old and worn out.
    D. The speaker dies of a broken heart.

14. What do lines 9 and 10 *most likely* describe?
    F. There are too many streetlights.
    G. The speaker is blinded by the moonlight.
    H. Tears are forming in the speaker's eyes.
    I. The speaker is holding a flashlight.

15. What is the speaker doing in this poem?
    A. riding in a taxi
    B. watching the taxi speed by
    C. calling out for her friend
    D. looking out the window of her home

16. How does the speaker feel in the poem?
    F. upset
    G. joyful
    H. calm
    I. terrified

Complete the following analogy.

17. FORTIFIED : VULNERABLE ::
    A. wistful : nostalgic
    B. famous : unknown
    C. bright : luminescent
    D. infinite : numerous

Below is the first part of a rough draft of an editorial for a school newspaper. Read the passage. Then answer the questions that follow.

1) We are very lucky to have a computer lab here at school that students can use at almost anytime of day. (2) Judging from the way some people use the lab, I don't think everyone sees the computer lab the way I do. (3) You need to be sure you act right in the lab.

4) I think we all need to show more respect for the equipment in the computer lab and for each other. (5) Eventhough our computers are fairly new and are good quality, sometimes I am amazed when I sit down and can actually start working. (6) So many students get up and move to a different computer if the screen freezes. (7) It is not polite or fair for students to leave a problem for others to figure out. (8) This is not fair because even if you are in hurry, how do you know someone else is not in hurry, too? (9) Also, when the printers jam or are not working, students sometimes leave the problem for the next person. (10) It has gotten to the point that I don't even bother to try to print at school, even though the lab just got three new printers last year.

18. Which of the following is the best way to rewrite part 3?
    F. We need to act better in the lab.
    G. We all need to be sure we observe good behavior in the computer lab.
    H. We all need to be sure we demonstrate our gratefulness and responsibility by behaving in the computer lab in a manner that is consistent with school rules and that meets the high expectations we set for ourselves.
    J. Correct as is

19. Which of the following identifies the likely audience for this passage?
    A. Other students at the school
    B. Teachers at the school
    C. Residents of the community
    D. Students at schools throughout the area

20. Which of the following is the <u>best</u> way to revise parts 5 and 6?
    F. Even though our computers are fairly new and are good quality, many students get up and move to a different computer if the screen freezes. Sometimes I am amazed when I sit down and can actually start working.
    G. Even many students get up and move to a different computer if the screen freezes, our computers are fairly new and are good quality and sometimes I am amazed when I sit down and can actually start working.
    H. Even though our computers are fairly new and are good quality, many students get up and move to a different computer if the screen freezes. I have to fix computers so frequently that I am amazed when I sit down and can actually start working right way.
    J. Correct as is

21. Which of the following is least relevant to the writer's topic and purpose?
    A. Part 3   C. Part 8
    B. Part 4   D. Part 10

Directions Read the passage. Then answer the questions that follows.

from *Don Quixote* by Miguel de Cervantes, translated by John Ormsby

In short, he [Quixote] became so absorbed in his books that he spent his nights from sunset to sunrise, and his days from dawn to dark, poring over them; and what with little sleep and much reading his brain shriveled up and he lost his wits. His imagination was stuffed with all he read in his books about enchantments, quarrels, battles, challenges, wounds, wooings, loves, agonies, and all sorts of impossible nonsense. It became so firmly planted in his mind that the whole fabric of invention and fancy he read about was true, that to him no history in the world was better substantiated.

22. Which of the following identifies the point of view used in this passage?
    F. first person point of view   H. third person point of view
    G. second person point of view   J. Author's point of view

23. What literary device does the author use when he states that the excessive time Quixote spent reading caused his brain to shrivel?
    A. personification   C. situational irony
    B. verbal irony   D. cliché

Read the passage. Then choose the word or group of words that belongs in each space.

I found a _____(24)_____ glass object in an antique store the other day. It was a beautiful dark green color and was shaped like a vase. However, it was _____(25)_____ than any vase I had ever seen before. I tried to imagine the _____(26)_____ kind of flower that might fit in its miniscule opening, but it was impossible. I finally decided to ask the owner of the shop what she knew about this mysterious object. She _____(27)_____ pulled a guide to antique glassware from a crowded shelf. Despite her efforts, she knew _____(28)_____ about the object than I. Finally, I bought the strange glass and went home with the _____(29) purchase I have ever made.

24. F. unique
    G. most unique
    H. more unique
    J. uniquest

25. A. small
    B. more small
    C. smaller
    D. small

26. F. tinier
    G. most tiny
    H. more tinier
    J. tiniest

27. A. quickly
    B. more quickly
    C. most quickly
    D. quick

28. F. least
    G. little
    H. less
    J. leastest

29. A. interesting
    B. most interesting
    C. more interesting
    D. interestinger

Practice Test 2

Directons: Read the following passages. Then answer the questions that follow.

from *Macbeth*, Act V, Scene V by William Shakespeare

MACBETH: Tomorrow, and tomorrow, and tomorrow,
Creeps in this petty pace from day to day,
To the last syllable of recorded time;
And all our yesterdays have lighted fools
The way to dusty death. Out, out, brief candle!
Life's but a walking shadow, a poor player
That struts and frets his hour upon the stage
And then is heard no more. It is a tale
Told by an idiot, full of sound and fury,
Signifying nothing.

1. What does this soliloquy tell the reader about Macbeth's state of mind?
   A. He feels overwhelmed by the many tasks he must accomplish in very little time.
   B. He believes he is surrounded by vain people who are shallow compared to him.
   C. He is irritated by an overwhelming boredom.
   D. He believes that life is short and meaningless.

2. The direct characterization provided by Macbeth's own words would appear as which of the following literary elements in a short story?
   F. theme   H. imagery
   G. dialogue   J. tone

[Untitled]

1) *Antigone* is a play by Sophocles. (2) It is an example of his sensitivity to the issues of his day. (3) He portrays these issues by having mortal people acting out there destinies, which are determined by the gods. (4) *Antigone* is one of three plays that has to do with the *dike*, or curse, that King Oedipus brings upon his family. (5) Oedipus has four children: Antigone, Ismene, Polynices, and Eteocles.

6) The basic dramatic confllict in *Antigone* occur between two characters with conflicting principles. (7) These characters are Creon, which represents the sate and Antigone, which represents the family and the laws of the gods. (8) At the end of the play, this conflict is tragically resolved.

9) Sophocles wrote *Antigone* in a time much like our own, when the traditional respect for laws was under scrutiny. (10) This age is filled with debates on custom, laws, and nature, the playwright doubtlessly was effected by such debates and worked them into his work.

3. Which of the following is the best order for the paragraphs?
   A. 2, 3, 1
   B. 1, 3, 2
   C. 3, 2, 1
   D. Correct as is

4. Which of the following sentences would add important information to the second paragraph?

   F. Ismene disagrees with her sister's plan.

   G. The conflict occurs when Creon refuses to allow the burial of Polynices, Antigone's brother.

   H. Creon is preoccupied with thoughts of money and power; his wordly concerns displease the gods and bring disaster to Thebes.

   J. Sophocles was influenced by the philosopher Heraclitus.

5. Which of the following is the <u>best</u> revision of the part 7?

   A. These characters are Creon, who represents the state, and Antigone, who represents the family and the law of the gods.

   B. These characters are Creon and Antigone, who represent the state, the family, and the law of the gods.

   C. Creon is representing the state and Antigone is representing her family and the law of the gods.

   D. These characters represent the state and the family and the law of the gods.

6. Which of the following is the <u>best</u> rewrite of part 1?

   F. *Antigone* was a great play by the Greek playwright, Sophocles.

   G. *Antigone* is play written by the Greek playwright, Sophocles.

   H. *Antigone* is famous tragedy written by the Greek playwright, Sophocles.

   J. Correct as is

7. Which of the following is the <u>best</u> rewrite of part 10?

   A. This age is filled with debates on custom, laws, and nature, and the playwright doubtlessly was effected by such debates and worked them into his writing.

   B. This age was filled with debates on custom, laws, and nature, and the playwright doubtlessly was affected by such debates and worked them into his work.

   C. This age was filled with debates on custom, laws, and nature; the playwright doubtlessly was affected by such debates and worked them into his writing.

   D. Correct as is

8. Which of the following is the <u>best</u> rewrite of part 3?

   F. He portrays these issues by having mortal people acting out thier destinies, which are determined by the gods.

   G. He portrays these issues by having mortal people acting out they're destinies, which are determined by the gods.

   H. He portrays these issues by having mortal people acting out his destiny, which are determined by the gods.

   J. Correct as is

9. Which of the following identifies the <u>most</u> likely audience for this passage?

   A. Students learning Greek

   B. Readers of a letters to the editor column

   C. Professors of Greek literature

   D. Students reading plays from different eras

10. Which of the following is the <u>best</u> title for this passage?
    F. Modern Drama
    G. The Timeless Issues of *Antigone*
    H. The Children of Oedipus
    J. The *Dike*

Historic Philadelphia

(1) Benjamin Franklin greatly influenced daily life in colonial Philadelphia. (2) In addition, between his efforts Philadelphia became the first city in the colonies to have street lights. (3) He helped establish the city's public library and fire department, as well as its first college.

(4) Philadelphia was an important center of activity during the period leading up to and at the time of the American Revolution. (5) It was here that the Declaration of Independence, establishing the United States as an independent nation, was written and signed.

(6) In Philadelphia today, you can still walk down the cobblestone streets and visit historic sites. (7) Benjamin Franklin operated his own print shop in Philadelphia many years ago. (8) Independence Hall (where the Declaration of Independence was signed), the Liberty Bell, and the home of Betsy Ross are within walking distance for tourists and history enthusiasts. (9) All of these features make Philadelphia the best tourist destination in the nation.

11. Which of the following changes is needed in the first paragraph?
    A. In part 1, change *in* to *within*.
    B. In part 3, change *city's* to *citys'*.
    C. In part 2, change *In addition* to *as well as*.
    D. In part 2, change *between* to *as a result of*.

12. Which of the following changes would help focus attention on the main idea in the third paragraph?
    F. Reverse parts 6 and 7   H. Reverse parts 7 and 8
    G. Delete part 7   J. Delete part 8

13. Which of the following parts should be revised to reduce unnecessary repetition?
    A. Part 3   C. Part 6
    B. Part 4   D. Part 8

14. Which of the following is the <u>best</u> rewrite of part 5?
    F. It was here in Independence Hall that the Declaration of Independence, establishing the United States as an independent nation, was written and signed.
    G. It was here in Independence Hall. The Declaration of Independence, establishing the United States as an independent nation, was written and signed.
    H. It was here in Independence Hall that the Declaration of Independence was written and signed, establishing the United States as an independent nation.
    J. Correct as is

15. Which of the following identifies the <u>best</u> order of sentences in the first paragraph?
    A. 2, 1, 3   C. 3, 1, 2
    B. 1, 3, 2   D. Correct as is

16. In which of the parts does the writer express an opinion?
    F. Part 2   H. Part 8
    G. Part 5   J. Part 9

17. Which of the following would be the <u>best</u> location for the following sentence?

    This institution was later named the University of Pennsylvania.
    A. After part 3
    B. After part 5
    C. After part 7
    D. The passage offers no good place to add this sentence.

Read the passage. Then answer the following questions by choosing the <u>best</u> way to rewrite the underlined sections.

18) <u>Paul's mom said they neede the rain for their garden. Had had a drought for many weeks.</u> Paul didn't agree. He just wanted to play basketball as he did every Saturday. (19) <u>To Paul, basketball was the better sport of all. In fact, he liked playing hoops better than he liked doing any other activity.</u> Paul's dad suggested that Paul read a book, but Paul didn't want to read a book. (20) <u>He felt mad. Saturday was the only day he could play basketball.</u> (21) <u>He knew he couldn't play on Sunday. Sunday was a day when all of the kids had family obligations.</u> (22) <u>Paul's dad was an avid reader. He came into the room. Paul's dad held a book.</u> (23) <u>Maybe you would like to read this book, he said.</u> He gave it to Paul and left the room. The book was about basketball strategies. Paul smiled. (24) <u>He realized that he couldn't play basketball today, he dived into the first chapter.</u> (25) <u>Before long he realized that reading about basketball could be just as enjoyable as to play basketball.</u>

18. F. Paul's mom said they needed the rain for their garden having a drought for many weeks.
    G. Paul's mom said they needed the rain for their garden because they had had a drought for many weeks.
    H. Paul's mom said they needed the rain for their garden, which they had had a drought for many weeks.
    J. Paul's mom said they needed the rain for their garden they had had a drought for many weeks.

19. A. To Paul, basketball was the best sport of all. In fact, he liked playing hoops better than him.
    B. To Paul, basketball was the better sport of all. In fact, he liked playing hoops better than they liked doing any other activity.
    C. To Paul, basketball was the best sport of all. In fact, he liked playing hoops better than he liked doing any other activity.
    D. To Paul, basketball was the better sport of all, he liked playing hoops best than he liked doing any other activity.

20. F. Feeling mad, Saturday was the only day he could play basketball.
    G. He felt mad since Saturday was the only day he could play basketball.
    H. Although Saturday was the only day he could play basketball, he felt mad.
    J. He felt mad Saturday was the only day he could play basketball.

21. A. He knew he couldn't play on Sunday unless all of the kids had family obligations.
    B. Knowing he couldn't play on Sunday, all of the kids had family obligations.
    C. He knew he couldn't play on Sunday all of the kids had family obligations.
    D. He knew he couldn't play on Sunday when all of the kids had family obligations.

22. F. Paul's dad, an avid reader, came into the room holding a book.
    G. Paul's dad was an avid reader who came into the room he held a book.
    H. Although Paul's dad was an avid reader, he came into the room holding a book.
    J. Coming into the room, Paul's dad was an avid reader who held a book.

23. A. Maybe you would like to read this book he said.
    B. "Maybe you would like to read this book, he said."
    C. "Maybe you would like to read this book," he said.
    D. "Maybe you would like to read this book." He said.

24. F. He realized that he couldn't play basketball today, diving into the first chapter.
    G. Realizing that he couldn't play basketball today, he dived into the first chapter.
    H. He realized that he couldn't play basketball today unless he dived into the first chapter.
    J. He realized that he couldn't play basketball today even though he dived into the first chapter.

25. A. Before long he was realizing that reading about basketball could be just as enjoyable as to play basketball.
    B. Before long he realized that to read about basketball could be just as enjoyable as playing basketball.
    C. Before long he realized that reading about basketball could be just as enjoyable as playing basketball.
    D. Before long he realized that reading about could be just as enjoyable as playing basketball.

Writing Prompt 1

What is the most important thing about students in your school that you would like other people to know? You might choose the interests, behavior, or abilities of the students in your school. Write an essay in which you identify and describe some important quality of your schoolmates. Be sure to tell why it is the most important characteristic, and give examples and reasons to support your idea.

Writing Prompt 2

Think about a person, place, animal, or object that you have known for a long period of time. What makes this subject important to you? How has the subject changed during the years you have known it? Write a paragraph in which you explain the importance of this person, place, animal, or object to you. Use specific sensory details to create a distinct mood and to give the reader a clear sense of your subject. Be sure to use transitional words and phrases to move effectively between past and present times.

PSAT PRACTICE TEST

CRITICAL READING
Section 1: Sentence Completion

Directions: *Each of the following questions consists of an incomplete sentence followed by five words or pairs of words. Choose that word or pair of words which, when substituted for the blank space or spaces, best completes the meaning of the sentence and mark the letter of your choice on your answer sheet.*

Example:

Because of widespread corruption and neglect of basic governmental functions, China's Qing dynasty fell into ---- by the late 1700s.

(A) agreement

(B) animosity

(C) malady

(D) supplication

(E) decline

1. Opera is considered both a visual and a(n) ---- medium, as audiences both watch the story unfold and listen to dramatic music.

   (A) anonymous

   (B) callous

   (C) auditory

   (D) cumulative

   (E) expressive

2. Hiking in the beautiful and remote Himalayas is ---- experience that holds great ---- for adventurous travelers.

   (A) an exotic..allure

   (B) an ethical..exuberance

   (C) a feasible..discretion

   (D) a reformatory..progression

   (E) impersonal..prestige

3. According to many environmentalists, the construction of dams has created a ---- of ecological disruption.

   (A) pinnacle

   (B) legacy

   (C) providence

   (D) statute

   (E) barricade

4. Contrary to popular belief, the idea of true romantic love based on steady emotion, rather than momentary ----, is a relatively recent and ---- invention in Western history.

(A) luxury..linear

(B) inclination..belated

(C) betrothal..parochial

(D) oblivion..nonchalant

(E) phenomenon..pictorial

5. Some ---- theorize that ---- integrated use of both sides of the brain decreases frustration and leads to a greater sense of happiness and well-being.

(A) experts..premature

(B) scientists..sedentary

(C) psychologists..habitual

(D) mathematicians..proficient

(E) researchers..pessimistic

6. Although the sculptor relied primarily on using metal and wood in his creations during his early career, he later switched to employing more ---- materials.

(A) pliable

(B) secure

(C) stolid

(D) thermal

(E) tiered

7. New York's elegant Seagram Building is recognized for its success in ---- elements of two architectural aesthetics, the Gothic and the classical.

(A) transfusing

(B) obliterating

(C) verifying

(D) unifying

(E) visualizing

8. Following the ---- of always showing the best side of things, the photographer chose to ---- the model's lustrous hair rather than highlight his broken nose.

(A) bane..emphasize

(B) rule..belittle

(C) saying..blur

(D) maxim..appropriate

(E) axiom..accentuate

9. Sensing a rising tide of skepticism among members of the audience, Dr. March ---- her arguments with a bevy of concrete facts.

(A) chagrined

(B) buttressed

(C) circumvented

(D) insured

(E) formulated

Name _____ Date _____

Section 2: Reading Comprehension

QUESTIONS 10–17 are based on the following two passages:

An excerpt from Device for Disabled Converts Brain Signals into Spoken Words

Invention also enables wheelchair to be controlled by signals from brain

Washington—Two young inventors are perfecting a device that gives back the power of speech to people who suffer from diseases or disabilities that have taken away their ability to talk.

The device, called the Audeo, translates thoughts— or, more precisely, brain signals sent to the vocal cords—into synthesized speech. Using the same technology, inventors Michael Callahan and Thomas Coleman also have created a mechanized wheelchair that moves, turns and stops in response to intercepted brain signals.

"If development goes well, it should give patients a full vocabulary, their ability to speak," Callahan said.

ALS—amyotrophic lateral sclerosis, or Lou Gehrig's disease—can rob people of their physical motor control and ability to produce speech. So can some other diseases, as well as traumatic brain injury, cerebral palsy, stroke and certain spinal cord injuries. Callahan and Coleman are anxious to help people with such conditions.

In fact, Callahan said, "our goal is to make [the Audeo] affordable to people who may or may not have health insurance, because we want the technology to get to everyone—so it will be priced accordingly."

"The technology is not finished, so the communication we can give them is limited but extremely useful where there are no other options," he said.

The Audeo uses sensors located in a neckband worn by the user to detect electrical impulses in the vocal cords and relay them to a nearby computer that converts the signals to speech. But users need not fear that the device can read their minds, Callahan said.

An excerpt from Music Therapy Helps People with Disabilities

Singing, MIDI software aid speech and motor recovery

Washington—Some stroke victims who have lost the ability to speak fluently often are able to sing, says a leading music therapist. But even when you have the beat, it is hard to play music if you cannot move.

Innovations in music technology are making it possible—and enjoyable—for people with severe physical disabilities to play and compose music. They also can help restore speech.

Research shows that music therapy is effective in promoting wellness among healthy people, and it has been shown to alleviate pain and improve the quality of life for persons with disabilities.

SINGING HELPS SPEECH RECOVERY

Singing and speaking are neurologically different functions, said Concetta M. Tomaino, who has a doctorate in music therapy. For example, stroke victims can sometimes sing entire lyrics of songs but are unable to speak a simple "Hello."

Clinical studies conducted by Tomaino and her colleagues, have shown that singing word phrases such as "Hello, how are you?" affects speech recovery by "rehearsing" speech. By putting common phrases into a musical context, patients are learning to say "Hello" and more.

LIVE AND DIGITAL MUSICAL INSTRUMENTS CAN IMPROVE MOTOR SKILLS

In addition to restoring speech, music therapy can improve motor skills and coordination, according to the American Music Therapy Association.

Most of the music therapy work incorporates live and recorded music and encourages patients to play actual musical instruments.

Companies equip musical instruments with devices that make it possible for individuals with disabilities to hold and play instruments. Now patients who need to increase strength and range of motion in their hands and arms can use digital drumsticks, Tomaino said.

10. Based on passage 1, why is the wheelchair invented by Callahan and Coleman special?

    (A) It is made of titanium.

    (B) It moves in response to brain signals.

    (C) It has three wheels.

    (D) It has the power to speak.

    (E) It records voices.

11. According to passage 1, which of the following statements does _not_ describe what the Audeo does?

    (A) It uses a computer to convert signals.

    (B) It converts brain signals into speech.

    (C) It reads the minds of the users.

    (D) It uses sensors located in a neckband worn by the user.

    (E) It will help many people who are unable to speak.

12. According to passage 1, who will be able to use the Audeo?

    (A) people who suffer from diseases and disabilities that have taken away their ability to talk

    (B) all people, whether or not they have health insurance

    (C) only people who have health insurance to cover to high cost of the Audeo

    (D) A and C

    (E) A and B

13. According to passage 2, which of the following statements is true?

    (A) Singing and speaking are neurologically the same.

    (B) To sing well, one must speak well.

    (C) Some stroke victims can sing an entire song, but they cannot say "hello."

    (D) Singing common phrases will not improve one's ability to speak common phrases.

    (E) Music therapy has no affect on motor skills.

14. According to passage 2, music therapy is able to do which of the following?

    (A) all of the following

    (B) promote wellness among healthy people

    (C) alleviate pain for people with disabilities

    (D) improve life for people with disabilities

    (E) restore speech for people with disabilities

15. According to passage 2, which of the following statement does _not_ describe the role of musical instruments in music therapy?

    (A) Patients are encouraged to play actual musical instruments.

    (B) Digital instruments are used by individuals who can not hold an instrument.

    (C) The use of musical instruments is not encouraged.

    (D) The instruments are often equipped with devices enabling people with disabilities to play.

    (E) B and C

16. Which of the following statements is true concerning passages 1 and 2?

   (A) Both passages discuss music therapies related to music for the disabled.

   (B) Both passages discuss using brain waves to help the disabled.

   (C) Research for both the device and therapy took place in New York.

   (D) Both passages are news articles, and both discuss things that will help people with disabilities.

   (E) Both the device and therapy have been used by people for several years.

17. What is the main purpose of passage 1 and passage 2?

   (A) to persuade those with disabilities to buy the new devices which are available

   (B) to inform the readers about new technology which will help those with disabilities

   (C) to inform the readers about the problems faced by people with disabilities

   (D) to persuade the readers to support legislation helping people with disabilities

   (E) to express the feelings of the authors

Directions: *The three passages below are followed by questions based on their content. Answer the questions on the basis of what is <u>stated</u> or <u>implied</u> in the passages.*

> There was never a sound beside the wood but one,
> And that was my long scythe whispering to the ground.
> What was it it whispered? I knew not well myself;
> Perhaps it was something about the heat of the sun,
> 5   Something, perhaps, about the lack of sound—
> And that was why it whispered and did not speak.
> It was no dream of the gift of idle hours,
> Or easy gold at the hand of fay or elf:
> Anything more than the truth would have seemed too weak
> 10   To the earnest love that laid the swale in rows,
> Not without feeble-pointed spikes of flowers
> (Pale orchises), and scared a bright green snake.
> The fact is the sweetest dream that labor knows.
> My long scythe whispered and left the hay to make.

—"Mowing," by Robert Frost

18. What does line 13 tell you about the speaker's attitude toward labor?

(A) The speaker enjoys daydreaming instead of working.

(B) The speaker loves his work and believes in its value.

(C) The speaker would rather sleep than work.

(D) The speaker dreams of finding more fulfilling work.

(E) The speaker is exhausted working in the heat.

19. Why does the scythe only whisper?

(A) The scythe does not want to frighten the speaker.

(B) The weather is too hot for the scythe to speak louder.

(C) The scythe is weakened by its heavy labor.

(D) The scythe does not want to disturb the silence.

(E) The scythe wants to conserve its energy.

Lightning is the result of a build-up of opposite electrical charges within a cumulonimbus cloud. Exactly how this happens is not yet clear, but it seems that ice crystals, which form in the upper part of the cloud, are generally positively charged while water droplets, which tend to sink to the bottom of the cloud, are normally negatively charged. It may be that updrafts carry the positive charges up and downdrafts drag the negative charges down.

As this build-up occurs, a positive charge also forms near the ground under the cloud and moves with the cloud.

—from "Lightning and Thunder," science text from
The Nature Company Guides: Weather

20. Which of the following cause-and-effect relationships is described in the passage?

(A) The build-up of opposite charges in a cumulonimbus cloud causes lightning.

(B) Ice crystals and water droplets combine to form clouds.

(C) A lightning bolt causes sound waves that we hear as thunder.

(D) Positive charges that form near the ground cause clouds to move.

(E) Updrafts cause positive charges, and downdrafts cause negative charges.

21. From the information in the passage, you can *best* conclude that

(A) scientists have fully explored the causes and effects of lightning

(B) only weather experts would be interested in reading this article

(C) the author is trying to renew interest in weather phenomena

(D) scientists are still trying to determine what causes lightning

(E) the author has an unusual theory about how lightning forms

My lords, the present occasion is too serious to allow me to follow the convention that a woman should not speak in a man's council. . . .

In my opinion, flight is not the right course, even if it should bring us to safety. It is impossible for a person, having been born into this world, not to die; but for one who has reigned it is intolerable to be a fugitive. May I never be deprived of this purple robe, and may I never see the day when those who meet me do not call me empress.

If you wish to save yourself, . . . there is no difficulty. . . . As for me, I agree with the adage that the royal purple is the noblest shroud.

—from Speech During the Invasion of Constantinople, by Empress Theodora

22. What does the speaker mean by the line "As for me, I agree with the adage that the royal purple is the noblest shroud"?

(A) She believes that purple best conveys the meaning of royalty.

(B) She would rather die in her robes than give them up.

(C) She holds the cowardly lords in contempt.

(D) She can achieve nobility only by dying.

(E) She believes that she is no longer worthy of wearing purple.

23. Which of the following sentences *best* explains why it would be "intolerable" for the speaker to be a fugitive?

(A) She would be uncomfortable living anywhere else.

(B) She would lose the power and respect that she is used to having.

(C) She could not bear to leave her family and friends.

(D) She fears that the life of a fugitive would be dangerous.

(E) She would no longer have the rights that she enjoys as a woman.

WRITING

Directions: *The sentences below contain errors in grammar, usage, word choice, and idiom. Parts of each sentence are underlined and lettered. Decide which underlined part contains the error and mark its letter on your answer sheet. If the sentence is correct as it stands, mark (E) on your answer sheet. No sentence contains more than one error.*

24. Even though <u>they were</u> tired and
　　　　　　　(A)
hungry, the <u>womens'</u> outlook
　　　　　　　(B)
<u>brightened considerably</u> when they
　　　(C)
noticed that the storm <u>had broken</u>.
　　　　　　　　　　　　(D)

<u>No error</u>
(E)

25. South of the Sahara, <u>their</u> <u>spreads</u> a
　　　　　　　　　　(A)　　**(B)**
vast <u>area</u> of grasslands <u>known as</u> the
　　　(C)　　　　　　**(D)**
savannas. <u>No error</u>
　　　　　(E)

26. After hearing that his sister <u>spent her</u>
　　　　　　　　　　　　　　　(A)
only day out of school <u>watching</u> talk
　　　　　　　　　　(B)
shows, Atietie scowled <u>at her</u> in
　　　　　　　　　　　(C)
disgust, as if she <u>was</u> the biggest fool
　　　　　　　　(D)
on earth. <u>No error</u>
　　　　　(E)

27. <u>Working quickly</u> and precisely, the
　　　(A)
window cleaners <u>stood upon</u> the
　　　　　　　　　(B)
scaffolding, <u>which hung</u> four
　　　　　　　(C)
hundred <u>feet above</u> the sidewalk
　　　　　　(D)
below. <u>No error</u>
　　　　(E)

28. After <u>sauntering casually</u> into the
　　　　　　(A)
reception hall, Dietrich <u>gazed around</u>
　　　　　　　　　　　　(B)
and <u>realized that</u> he was dressed
　　　　(C)
<u>improper</u>. <u>No error</u>
　(D)　　**(E)**

29. Howard and Dorothy <u>clasped</u> hands
　　　　　　　　　　　(A)
and <u>proclaimed loudly</u> that nothing
　　　　(B)
so <u>trivial would</u> come <u>among them</u>
　　(C)　　　　　　**(D)**
again. <u>No error</u>
　　　　(E)

30. A Chinese <u>general named</u> Zhao
　　　　　　　(A)
<u>Kuangyin, he</u> established the Song
　(B)
dynasty and <u>reduced the</u> power of
　　　　　　(C)
the military in <u>his country's</u>
　　　　　　　(D)
government. <u>No error</u>
　　　　　　(E)

31. <u>Either Bill</u> or Leslie—I don't
　(A)
<u>remember which</u>—<u>were</u> unable to
　　(B)　　　　**(C)**
<u>arrange for</u> transportation to the
　(D)
research center. <u>No error</u>
　　　　　　　(E)

32. "I <u>absolutely refuse</u> to patronize an
       (A)
   establishment <u>whose owners</u> are
                       (B)
   such obnoxious bigots," Claude

   <u>declared</u>, wringing <u>his hands</u>.
       (C)   **(D)**
   <u>No error</u>
       (E)

33. <u>We</u> test-drove <u>every car</u> at the
    (A)   **(B)**
   dealership, <u>accept</u> the rusted-out
                  (C)
   <u>black</u> sedan. <u>No error</u>
    (D)   **(E)**

34. <u>Our</u> public <u>library</u> owns <u>far less</u>
    (A)   **(B)**   **(C)**
   copies of N. Scott Momaday's

   House Made of Dawn <u>than of</u> Louise
                          (D)
   Erdrich's *The Blue Jay's Dance*.

   <u>No error</u>
       (E)

35. <u>When</u> purchasing <u>her new</u> rock-
    (A)   **(B)**
   climbing equipment, <u>she frequently</u>
                          (C)
   asked Silko <u>and I</u> for advice.
                 (D)
   <u>No error</u>
       (E)

36. The Park Service <u>refused</u> to hire
                      (A)
   Rufus—<u>who is</u> an amazingly hard
            (B)
   worker, <u>by the way</u>—for trail
              (C)
   maintenance because he is younger

   <u>then</u> sixteen. <u>No error</u>
    (D)   **(E)**

37. I want <u>to spend</u> my entire vacation
           (A)
   <u>scuba diving</u> in the clear waters
       (B)
   <u>of the gulf</u>, wandering through ancient
       (C)
   ruins, and <u>to read</u> old magazines.
                 (D)
   <u>No error</u>
       (E)

38. If <u>you thrust</u> your hand <u>in front of</u>
        (A)   **(B)**
   <u>a alligator</u> snapping turtle, it is likely
       (C)
   to <u>bite you</u>. <u>No error</u>
        (D)   **(E)**

39. A <u>traditional</u> Japanese art form,
       (A)
   woodblock printing <u>use</u> carved
                        (B)
   wooden <u>blocks covered</u> with ink to
            (C)
   <u>produce images</u> on paper. <u>No error</u>
       (D)   **(E)**

40. Disorganized and reeling <u>after its</u> last
                              (A)
   defeat, <u>the team</u> of determined
            (B)
   hockey players <u>passed</u> the puck
                    (C)
   rapidly, and to great <u>affect</u>. <u>No error</u>
                          (D)   **(E)**

41. Jason <u>stumbled over</u> a rock, <u>tried</u> to
          (A)   **(B)**
   <u>regain his</u> balance, and pitched
       (C)
   <u>forward into</u> a cluster of cactus.
       (D)
   <u>No error</u>
       (E)

42. Many traditional <u>Mexican</u> cooks
                      (A)
   <u>have began</u> using metal presses
       (B)
   to <u>pat</u> down <u>their</u> tortillas. <u>No error</u>
        (C)   **(D)**   **(E)**

Directions: *The sentences below contain problems in grammar, sentence construction, word choice, and punctuation. Part or all of each sentence is underlined. Select the lettered answer that contains the best version of the underlined section. Answer (A) always repeats the original underlined section exactly. If the sentence is correct as it stands, select (A).*

43. Howard Sanchez arrived late to the business <u>meeting, his right-rear car tire</u> was punctured by a rusty nail.

   (A) meeting, his right-rear car tire

   (B) meeting, you see his right-rear car tire

   (C) meeting because his right-rear car tire

   (D) meeting—for the right-rear tire of his car

   (E) meeting; because his car, its tire

44. Oh, I think she enjoys the company of almost <u>everyone who speaks polite</u>.

   (A) everyone who speaks polite

   (B) everyone who speak polite

   (C) everyone whom speak politely

   (D) everyone who speaks politely

   (E) everyone whom speak polite

45. Jared says that nobody with pets should <u>come, but I disagree</u>.

   (A) come, but I disagree

   (B) come however, I disagree

   (C) come, though, I disagree

   (D) come but, I disagree

   (E) come, however, I disagree

46. I'm offended that the financial aid department failed to offer <u>scholarships to Jamie and I</u>.

   (A) scholarships to Jamie and I

   (B) scholarships unto me and Jamie

   (C) scholarships to Jamie and me

   (D) scholarships to I and Jamie

   (E) scholarships unto I and Jamie

47. Cheryl <u>strode confident into</u> the crowded auditorium to deliver a speech against reducing federal funding for the arts.

   (A) strode confident into

   (B) strided confident into

   (C) strided confidently into

   (D) stride with a degree of confidence into

   (E) strode confidently into

48. The doctor assured us that the new medication would be as <u>safe as, if not safer than the</u> old one.

   (A) safe as, if not safer than the

   (B) safe as, if not safer, than the

   (C) safe, if not safer, as the

   (D) safe as, if not safer than, the

   (E) safe, if not safer, than the

49. The things that most impress me about him are his earnestness, his sharp <u>wit, and the way in which he speaks</u>.

   (A) wit, and the way in which he speaks

   (B) wit, and his speaking ability

   (C) wit, and his way with speaking

   (D) wit, and how he makes a speech

   (E) wit, and the method he has of speaking powerfully

50. Tomás <u>seemed to be inferring</u> that he wants to move to Cedar Rapids, Iowa.

   (A) seemed to be inferring

   (B) will seem to infer

   (C) seemed to be implying

   (D) has seemed to infer

   (E) will have seemed to imply

Directions: *Questions 51–56 are based on a passage that might be an early draft of a student's essay. Some sentences in this draft need to be revised or rewritten to make them both clear and correct. Read the passage carefully; then answer the questions that follow it. Some questions require decisions about diction, usage, tone, or sentence structure in particular sentences or parts of sentences. Other questions require decisions about organization, development, or appropriateness of language in the essay as a whole. For each question, choose the answer that makes the intended meaning clearer and more precise and that follows the conventions of standard written English.*

(1) Pet overpopulation is a terrible problem throughout the United States. (2) It is tragic that so many potentially loving pets end up in animal shelters or are euthanized because they are unwanted. (3) Not enough pets are spayed or neutered, which is the tragedy and it should be improved.

(4) Unfortunately, many people object to spaying and neutering. (5) Some people think that their animals will not develop properly if they do not reproduce; this thought is contradicted by veterinarians, who have disproved this idea. (6) Other people maintain a romantic notion that their dog or cat should experience "motherhood" at least once. (7) Some people believe that spaying and neutering animals is unnatural, they fear that their pets will become obese if altered. (8) However, spaying and neutering pets is far healthier than putting them to sleep by the thousands in animal shelters. (9) In addition, veterinary studies show, which female dogs and cats live longer and have a reduced risk of cancer if they are spayed before going into heat or giving birth.

(10) Some animals reproduce freely. (11) This is due to their becoming feral. (12) This means that they have escaped domesticity to become wild. (13) Skillful hunters, feral cats feed themselves easily, reproduce quickly, and spread deadly feline diseases to pet populations. (14) The easiest and most effective way that people can prevent cats and dogs from becoming feral is to spay and neuter their pets and to never allow unwanted pets to roam free.

(15) Finally, some animals are not spayed or neutered because their human companions cannot afford the procedure. (16) In this instance, communities need to provide adequate low-cost spay/neuter clinics so that every member of the community can participate in reducing the tragic problem of pet overpopulation.

51. Which is the *best* revision of Sentence 3?

(A) This here is a tragic situation, one that requires people to spay and neuter their pets.

(B) The primary reason for this tragedy is that too few pets are spayed and neutered.

(C) In such a tragic circumstance there is an answer, and this answer is spaying and neutering.

(D) With such tragedies about, people need to spay and neuter their pets.

(E) Pets need to be spayed and neutered.

52. Which is the *best* revision of Sentence 5?

(A) Their objections are based on the idea that their animals will not develop although they have been disproved by veterinarians.

(B) Some people think that animals will not develop properly and that reproducing is the problem, though veterinarians believe that's not true.

(C) Some people think that their animals will not develop properly if they do not reproduce, although veterinarians have disproved this idea.

(D) Veterinarians and people who want their pets to reproduce disagree about whether animals need to reproduce in order to develop properly.

(E) These people feel that their pets need to reproduce, although veterinarians disagree that the reason is because of a lack of proper development.

53. Which is the *best* revision of Sentence 7?

(A) Spaying and neutering is unnatural, which is why it may cause pets to become obese.

(B) Some people believe that spaying and neutering animals will unnaturally cause obesity.

(C) People fear unnatural things like spaying and neutering and believe that obesity will result.

(D) Some people believe that spaying and neutering animals is unnatural and that obesity will result if alteration takes place.

(E) Some people believe that spaying and neutering animals is unnatural, and that their pets will become obese if altered.

54. Which is the *best* revision of the underlined part of Sentence 9?

(A) veterinary studies show that female dogs and cats

(B) veterinary studies show, that female dogs and cats

(C) veterinary studies have been known to show that female dogs and cats

(D) veterinary studies also show that female dogs and cats

(E) veterinary studies, show which female dogs and cats

55. Which is the *best* way to combine Sentences 10 and 11?

(A) Some animals reproduce freely; this is due to their becoming feral.

(B) Animals will reproduce freely under some circumstances, such as having become feral.

(C) Some animals reproduce freely and that's because they have become feral.

(D) Some animals reproduce freely because they have become feral.

(E) Becoming feral, that's another reason why some animals reproduce freely.

56. Which of the following would be the *best* way to improve the essay?

(A) Add information about other kinds of pets.

(B) Switch the order of the second and fourth paragraphs.

(C) Add a concluding statement.

(D) Add more transitional words and phrases.

(E) Change the tone to one of complete neutrality.

Prompt 1

Directions: *Think carefully about the issue presented in the following passage and the assignment below.*

In "At Harvesttime," Maya Angelou writes about the life principle that people reap what they sow. In other words, if you treat people well, they are likely to treat you well in return. Angelou's words remind people to think about the consequences of all of their actions.

Assignment: What is your view on the idea that you get back from others what you give to them? Plan and write an essay in which you develop your point of view on this issue. Support your position with reasoning and examples taken from your reading, studies, experience, or observations.

Prompt 2

Directions: *Think carefully about the issue presented in the following passages and the assignment below.*

1. Honor-roll students should be exempt from taking final exams. They have shown responsibility and dedication, and they have demonstrated that they know the material. In addition, enacting this policy would inspire other students to work harder to earn the privilege of not taking final exams.

2. Honor-roll students should *not* be exempt from taking final exams. This policy would be unfair to other students and would create resentment in the classroom. In addition, honor-roll students are already rewarded with public acknowledgement and certificates; these rewards are sufficient for inspiring other students to work harder.

Assignment: Is exempting honor-roll students from taking final exams unfair to other students or a just reward? Plan and write an essay in which you develop your point of view on this issue. Support your position with reasoning and examples taken from your reading, studies, experience, or observations.

Answer Sheet
Screening Test

Practice Test 1

1.	Ⓐ	Ⓑ	Ⓒ	Ⓓ	
2.	Ⓕ	Ⓖ	Ⓗ	Ⓙ	
3.	Ⓐ	Ⓑ	Ⓒ	Ⓓ	
4.	Ⓕ	Ⓖ	Ⓗ	Ⓙ	
5.	Ⓐ	Ⓑ	Ⓒ	Ⓓ	
6.	Ⓕ	Ⓖ	Ⓗ	Ⓙ	
7.	Ⓐ	Ⓑ	Ⓒ	Ⓓ	
8.	Ⓕ	Ⓖ	Ⓗ	Ⓙ	
9.	Ⓐ	Ⓑ	Ⓒ	Ⓓ	
10.	Ⓕ	Ⓖ	Ⓗ	Ⓙ	
11.	Ⓐ	Ⓑ	Ⓒ	Ⓓ	
12.	Ⓕ	Ⓖ	Ⓗ	Ⓙ	
13.	Ⓐ	Ⓑ	Ⓒ	Ⓓ	
14.	Ⓕ	Ⓖ	Ⓗ	Ⓙ	
15.	Ⓐ	Ⓑ	Ⓒ	Ⓓ	
16.	Ⓕ	Ⓖ	Ⓗ	Ⓙ	
17.	Ⓐ	Ⓑ	Ⓒ	Ⓓ	
18.	Ⓕ	Ⓖ	Ⓗ	Ⓙ	
19.	Ⓐ	Ⓑ	Ⓒ	Ⓓ	
20.	Ⓕ	Ⓖ	Ⓗ	Ⓙ	
21.	Ⓐ	Ⓑ	Ⓒ	Ⓓ	
22.	Ⓕ	Ⓖ	Ⓗ	Ⓙ	
23.	Ⓐ	Ⓑ	Ⓒ	Ⓓ	
24.	Ⓕ	Ⓖ	Ⓗ	Ⓙ	
25.	Ⓐ	Ⓑ	Ⓒ	Ⓓ	
26.	Ⓕ	Ⓖ	Ⓗ	Ⓙ	

Screening Test

1. Ⓐ Ⓑ Ⓒ Ⓓ
2. Ⓕ Ⓖ Ⓗ Ⓙ
3. Ⓐ Ⓑ Ⓒ Ⓓ
4. Ⓕ Ⓖ Ⓗ Ⓙ
5. Ⓐ Ⓑ Ⓒ Ⓓ
6. Ⓕ Ⓖ Ⓗ Ⓙ
7. Ⓐ Ⓑ Ⓒ Ⓓ
8. Ⓕ Ⓖ Ⓗ Ⓙ
9. Ⓐ Ⓑ Ⓒ Ⓓ
10. Ⓕ Ⓖ Ⓗ Ⓙ
11. Ⓐ Ⓑ Ⓒ Ⓓ
12. Ⓕ Ⓖ Ⓗ Ⓙ
13. Ⓐ Ⓑ Ⓒ Ⓓ
14. Ⓕ Ⓖ Ⓗ Ⓙ
15. Ⓐ Ⓑ Ⓒ Ⓓ
16. Ⓕ Ⓖ Ⓗ Ⓙ
17. Ⓐ Ⓑ Ⓒ Ⓓ
18. Ⓕ Ⓖ Ⓗ Ⓙ
19. Ⓐ Ⓑ Ⓒ Ⓓ
20. Ⓕ Ⓖ Ⓗ Ⓙ
21. Ⓐ Ⓑ Ⓒ Ⓓ
22. Ⓕ Ⓖ Ⓗ Ⓙ
23. Ⓐ Ⓑ Ⓒ Ⓓ
24. Ⓕ Ⓖ Ⓗ Ⓙ
25. Ⓐ Ⓑ Ⓒ Ⓓ
26. Ⓕ Ⓖ Ⓗ Ⓙ
27. Ⓐ Ⓑ Ⓒ Ⓓ
28. Ⓕ Ⓖ Ⓗ Ⓙ
29. Ⓐ Ⓑ Ⓒ Ⓓ

All-in-One Workook: Standardized Test Practice